FAVOURITE
ASIAN MEALS

FAVOURITE
ASIAN MEALS

TIMES BOOKS
International

Marshall Cavendish

Photographs Andrew Merewether

UK edition jointly published
1985 by Times Books International, Singapore
and Marshall Cavendish Books Limited, London

© Times Books International 1979
No 1 New Industrial Road
Singapore 1953

Cover copyright: Marshall Cavendish Limited 1985

Printed and bound in Hong Kong by Dai Nippon

ISBN 0 86307 421 9

Preface

This book is specially written for busy men and women whose lives are rushed. Yet there is no reason why they should not be able to enjoy well-balanced gourmet meals in the comfort of their own homes.

Every recipe in *Favourite Asian Meals* has been 'proved' through cooking lessons given over a 20-year period. All the ingredients and the time taken for preparation and cooking have been carefully measured. Short cuts and cooking tips are included wherever possible. I have often mentioned to my pupils the usefulness of modern gadgets as an aid to quick meals. Use them. Asian meals can be served within minutes.

Creating recipes has always been my passion. I have included several in this book for you to add to your collection. Some will be found in the chapters on Claypot Specials and Desserts and Savouries. The old favourites have not been forgotten. Some of them, like those in the chapter on Pickles and Dips, are old secrets learned in my mother's and mother-in-law's kitchens.

Whether an experienced cook or a novice, I would suggest you make full use of the Buying, Storage and Food Preparation Guide which follows. The colour pictures of miscellaneous ingredients, vegetables and spices as well as the glossary at the back of the book have been included for the benefit of those not too familiar with Asian ingredients.

My good wishes go with you in your cooking adventures!

Dorothy Ng

Contents

Nonya (Straits Chinese)

Indian and Sri Lankan

Rice and Noodles

Tasty Soups

Claypot Specials

Hawker Favourites

Equipping an Asian Kitchen

Most of the equipment needed for Asian cooking will be found in an average Western kitchen. The exceptions, given below, are few and may be acquired at very little cost.

Wok

Used in China and throughout Southeast Asia, the shape of a wok allows rapid stir-frying of ingredients and the minimal use of oil. An iron wok is considered far superior to an aluminium one as it retains greater heat and prevents food from burning easily. A new wok is seasoned by heating it gently, then rubbing oil all over with an absorbent cloth pad. Traditional Chinese rub a heated wok with sliced ginger, long pieces of chive and a solid lump of lard. (Supposedly, chives remove rust and ginger a "certain smell" while lard does the actual seasoning.) Once seasoned, a wok must never be scoured – only a sponge and hot water with a non-abrasive detergent are necessary.

Mortar and Pestle

Get a large mortar as small ones are inadequate for pounding more than very small quantities of *rempah*. The time and energy saving electric blender is fast replacing the stone mortar and pestle in many Asian homes, but old diehards insist that sambals and curries can never be *shiok* (in the food context, "tasty" or "scrumptious" are pale translations of this Malay word) unless the *rempah* has gone through some stone grinding or pounding implement. Season a new mortar by pounding sand in it till the surface is reasonably smooth.

Grinding Block and Rolling Pin

It takes some skill to use the heavy granite rolling pin without expending too much energy. The mortar and pestle will do the job as well if less quickly.

Roti Jala Cup

This is illustrated on page 26. The cup works like a multiple icing sugar nozzle, allowing the batter to drop in thin streams into the frying pan to form a lacy pancake.

Cendol Mould or Frame

Cendol moulds are sold by Cheong-Leen (see page 180), but a colander or an icing sugar nozzle can be used instead to produce the spaghetti-shaped strips (see illustration page 149).

Clay Pot and Yunan Pot

Nothing beats a clay pot for retaining the flavour of stewed meat and chicken. Special care is required in handling a clay pot as it breaks easily. For more details on how to use a Yunan pot, see page 118. Season a clay pot by frying grated coconut in a little oil for about 10 minutes over low heat.

Slotted and Wire-mesh Spoons

Two such spoons will be necessary, a shallow slotted spoon for frying fish and a deeper wire-mesh spoon for stirring and lifting out noodles or vegetables when scalding.

Colanders

Most Asian kitchens will have two or three plastic ones. Food prepared would be washed and left in a colander to drain dry before being cooked.

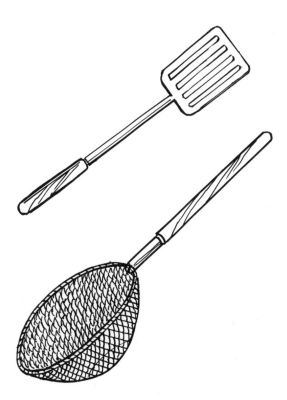

Chopsticks

(1) Wooden/Bamboo Chopsticks
   are recommended to be used for cooking as they can withstand boiling water and hot cooking oil.
(2) Ivory/Plastic Chopsticks
   are recommended to be used for serving.
   Ivory chopsticks are ideal for special occasions while plastic ones are for daily use.
   Ivory chopsticks must never be washed in hot water – rinse under cold tap.

How To Use:
(1) The first chopstick is to be rested between the thumb and the ring finger. (This chopstick should be in fixed position.)
(2) The other chopstick is to be gripped between tip of the first finger and the index finger with the tip of the thumb resting on it. (This chopstick should be able to move freely in order to touch the other chopstick and grasp the food.)

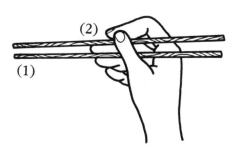

Buying, Storage and Food Preparation Guide

Agar-Agar

Agar-agar is a seaweed used widely in Asia for making jellies. It has better setting qualities than gelatin and sets without refrigeration. It is available in powder form in packets, or in strands from Chinese grocery stores or health food stores.

Bamboo Shoots

Canned bamboo shoots are already parboiled and need only be scalded in boiling water before slicing. Fresh Bamboo shoots have a thick black furry skin. Cut through the skin and peel away, then slice off the tough fibrous layer beneath the skin and the base of the bamboo shoot. Halve each shoot and boil with ½ teaspoon salt and 2-3 teaspoons sugar for about 30 minutes. Change water and boil for another 15 minutes. Slice into wedges if using as a curry or if frying and shred for soups and spring rolls. Always cut across the grain. If not using immediately, freeze in a plastic box for up to two weeks. All measurements for bamboo shoots in this book are based on parboiled weights, as the amount of edible shoot varies according to the quality of the raw material.

Bean Curd (Soy Bean Cakes)

Are made from Soy Beans. They should be used fresh and are best within one day of purchase.

Firm Soy Bean cakes – best for braising, stewing or frying.

Soft Soy Bean cakes – best for making soup.

Bittergourd

Rub salt into cut bittergourd to lessen its bitter taste.

Butter

Always mix butter with a little corn oil as butter burns very quickly.

Buying Vegetables

(a) Leafy vegetables should look fresh and have crisp leaves. Avoid wilted ones or vegetables with holes in leaves.
(b) Celery, Chinese parsley and spring onions should break easily and have fresh foliage.
(c) The tips of lady's fingers should break easily when bent.
(d) Cauliflower should be firm and white with no black spots.
(e) Tomatoes, cucumber, marrows, pumpkin and aubergines should be smooth, firm and rich in colour. Look out for tiny holes in aubergines – a sure sign of internal worm rot.
(f) Good onions, garlic and shallots are hard and have shining skins. They should have no rotting smell.
(g) The skin of fresh radish, carrot, tapioca, sweet potato, yam bean and potatoes is smooth, firm and free from specks, never broken. Medium-sized ones are better buys.
(h) Fresh mushrooms have stems attached, look clean and firm.

Candlenuts

If not available, use macademia nuts, blanched almonds or cashew nuts.

Chinese Parsley

This is another name for coriander leaves and it is used in much the same way as parsley, for flavouring and garnishing.

Chinese Sausages

Seasoned lean meat and pork fat are used to make Chinese sausages which are then dried in the sun so that they can keep without refrigeration. To cook, either steam or fry them. They are available from Chinese grocers.

Coconut Milk

Coconut milk (*santan*) is obtained by squeezing the grated kernel. Coconut water is the clear liquid found in the cavity of a coconut and must not be mistaken for coconut milk. Thick coconut milk, called "coconut creme", "*pati santan*" or "the first squeeze" in some books, is obtained by squeezing and straining through muslin before water is added to grated coconut. To squeeze out milk more easily I have always added a few tablespoons of water to grated coconut and squeezed a handful at a time. Thin coconut milk or "the second squeeze" is obtained in exactly the same way, only more water is added first.

Grated coconut and coconut milk sours quickly if kept at room temperature. Add a pinch of salt to both and refrigerate if using later in the day. Otherwise freeze in a plastic bag for a week or longer. Add hot water to thaw out and squeeze for milk. Personally I have found that coconut kept refrigerated gives up less milk than fresh grated coconut at room temperature. I usually squeeze out the milk then refrigerate with a pinch of salt.

Canned coconut milk can be used as "thick coconut milk". Add an equal quantity of water to obtain "thin coconut milk". In some places, like Australia, solid slabs of coconut creme can be obtained easily. In fact this is better than canned coconut milk. Chop a piece and let it melt in hot gravy if using as thick coconut milk or add boiling water to chopped pieces for thin coconut milk.

Cooking Rice

When cooking plain rice, "old" rice is preferable to "new" rice (old rice has slightly yellower grains) as one can see firm whole grains after cooking. Remove unwanted particles. Keep a sharp lookout for small white stones which can give an awful jar if you happen to crunch on one!

Wash rice and add cold water. The proportion is 1½ cups water to every cup of rice if you are using the ordinary thin aluminium pot. If a heavy-bottomed pot is used add a little less water, for rice cooks more slowly then. Cook over moderate heat till water is absorbed, then turn to very low heat, with lid tightly closed and continue cooking till dry. Loosen rice grains with a fork or a pair of chopsticks before serving.

Crispy Anchovies

Remove unwanted particles. Wash to remove excessive saltiness and sun or warm in an oven till absolutely dry. Deep-fry in hot oil till crisp and leave on absorbent paper to cool before storing in an airtight container.

Crispy Garlic

Deep-fry sliced or minced garlic in hot oil over low heat, stirring constantly till it turns light brown. Increase heat just before removing crispy shallots or garlic from the wok so that they do not retain too much oil. Scoop up with a perforated ladle and leave on absorbent paper. When cool, store in an airtight bottle.

Crispy Shallots

Slice shallots thinly across. Deep-fry in hot oil over low heat, stirring briskly all the while. Add a pinch of salt while frying. Turn off heat as soon as they turn a pale brown. Remove with a perforated ladle on to absorbent paper to cool, then pack in a dry airtight bottle. Use for garnishing.

Croutons

Cube one day old bread. Sun bread cubes till dry. If the weather does not permit this, grill for 30 minutes. Deep-fry in hot oil in a wok or non-stick pot till light gold. Scatter on absorbent paper to remove oil and store in an airtight container when cooled to room temperature.

Cucumber

Always cut away about 2½ cm (1 in) from the ends of cucumber. Rub cut ends together to bring up the sap. This removes a bitter taste from the ends of cucumber.

Damp Rice Flour

Damp rice flour is freshly ground rice flour which is superior in flavour to the dried flour. To prepare damp rice flour, soak rice overnight, grind in a blender until it is very fine, and pass through a hair-sieve. Pour into a calico bag and allow to drip dry.

Dhal

Lentils, which are a type of dhal, are found in many varieties in India and form an important part of the diet.

Substitute with any type of lentil obtainable in the West if the Indian types mentioned are unobtainable.

Dried Chinese Mushrooms

They are dried and are either black in colour or very dark brown with white markings. Good quality mushrooms are evenly sized and are thick. These mushrooms have a flavour that is distinct from any other mushroom.

Before cooking, soak the mushrooms in boiling water for 15-20 minutes until soft, discard the stems; slice or use whole.

Eggs

When a recipe calls for egg yolks only, do not throw away the whites. Store in a lidded jar in the refrigerator and use for meringues within 2 weeks. If you forget how many egg whites have been stored, remember 4 egg whites make about 1 cup (250 ml or 8 fluid ounces). Whisk 1 cup egg whites with 200 g castor sugar to get a good meringue.

Fish

Most of the specialist varieties of fish mentioned are imported into this country and are available frozen or dried at Chinese supermarkets (see list of stockists, p.180). These include salt fish (*ikan asin*), white pomfret (*ikan bawal putih*), black pomfret (*ikan bawal hitam*), ray fish (*ikan pari*), and squid. In season red snapper (*ikan merah*) is sold by good fishmongers. Substitutes such as sea bass, mullet, turbot, cod, tuna, plaice, or mackerel can usually be used instead, depending on the recipe. A list of substitutes is given below:

Blue crabs:	any crabs available at fishmongers
Grouper:	mullet or sea bass
Salt fish bones:	bones of any fish
Spanish mackerel:	tuna or mackerel
Threadfin:	mullet or sea bass, or cod, rock cod or mackerel
Wolf herring (also known as horse mackerel):	mackerel

Five-Spice Powder

This is a mixture of ground star anise, cloves, fennel, aniseed and cinnamon, and is sold ready mixed in oriental stores.

Frying Fish

The wok or pan used for frying fish must be scrupulously clean. Pour in oil only when the utensil is hot. When oil is smoking hot, slide in fish. Use just enough oil to cover one side of the fish. A little salt rubbed over fish will prevent fish from sticking to the pan.

Frying *Rempah*

The best pot for frying *rempah* is the Indian clay pot or *belanga*. If a wok is used, turn heat to very low or some ingredients may be burnt. When utensil is hot, add *rempah* and sufficient oil to cover. Stir-fry briskly, sprinkling in a little of any liquid used in cooking (like tamarind juice or coconut milk) as you fry. Add more liquid or other ingredients only when *rempah* is aromatic and oil separates from it.

Galingale

This rhizome of the ginger family, also known as "black ginger", is a very popular flavouring used in Malaysian cookery. It has a shiny off-white skin with brown markings. It can be sliced, dried and stored. Use green root ginger as a substitute.

Green Aubergine

This fruit has a tougher skin than the purple aubergine, but the flavour is the same.

Green Ginger

This is the fresh root ginger which is used as a flavouring in many different dishes. It has a mildly pungent flavour. If fresh ginger is not available, use ground ginger.

Grinding or Pounding *Rempah*

The order in which *rempah* ingredients should be ground is given below. Grind or pound each ingredient till fine (unless instructed otherwise in the recipe) before adding the next. If the gravy has a tamarind base, as in Masak Nanas Pedas, shallots should be pounded coarsely. For curries using a coconut milk base, all ingredients should be pounded finely. If possible, use an electric blender. Blend all ingredients finely with a little water and add shallots and

fresh chillies towards the end for just half a minute.

(a) Turmeric, sliced thinly or shredded
(b) Lemon grass, shredded
(c) Galingale, shredded
(d) Candlenuts (if not ground very finely, bits will float in gravy)
(e) Dried chillies, soaked in hot water to soften
(f) Dried shrimp paste
(g) Fresh chillies, sliced coarsely
(h) Shallots, sliced coarsely
(i) Garlic, sliced coarsely

Indonesian Black Nuts

Brush the nuts with an old brush, then boil in water for 30 minutes. The nuts will be really clean. Bring a pestle down sharply on the smooth semi-circular end to crack open a "mouth" just wide enough to insert the narrow handle of a teaspoon.

Kiamchye

This is salted kale (*kuakchye*) and can be bought in tins from oriental supermarkets.

Kuakchye

This is another name for kale.

Lard Oil

The best results are obtained when you fry vegetables in lard oil as it gives a shine. To prepare the oil, cut lard into small cubes. It is safer to use a pot than a wok. Add a little corn oil to make frying easier. Stir frequently and if pot gets too hot, turn off heat – burnt lard cubes taste bitter. Drain oil into a glazed pot and keep crisp brown cubes for frying with vegetables and noodles.

Leafy Vegetables

Separate leaves from stalks and add stalks to the pot first as they take longer to cook. The wok must be very hot when frying vegetables. Stir-fry vegetable in oil first, sprinkling in a little water if necessary. Add more water only when the colour deepens a little. To preserve greenness of leafy vegetables in soup, add one teaspoon baking soda to every eight cups boiling water. Kale (*kai lan*) is tastier if Chinese rice wine and sugar are added to the cooking oil or water.

Lemon Grass

This is a tall grass with very fleshy leaf-bases that are used for flavouring food, especially curries. Use only 4 inches (10 cms) to 5 inches (12 cms) of the slightly swollen leaf-bases. When sliced and dried, they keep very well. Lemon grass is also sold in powder form. If it is not available grated lemon rind can be used in its place.

Long Beans

These beans are sometimes known as string beans. Each bean measures 15 to 20 inches (37½ to 50 cms) and is about ¼ inch (½ cm) to ½ inch (1 cm) in diameter.

Maizena

Cornflour can be used as a substitute.

Noodles

EGG NOODLES are available in both thick and thin strands, coiled into little heaps.

DRIED EGG NOODLES are available from Chinese groceries, supermarkets and food emporiums. They are yellow-coloured noodles either in round cakes of about 2½ inches (6½ cms) diameter, or rectangular pieces of about 3 inches (7½ cms) square. Some are also sold in straight sticks very much like spaghetti.

FRIED EGG NOODLES are loosely packed, round pieces of yellowish, pinkish noodles. They are very crisp and break easily.

RICE VERMICELLI are white strands of dried noodles.

Thin Vermicelli ('Mee Fun') or Thick Vermicelli ('Lai Fun') can both be fried or cooked in soup whilst Flat Rice Noodles ('Ho Fun') are ideal for cooking in soup.

YELLOW NOODLES are a bright yellow colour and are coated very lightly with oil to prevent them sticking to each other and to give them a slight sheen. They are available in thick and thin strands.

Palm Sugar

This sugar is very sweet. The nearest substitutes are brown sugar and molasses, or treacle will do.

Rempah

This is the mixture of ground spices, herbs and seasoning which gives Indian cooking its distinctive flavour. Different ingredients can be combined so that each dish has its own *rempah*. See "Grinding or Pounding *Rempah*" and "Frying *Rempah*" on page 15.

Rice Wine

Shiu Hing Rice Wine is very good for cooking but dry sherry can be used instead.

Roasting Peanuts

Pick out stones and grit, then spread out in a tray under a preheated grill. Cook for 15 minutes under a very hot grill, stirring from time to time, then turn heat to low and grill for another 10 minutes. Leave for 5 minutes to cool, then rub to separate skin. When cooled to room temperature, store in an airtight container. You can also roast peanuts in a dry wok. Stir constantly over low heat till golden brown, turning off heat if wok gets too hot.

Rock Sugar

These are lumps of sugar crystals that are sweeter than granulated sugar.

Salted Duck's Eggs

To remove black earth packed around the eggs, soak in a basin of cold water for ten minutes, then scrape away softened earth. Eggs that float have not been successfully seasoned. Throw them away.

Scalding Noodles

To prevent dried yellow noodles from becoming soggy, scald in its block form, then drain away water and loosen slightly with a pair of chopsticks just before frying. It is necessary to dip quickly in cold water to stop the cooking process.

Prevent rice vermicelli from breaking when frying Meesiam by soaking in cold water to soften. Take care not to soak too long or it becomes soggy. Drain in a colander.

Flat rice noodles must never be washed. Sprinkle in a little water as you fry if it becomes too dry.

Screwpine Leaves

These bright green leaves are stiff, long, and narrow, with a pronounced furrow down the centre. When cooked with food they impart a lovely flavour. The leaves are pounded and the green juice extracted to be added to food for colouring as well as flavouring.

Shallots

If peeling shallots makes you cry, slice away just enough of the root and tip to expose shallots and soak in water to soften skin. Rub away skin and dry with a tea towel before storing in a dry plastic container. Shallots keep refrigerated for a week this way.

Small Sour Starfruit (Belimbing Buloh)

If these are not available, use lemon juice. The strength of five *belimbing* would be roughly that of half a lemon.

Soy Sauce

There is the light sauce (*kicap putih putih*) and the dark (*kicap hitam*). The former is normally used for flavouring, while the dark sauce is used not only for flavouring but also to give colour. Both are available at most Chinese or Oriental food stores.

Spices

It is advisable to buy spices in whole pieces rather than in the ground or powdered form. Keep in airtight plastic boxes in the refrigerator and grind small quantities each time, remembering to sun and roast those which require such treatment first.

Sugar Peas or Garden Peas

These are green peas in the pod that need very little cooking and are very tender. Use mange tout when in season.

Tamarind

Tamarind is the brown pulp and black seeds of the assam fruit and is used to give a sour taste to food. It is sold in packets. The brown-coloured tamarind is fresher than the black.

Tea

Chinese people are very particular about which type of tea leaves to choose as it is very important to serve a good cup of tea after each meal.

There is a wide variety of different tea leaves in China but the most common types used in the West are:

(a) Compressed Tea ('peu-erh') –
    Fairly strong but good for combating oily food.
(b) 'Lai-Chee' Black Tea –
    Fairly light with fragrance.
(c) Jasmine Tea –
    Very light and fresh.

Tung Chye

Tung Chye, made from cabbage, is sprinkled on oriental dishes as a flavouring. It can be purchased in oriental supermarkets.

Yam Bean

This is a tuberous root which has a brown skin that can be peeled away from the sweet white flesh.

Weights and Measures

Generally Speaking

Metric and imperial measures are used throughout this book. As far as possible, volume measures are given for both liquids and solids. All cup and spoon measures are level ones. A pinch is literally what can be picked up between thumb and forefinger. Salt and sugar measures for food dishes can be changed to suit individual taste.

Matching Spoonfuls

1 tablespoonful	3 teaspoonfuls
1 tablespoonful	2 dessertspoonfuls
1½ teaspoonfuls	1 dessertspoonful
12 tablespoonfuls	1 cup (250 ml)

Cup Equivalents

1 cup cooking oil	250 ml	8 fl oz
1 cup plain flour	125 g	4 oz
1 cup sugar	210 g	8 oz
1 cup rice	210 g	8 oz

Oven Temperatures

	°C	°F	Gas Regulo
Low	150	300	4
Moderately low	165	325	5
Moderate	175	350	6
Moderately hot	190	375	7
Hot	205	400	8
Very Hot	220	425	9

Temperatures vary according to the make of oven. Use an oven thermometer to determine the correct temperature according to the gas mark.

Servings

Recipes in this book will serve 6-8 people.

Malay and Indonesian

Mutton Rendang

Preparation: 30 minutes
Cooking: 1½-2 hours

1¼ kg (2½ lb) mutton
2 L (2 qt) water
1¼ coconuts, grated
1 teaspoon tamarind
250 ml (8 fl oz) water
2 turmeric leaves, torn into big pieces
4 lime leaves, shredded
2 teaspoons sugar
1 teaspoon salt

Rempah
30 dried chillies
10 red chillies (bird chillies if preferred spicier)
25 shallots
5 cloves garlic
5 cm (2 in) piece turmeric *or* 2 teaspoons ground turmeric
10 slices galingale *or* green root ginger
8 slices ginger
3 stalks lemon grass

Cut mutton into bite-size pieces. Add 250 ml (8 fl oz) water to coconut. Squeeze and strain for thick coconut milk. Add another 1.75 L (3½ pt) water to the residue and squeeze and strain to obtain thin coconut milk. Mix tamarind and 250 ml (8 fl oz) water. Sqeeze and strain to obtain juice.

Simmer thin coconut milk with mutton and *rempah* in an uncovered wok. Add turmeric and lime leaves. Add water if necessary during cooking to prevent meat drying out. Stir constantly till half the liquid has evaporated.

When meat is tender, add thick coconut milk, tamarind juice, sugar, and salt. Simmer till meat is very soft and gravy has thickened.

Indonesian Beef Rendang

Preparation: 20 minutes
Cooking: 3 hours

2½ coconuts, grated
2¼ L (2¼ qt) water
1¼ kg (2¾ lb) beef, sirloin *or* rump, cut into
    5 × 7½ cm (2 × 3 in) pieces
2 onions, sliced lengthwise
2 teaspoons sugar
2 teaspoons salt
6 lemon leaves

Rempah
2 stalks lemon grass
4 cm (1½ in) piece galingale *or* green root ginger
20 dried chillies or 2 tablespoons ground chilli
15 red chillies (bird chillies if preferred spicier)
25 shallots
2 cloves garlic
15 black peppercorns
3 tablespoons coriander, roasted
1 teaspoon cummin *or* ¾ teaspoon ground cummin
1 teaspoon fennel *or* ¾ teaspoon ground fennel

Mix coconut and water. Squeeze and strain to obtain coconut milk.

Put beef, onions, seasoning, lemon leaves, *rempah* and half the coconut milk in a pot. Cook over low heat for 1½ hours (or in a pressure cooker for 40 minutes).

At the end of that time, add remaining coconut milk and simmer, stirring occasionally, till meat is tender and very little gravy remains.

Kurmah

Preparation: 20 minutes
Marinating: 1 hour
Cooking: 1 hour for chicken, 2¹/₂ hours for beef
*   or mutton*

1½ kg (3⅓ lb) beef, mutton or chicken
¾ cup kurmah curry powder (p.143)
1½ teaspoons salt
1½ coconuts, grated
3 L (6¼ pints) water
150 ml (¼ pint) fresh milk
juice of 1 lemon
2 tablespoons ghee *or* clarified butter
250 ml (8 fl oz) oil
20 shallots, sliced thinly
2 cloves garlic, sliced thinly
4 stalks curry leaves
8 cardamoms
1 star anise
5 cm (2 in) cinnamon stick
8 cloves
6 potatoes, halved
2 tomatoes, halved
6 red chillies, cut into long strips
2 green chillies, cut into long strips
1 big onion, quartered
12 cashew nuts, ground finely
10 almonds, ground finely
2 tablespoons poppy seeds, ground finely
2 tablespoons oil
¾ teaspoon mustard seeds
2 sprigs coriander leaves

Cut meat into bite-size pieces and season in kurmah powder and salt for at least an hour.

Squeeze and strain grated coconut to obtain thick coconut milk. Add 3 L (6¼ pints) water (less if cooking chicken) to residue to obtain thin coconut milk.

Curdle fresh milk with lemon juice.

Heat ghee and oil in a wok. Stir-fry shallots, garlic and curry leaves for 2 minutes, then add cardamoms, star anise, cinnamon, cloves and meat with seasoning.

Stir-fry for 2 minutes, then add thin coconut milk a little at a time, stirring frequently to prevent burning.

When meat is almost cooked, add potatoes, tomatoes, chillies, onion, curdled milk and ground ingredients.

When meat is tender, add thick coconut milk. Simmer for another 5 minutes.

During the last 2 minutes of cooking meat, heat 2 tablespoons oil in a clean pan and fry mustard seeds. Pour over Kurmah, throw in coriander leaves and remove from heat.

Mutton, Lamb or Beef Satay

Preparation: 25 minutes
Marinating: 4 hours
Cooking: 20-25 minutes

1¼ kg (3 lb) mutton, lamb or beef
1 tablespoon tamarind
5 tablespoons water
3 tablespoons ginger juice from 7½ cm (3 in) piece
    ginger, pounded
5 tablespoons sugar
¾ teaspoon salt
1 tablespoon black soy sauce

Rempah

3 teaspoons ground turmeric
2 stalks lemon grass
3 tablespoons coriander, pounded roughly
½ teaspoon fennel
½ teaspoon cummin

Slice meat into thin 2½ cm (1 in) squares. Mix tamarind with 5 tablespoons water. Squeeze and strain for tamarind juice.

Mix meat with *rempah*, ginger juice, sugar, salt and black soy sauce. Marinate for at least 4 hours.

Thread meat onto satay sticks or skewers, leaving the smaller pieces to cover the ends of the stick. Preheat the grill to high, put the meat with sticks on the rack in the grill and turn over once in a while; grill until meat is cooked.

Daging Cabe (Chilli Beef)

Preparation: 15 minutes
Advance cooking: 1 hour
Final cooking: 45 minutes

900 g (2 lb) rump steak, in one piece
1.2 L (2 pints) water
1¼ coconuts, grated
250 ml (8 fl oz) water
1 tablespoon tamarind
60 ml (2 fl oz) water
300 g (10 oz) palm sugar
2 teaspoons salt
½ teaspoon sugar
6 tablespoons oil
2 big onions, sliced coarsely
3 tomatoes, quartered

Rempah
15 shallots
2 cloves garlic
1 teaspoon dried shrimp paste
25 dried chillies, seeded
8-10 bird chillies

Prepare the meat a day in advance. Boil rump steak, whole, in 1.2 L (2 pints) water for 1 hour till meat is just tender. Add more water during cooking if necessary. When cold, slice meat across the grain into ½ cm (¼ in) thick pieces.

Rempah can also be prepared a day earlier. Pound the ingredients in the order given, making sure each item is fine before adding the next one. Store in a plastic box in the refrigerator for use the next day.

Mix grated coconut with 250 ml (8 fl oz) water. Squeeze and strain for 420 ml (¾ pint) coconut milk. Mix tamarind with 60 ml (2 fl oz) water to obtain tamarind juice.

Put sliced beef wih coconut milk, tamarind juice, palm sugar, salt, sugar and *rempah* in a saucepan. Bring to a boil and simmer till meat is very tender and gravy is almost dry. Stir every now and then or the *rempah* will burn at the bottom of the saucepan. (A non-stick pan prevents this.) Drain meat for 30 minutes before frying to prevent oil from spluttering. Keep the gravy.

Fry beef slices in 4 tablespoons oil, a few pieces at a time. Remove and set aside. Heat another 2 tablespoons oil and fry onions and tomatoes for about 1 minute. Add fried beef slices and thick gravy. Stir-fry for 1 minute over low heat. Serve immediately.

Daging Cabe goes beautifully with plain rice or bread.

Ayam Panggang (Indonesian Grilled Chicken)

Preparation: 20 minutes
Marinating: 2 hours
Cooking: 40 minutes

1¼ kg (3 lb) young chicken
2 teaspoons sugar
¾ teaspoon salt
lime juice from 1 large green lime
1½ coconuts, grated
3 tablespoons oil

Rempah
5 red chillies
10 bird chillies
2 cloves garlic
12 shallots
2 stalks lemon grass
4 slices galingale
15 peppercorns
2½ cm (1 in) piece turmeric or ½ teaspoon ground turmeric

Quarter chicken for grilling. Marinate in sugar, salt and lime juice for at least 2 hours. Grill chicken till golden brown. In the meantime, squeeze coconut to obtain about 350 ml (12 fl oz) thick coconut milk.

Heat oil in a wok and fry *rempah* till fragrant. Add thick coconut milk and grilled chicken and simmer till dry. Turn the chicken constantly so that all parts are evenly cooked in gravy.

Chop into bite-size pieces before serving.

Dry Curry Chicken (for Roti Jala)

Preparation: 15 minutes
Cooking: 30 minutes

1¾ kg (4 lb) chicken
¾ coconut, grated
500 ml (18 fl oz) water
6 tablespoons oil
20 shallots, sliced
4 cloves garlic, chopped
2½ cm (1 in) cinnamon stick
4 segments star anise
1 teaspoon cardamom seeds
1½ teaspoons salt
3 tablespoons light soy sauce
5 potatoes, diced into 1 cm (½ in) cubes
3 big onions, diced into 1 cm (½ in) cubes
juice of ½ lime

Rempah
20 dried chillies, seeded
6 red chillies
4 tablespoons coriander, roasted till fragrant
1 tablespoon fennel
1 tablespoon ground cummin
20 white peppercorns
10 black peppercorns
2½ cm (1 in) piece turmeric
1 stalk lemon grass
6 slices galingale
1 × 1 cm (½ × ½ in) piece ginger
4 tablespoons white grated coconut, roasted
1 tablespoon rice grains, roasted
½ piece nutmeg or ¼ teaspoon ground nutmeg

Cut chicken into bite-size pieces. Mix coconut with 4 tablespoons water. Squeeze and strain for 120 ml (4 fl oz) thick milk. Add 420 ml (¾ pint) water to residue. Squeeze and strain for 600 ml (1 pint) thin coconut milk.

Heat oil in a wok till smoking hot and fry shallots, then garlic till quite brown. Add *rempah* and stir-fry till fragrant, then add cinnamon, star anise and cardamom.

After stirring the contents of the wok for 1 minute, add chicken and about 120 ml (4 fl oz) of the thin coconut milk. Stir-fry for 5 minutes, then add salt, soy sauce and remaining thin coconut milk.

Simmer, stirring constantly, for 15 minutes. When chicken is quite tender, add potatoes. Cook for 6 more minutes before adding thick coconut milk. Stir-fry till potatoes are cooked, then add diced onions and cook until curry is quite dry.

Squeeze lime juice over the curry and serve with Roti Jala (p.35).

Chicken Satay

Preparation: 25 minutes
Marinating: 30 minutes
Cooking: 20-25 minutes

2¼ (5 lb) chicken
4 tablespoons coriander seeds, roasted and ground
    or 2 teaspoons ground coriander
2½ cm (1 in) piece turmeric, pounded or 1
    teaspoon ground turmeric
½ teaspoon pepper
1 tablespoon light soy sauce
salt to taste
4 tablespoons thick coconut milk from ⅓ coconut,
    grated
3 tablespoons oil to baste meat when grilling

Slice meat into thin 2½ cm (1 in) squares and score lightly to tenderize.

Season meat for 30 minutes in coriander, turmeric, pepper, soy sauce and salt. Thread meat onto satay sticks or skewers, leaving the smaller pieces to cover the ends.

Brush meat with thick coconut milk. Preheat grill to high. While grilling, brush meat several times with oil. Grill until meat is cooked.

Penang Curry Kapitan

Preparation: 25 minutes
Cooking: 40 minutes

1 coconut, grated
1.2 L (2 pints) water
2 rounded tablespoons tamarind
6 tablespoons water
4 tablespoons oil
1¾ kg (4 lb) chicken, cut into bite-size pieces
sugar to taste
salt to taste

Rempah
15 dried chillies
30 shallots
2 cloves garlic
2 stalks lemon grass
5 × 2½ cm (2 × 1 in) piece galingale
4 candlenuts *or* blanched almonds
2½ cm (1 in) piece turmeric
1 teaspoon dried shrimp paste
1 teaspoon ground coriander

Mix grated coconut with 250 ml (8 fl oz) water. Squeeze and strain to obtain thick coconut milk. Add 1 L (1¾ pints) water to coconut residue. Squeeze and strain to obtain thin coconut milk.

Mix tamarind with 6 tablespoons water. Squeeze and strain to obtain juice.

Heat oil in a wok, fry *rempah* till fragrant, then add chicken and stir-fry for 5 minutes.

Pour in 250 ml (8 fl oz) thin coconut milk and stir upwards to prevent curdling. When simmering, add tamarind juice and seasoning. Continue adding thin coconut milk till used up.

When meat is tender, add thick coconut milk and simmer till gravy is quite thick.

Curry Kapitan goes very well with plain white rice.

Indonesian Chicken Kurmah

Preparation: 12 minutes
Cooking: 35 minutes

1¾ kg (4 lb) chicken
4 potatoes
1½ coconuts, grated
1 L (1¾ pints) water
5 tablespoons evaporated milk
2 tablespoons juice of limes
175 ml (6 fl oz) oil
3 tomatoes, quartered
4 lime leaves
90 g (3 oz) ground almonds
1 teaspoon sugar
1 teaspoon salt

Rempah
1½ teaspoons ground turmeric
1 teaspoon black pepper
½ teaspoon white pepper
6 candlenuts *or* 10 blanched almonds
18 shallots
3 cloves garlic
1 tablespoon dried shrimp paste
1 stalk lemon grass
6 slices galingale

Cut chicken into bite-size pieces. Peel and quarter potatoes. Squeeze and strain grated coconut for 250 ml (8 fl oz) thick milk. Add 1 L (1¾ pints) water to residue to obtain thin coconut milk.

Curdle evaporated milk with lime juice.

Heat oil in a saucepan or clay pot and stir-fry *rempah* for 2 minutes. Add chicken and thin coconut milk in 4 portions, each every 5 minutes, stirring all the time till all the thin coconut milk has been added.

Add tomatoes, lime leaves and the thick coconut milk. After simmering for a few more minutes, add curdled milk, ground almonds, sugar and salt. Continue to simmer for another 5 minutes and the kurmah is ready.

23

Ayam Goreng (Spicy Indonesian Fried Chicken)

Preparation: 10 minutes
Cooking: 30 minutes

2 kg (4½ lb) chicken, cut into bite-size pieces, *or* 14
   chicken wings, halved
1 teaspoon salt
1 teaspoon sugar
1½ coconuts, grated
175 ml (6 fl oz) water
1 stalk lemon grass, bruised
2 teaspoons ground coriander
oil for deep-frying

Rempah
8 red chillies
20 dried chillies
10 bird chillies
3 cm (1¼ in) piece turmeric *or* ¾ teaspoon ground
   turmeric
6 slices galingale *or* 6 slices green root ginger
15 black peppercorns
2 cloves garlic
10 shallots

Rub chicken pieces with salt, and sugar. Mix coconut with 175 ml (6 fl oz) water and squeeze and strain to obtain milk.

Put coconut milk, *rempah*, lemon grass and coriander in a large saucepan and bring to a boil, stirring frequently. Add chicken and simmer for 20 minutes, stirring occasionally. Remove chicken from gravy, drain, then deep-fry in hot oil till golden. Drain and put on a serving dish.

Simmer gravy over moderate heat to thicken and serve in a separate bowl.

Sambal Telur (Egg Curry)

Preparation: 15 minutes
Cooking: 20 minutes

1 tablespoon tamarind
120 ml (4 fl oz) water
5 tablespoons oil
8 hardboiled eggs, shelled
1 teaspoon salt
1 teaspoon sugar

Rempah
15 dried chillies, seeded
4 red chillies
10 shallots
1 tablespoon dried shrimp paste

Mix tamarind with water. Squeeze and strain to obtain tamarind juice.

Heat oil in a wok. Stir-fry *rempah* for 3 minutes till fragrant. Add tamarind juice, hardboiled eggs, salt and sugar. Stir-fry for another 3 minutes.

Leave contents of wok to simmer for 5 more minutes till red oil floats on top. Serve with Lontong (p.100.)

Indonesian Fish Frikkadels

Preparation: 20 minutes
Cooking: 8-10 minutes

600 g (1⅓ lb) fish, preferably Mackerel
1 teaspoon butter
300 g (10oz) potatoes, boiled and mashed
¼ teaspoon grated nutmeg
¼ teaspoon salt
¼ teaspoon sugar
½ teaspoon pepper
1 egg yolk, beaten
3 teaspoons tapioca flour
1 stalk spring onion (white portion only), chopped
2 egg whites, beaten slightly
oil for deep-frying

Steam fish till cooked. When cool, remove bones and pound fish till fine.

Mix fish with butter, mashed potatoes, nutmeg, salt, sugar, pepper, egg yolk, tapioca flour and chopped spring onion.

Make round balls (the size of ping pong balls), then flatten slightly. Dip cutlets in beaten egg white and deep-fry in hot oil till a light golden brown.

Variation
Dip cutlet in beaten egg white or whole beaten egg and dip in breadcrumbs. Deep fry till golden brown.

Malay Satay (p. 20) with Satay Sauce (p. 142) and Ketupat (p. 100)

Roti Jala (p. 35) wih Dry Curry Chicken (p. 22) and Sambal Sotong (p. 31)

26

Clockwise from top: Lontong (p. 100), Sambal Udang (p. 29), Coconut Serondeng
(p. 32), Sambal Telur (p. 24, Indonesian Beef Rendang (p. 19) and Sayur Lodeh (p. 31)

Ikan Masak Bali (opposite)

Ikan Masak Bali

Preparation: 10 minutes
Cooking: 20 minutes

2 tomatoes
4 tablespoons oil
10 shallots, chopped
3 cloves garlic, pounded
¼ lime peel, grated
2 tablespoons palm sugar
4 tablespoons lemon juice
4 tablespoons black soy sauce
1 Red Snapper, about 1½ kg (3⅓ lb)
½ teaspoon salt
oil for deep-frying
2 tomatoes, sliced
1 cucumber, sliced

Rempah
6 red chillies
1 teaspoon dried shrimp paste
2 stalks lemon grass
1 cm (½ in) piece ginger
2½ cm (1 in) piece galingale *or* green root ginger

Boil 2 tomatoes, peel off skin and chop.
Heat 4 tablespoons oil in a saucepan and fry shallots and garlic for 1 minute, then add *rempah* and fry till fragrant.

Put in chopped tomatoes, grated lime peel, palm sugar, lemon juice and black soy sauce.

Simmer, stirring constantly, till gravy is thick.

Season fish with salt and deep-fry in hot oil till crisp.

Place fish on a serving dish, pour hot gravy on top and decorate with slices of tomato and cucumber.

Malay Sambal Udang (Malaysian Prawn Curry)

Preparation: 8 minutes
Cooking: 6 minutes

600 g (1⅓ lb) small prawns
4 tablespoons water
¼ coconut, grated
1 teaspoon tamarind
4 tablespoons water
4 tablespoons oil
1 big onion, sliced lengthwise
¼ teaspoon salt
½ teaspoon sugar
1 cucumber

Rempah
18 dried chillies
2 red chillies
3 slices galingale *or* green root ginger
1 stalk lemon grass
2½ × 6 cm (1 × 2¼ in) piece dried shrimp paste
12 shallots
2 cloves garlic

Shell the prawns. Add water to grated coconut and squeeze for thick coconut milk. Strain and discard residue. Mix tamarind with water, squeeze, then strain and discard pulp and seeds.

Heat oil in an earthenware pot or a non-stick pan, and fry *rempah* till fragrant.

Add half the coconut milk, prawns and sliced onion. Stir-fry over moderate heat for a few minutes, taking care not to overcook the prawns.

Add salt, sugar, tamarind juice and the remaining coconut milk. Simmer for a few moments till the oil floats on top.

Serve with cucumber cut into wedges.

Sambal Udang Kering

Preparation: 12 minutes
Cooking: 15 minutes

300 g (10 oz) dried prawns, soaked in cold water
2 tablespoons tamarind
4 tablespoons water
120 ml (4 fl oz) oil
3 tablespoons sugar
½ teaspoon salt
5 red chillies, sliced
3 green chillies, sliced

Rempah
15 dried chillies
6 red chillies
2½ cm (1 in) piece turmeric *or* ½ teaspoon ground
   turmeric
10 shallots
5 cloves garlic
2 stalks lemon grass
1½ tablespoons dried shrimp paste

Grind in electric blender or pound dried prawns till quite fine. Mix tamarind with water and squeeze. Strain and discard pulp and seeds.

Heat oil in a wok and fry *rempah* for 2 minutes till fragrant, then add ground dried prawns. Stir-fry for 3 minutes, then add tamarind juice, sugar and salt. Simmer for 1-2 minutes, add fresh red and green chillies, then stir-fry till sambal is quite dry. Serve with Lontong (p.100).

Indonesian Prawn Kroket

Preparation: 8 minutes
Cooking: 10 minutes

600 g (1⅓ lb) prawns
8 shallots, sliced
1 tablespoon oil
4-6 medium-sized potatoes
2 tablespoons butter
½ teaspoon white pepper
½ teaspoon salt
2 teaspoons tapioca flour
1 teaspoon plain white flour
600 g (1⅓ lb) minced pork
2 slices (approx. 50 g or 1¾ oz) cooked sandwich
   ham, minced
2 tablespoons milk
3 egg whites, beaten slightly
8 tablespoons breadcrumbs (or more as required)
oil for deep-frying

Peel prawns and chop coarsely. Fry sliced shallots in 1 tablespoon oil till crisp, add prawns and fry for 2 minutes. Remove and set aside.

Peel and boil potatoes for 15 minutes or till soft, then mash.

Mix mashed potatoes with butter, pepper, salt, tapioca flour, plain white flour, pork, ham, milk, prawns and fried shallots. Mix well with the hands.

Shape the mixture into little round patties, first rolling it into balls, then flattening them to patties of 2½ cm (1 in) thickness. Dip in beaten egg white, coat with breadcrumbs and deep-fry in hot oil till krokets are golden brown.

Indonesian Prawn Cutlet

Preparation: 10 minutes
Cooking: 15 minutes

600 g (1⅓ lb) prawns
900 g (2 lb) potatoes
5 shallots, sliced and fried
1 egg yolk
3 teaspoons plain white flour
salt to taste
pepper to taste
2 stalks spring onion, chopped
2 egg whites, lightly beaten
30 g (1 oz) fresh breadcrumbs
oil for deep-frying

Peel prawns and chop finely. Peel and boil potatoes for 15 minutes and mash till smooth.

Mix prawns with mashed potatoes, fried shallots, egg yolk, flour, salt, pepper and spring onion.

Shape into round balls 5 cm (2 in) in diameter, then flatten to 2½ cm (1 in) thick cutlets. Dip cutlets in beaten egg white and coat with breadcrumbs. Deep-fry till golden brown.

Sambal Sotong

Preparation: 10 minutes
Cooking: 10 minutes

600 g (1⅓ lb) cuttlefish
3 tablespoons tamarind blended with 6 tablespoons
    water *or* juice of ¾ lemon
7 tablespoons oil
2 onions, cut into ½ cm (¼ in) rings
1½ teaspoons sugar
¾ teaspoon salt
2 tomatoes, quartered

Rempah
15 dried chillies *or* 2 tablespoons ground chilli
10 shallots
2 cloves garlic
1 tablespoon dried shrimp paste

Clean cuttlefish, removing ink sac and bone. Cut into ½ cm (¼ in) rings.

If tamarind is used, squeeze with water and strain to obtain juice.

Heat oil in a wok and stir-fry *rempah* till oil separates from *rempah*. Add onion rings and cuttlefish.

Stir-fry for just 5 minutes, then add 5 tablespoons water. Cook cuttlefish for another minute.

Add seasoning and tomatoes and stir-fry just one more minute. Pour in lime juice or tamarind juice.

Sayur Lodeh (Vegetable Curry)

Preparation: 10 minutes
Cooking: 18 minutes

1¼ kg (2½ lb) yam bean
600 g (1⅓ lb) long beans
750 g (1½ lb) green aubergines
450 g (1 lb) cabbage
8 firm soybean cakes
4 fermented soybean cakes
225 g (8 oz) dried prawns
225 g (8 oz) dried anchovies
900 g (2 lb) small prawns
750 ml (1¼ pints) water
300 g (10 oz) dried anchovies for stock
400 ml (14 fl oz) water
2 coconuts, grated
175 ml (6 fl oz) cooking oil
1 teaspoon salt

Rempah
5 cm (2 in) piece fresh turmeric (or 1 teaspoon
    ground turmeric)
20 shallots
10 slices galingale *or* green root ginger
3 teaspoons dried shrimp paste
8 candlenuts *or* 12 blanched almonds
4 fresh red chillies
20 dried chillies, seeded

Slice yam beans into 1 × 5 cm (½ × 2 in) strips. Cut long beans into 2 ½ cm (1 in) lengths and aubergines into wedges. Cut cabbage into 2½ cm (1 in) squares.

Cut each firm soybean cake into 3 pieces. Slice each fermented soybean cake into quarters, then into 8 pieces.

Pound the dried prawns coarsely and the dried anchovies as fine as grains of sand. Shell fresh small prawns and keep shells for stock.

Boil dried anchovies (for stock) and prawn shells in 750 ml (1¼ pints) water for about 10 minutes, tthen strain to obtain clear stock.

Add 400 ml (14 fl oz) water to grated coconut. Squeeze and strain to obtain thick coconut milk. Add another 2.75 L (5 pints) water to residue and squeeze and strain to obtain thin coconut milk.

Add thin coconut milk to clear stock. Bring to a boil and simmer for 5 minutes.

Heat oil in a wok and deep-fry fermented soybean pieces slightly. Remove and drain. Fry firm soybean pieces slightly and set aside.

Heat 4 tablespoons oil and fry *rempah* together with the pounded dried prawns and dried anchovies for 3 minutes. Add stock and coconut milk mixture and boil for 10 minutes.

Add vegetables in the order listed and cook for not more than 1 minute, then add fried fermented soybean pieces and firm soybean pieces.

Simmer for 3 minutes, then pour in thick coconut milk and salt. Continue to boil, this time stirring constantly to prevent milk from curdling.

After 5 minutes, when the red oil floats to the top the Sayur Lodeh is ready to serve with Lontong (p.100) and other side dishes.

Taukwa Goreng (Fried Soybean Cake)

Preparation: 10 minutes
Cooking: 12 minutes

oil for deep-frying
4 firm soybean cakes
300 g (10 oz) beansprouts
1 cucumber, peeled and shredded finely

Sauce
5 red chillies
5 bird chillies
2 cloves garlic
85 g (3 oz) roasted peanuts
2 tablespoons palm sugar
2 teaspoons preserved soy beans
1 teaspoon vinegar *or* 2 tablespoons tamarind juice
    from 1 tablespoon tamarind

Heat oil in a wok till hot. Fry soybean cakes whole, then cut each cake into 9 cubes.

Scald beansprouts in boiling water. Drain and pile over soybean cakes. Add shredded cucumber.

Pour sauce over soybean cakes just before serving.

Sauce
Grind chillies, garlic and peanuts together, then add palm sugar, preserved soy beans and vinegar or tamarind juice.

Tempe Goreng (Fried Fermented Soybean Cake)

Preparation: 4 minutes
Marinating: 30 minutes
Cooking: 3 minutes

6 fermented soybean cakes
1 teaspoon tamarind juice
1 teaspoon ground turmeric
½ teaspoon salt
120 ml (4 fl oz) oil

Cut fermented soybean cakes into pieces 2½ cm (1 in) square. Soak in tamarind juice, ground turmeric and salt for 30 minutes.

Heat oil in a wok till smoking hot, then fry fermented soybean pieces till golden brown.

Serve immediately with other dishes to accompany Lontong (p.100).

Coconut Serondeng

Preparation: 5 minutes
Cooking: 10-12 minutes

1 coconut, black skin removed, grated
1-2 tablespoons Fried Sambal Blacan (p.140)
3 teaspoons sugar
½ teaspoon salt

Fry coconut slowly in a dry wok or non-stick pan for 5 minutes, stirring all the time. Add all the other ingredients and stir-fry over moderate heat till golden.

Sayur Assam Putih (Indonesian Vegetable in Tamarind Sauce)

Preparation: 8 minutes
Cooking: 15 minutes

300 g (10 oz) prawns
900 g (2 lb) water convolvulus *or*
   a mixed vegetable combination of:
   ⅓ cabbage, cut into 4 cm (1½ in) squares
8 long beans, cut into 4 cm (1½ in) lengths
2 aubergines, cut into wedges
4 tablespoons tamarind
120 ml (4 fl oz) water
1.6 L (2¾ pints) fish or prawn stock

Rempah
8 bird chillies (red chillies can be used if milder taste
   is preferred)
2 green chillies
4 slices galingale *or* green root ginger
4 candlenuts *or* 6 blanched almonds
4 shallots
1 teaspoon dried shrimp paste
2 cloves garlic

Side Dishes for Sayur Assam Putih
10 prawn crackers
oil for deep-frying
4 salted duck's eggs
5 × 1 cm (2 × ½ in) piece salt fish (*Ikan Kurau*)
6 tablespoons oil
Sambal Blacan (p.139)

Peel the prawns (shells can be used to make stock). Clean and cut water convolvulus into 5 cm (2 in) lengths, or prepare mixed vegetables. Mix tamarind and water, then squeeze for juice. Strain and discard pulp and seeds.

Mix 250 ml (8 fl oz) stock and *rempah* and simmer for 5 minutes. Stir, then pour in tamarind juice and remaining stock. Cover and bring to a boil. Simmer for 3 minutes, then add water convolvulus or prepared vegetables.

When vegetables are quite soft, add prawns and simmer for 2 minutes, taking care not to overcook prawns.

Side Dishes for Sayur Assam Putih
Dry prawn crackers in the sun for 3 hours, or dry in a very slow oven. Deep-fry in hot oil. Drain excess oil on absorbent paper and store in an airtight tin.

Scrape away black earth from salted duck's eggs. Boil for 15 minutes, then cut into quarters after cracking and peeling off shell or cut into quarters with the shell still on and scoop out the egg when eating.

Slice salt fish very thinly into 3 mm or ⅛ in squares and fry in 6 tablespoons oil till crisp.

Kobis Masak Lemak (Cabbage Cooked in Coconut Milk)

Preparation: 10 minutes
Cooking: 15 minutes

300 g (10 oz) cabbage
300 g (10 oz) small prawns
¾ coconut, grated
1 L (1¾ pints) water
½ teaspoon salt

Rempah
5 red chillies
5 shallots
1 clove garlic
2 cm (¾ in) piece turmeric *or* ½ teaspoon ground
   turmeric
1 teaspoon dried shrimp paste

Cut cabbage into 2½ cm (1 in) cubes. Peel prawns. Mix coconut with 120 ml (4 fl oz) water. Squeeze and strain for thick milk. Add 1 L (1¾ pints) water to residue. Squeeze and strain thin coconut milk.

Put thin coconut milk and *rempah* in a saucepan and bring to a boil. Simmer for 10 minutes, then add cabbage. When cabbage is quite soft, add salt, prawns and thick coconut milk. Simmer for 3 minutes till prawns are cooked.

Gado-Gado

Preparation: 1 hour
Cooking: 1 hour

10 long beans, cut into 2½ cm (1 in) lengths
600 g (1⅓ lb) cabbage, cut into 2½ cm (1 in) squares
300 g (10 oz) beansprouts, straggly roots discarded
1¼ kg (2¾ lb) water convolvulus, young stems cut into 2½ cm (1 in) lengths (available from Chinese supermarkets)
½ teaspoon baking powder
oil for deep-frying
2 fermented soybean cakes, quartered
4 firm soybean cakes, each cut into 16 pieces
20 prawn crackers
10 shallots, sliced thinly
10-12 potatoes peeled, boiled and sliced
2 cucumbers, cut into wedges
10 hardboiled eggs, sliced

Sauce
1-2 bottles (340 g/12 oz) peanut butter or 1¼ kg (2¾ lb) peanuts
5 × ½ cm (2 × ¼ in) piece dried shrimp paste
30 dried chillies, steamed
10 bird chillies, steamed
1 coconut, grated
1 L (1¾ pints) water
1 teaspoon salt
225 g (8 oz) tamarind
250 ml (8 fl oz) water
120 g (4 oz) palm sugar
4 tablespoons granulated sugar

Boil water in a deep pot to cook vegetables separately. First put in long beans. Remove after 2 minutes. Cook cabbage for 1 minute and beansprouts for ½ minute.

After removing beansprouts, put in water convolvulus and cook for 1 minute. At the end of this cooking time, stir in baking powder.

Heat oil in a wok. Deep-fry fermented soybean cakes and firm soybean pieces for 3 minutes each, separately. Remove to a dish.

Next, fry prawn crackers. Leave on absorbent paper. Fry sliced shallots till golden brown.

To serve Gado-Gado, place potato slices at the bottom of a serving dish, then cabbage, water convolvulus, long beans, cucumber, fermented soybean cake, beansprouts and firm soybean pieces.

Pour sauce over Gado-Gado and garnish with egg slices, fried shallots and crushed prawn crackers.

Sauce
If peanuts are being used, fry in a non-stick wok over moderate heat till dark brown. Rub off skin and pound coarsely.

Grill or toast dried shrimp paste for 2-3 minutes on each side, then pound or grind with steamed chillies.

Mix grated coconut and 1 L (1¾ pints) water. Squeeze and strain to obtain coconut milk. Stir in salt.

Mix tamarind and 250 ml (8 fl oz) water. Squeeze and strain to obtain juice.

Scrape palm sugar into an enamel pot. Add granulated sugar, shrimp and chilli paste, tamarind juice and half the peanut butter or pounded peanuts. Cook over moderate heat, stirring constantly for 4 minutes.

Stir in coconut milk, bring to a boil and simmer, stirring for 3 minutes.

Thicken sauce with remaining peanut butter or pounded peanuts. Season to taste.

Refrigerate for 2 hours before serving.

Note: Gado-Gado sauce can be kept refrigerated for at least a week. If too thick, add a little boiled water.

Roti Jala (Lacy Pancakes)

Preparation: 25 minutes
Cooking: 35 minutes

1 coconut, grated
350 ml (12 fl oz) water
225 g (8 oz) plain flour, sifted
4 eggs, beaten well
1½ teaspoons fine salt
2 teaspoons oil
Roti Jala mould
6 screwpine leaves (available in Chinese
   Supermarkets) cut into 5 × 3 cm (2 × 1¼ in)
   strips

Blend coconut with 120 ml (4 fl oz) water.
Squeeze and strain for thick coconut milk. Add
250 ml (8 fl oz) water to coconut milk residue,
squeeze and strain for thin coconut milk.

Pour flour into a bowl and make a well in the
centre. Pour thin coconut milk and beaten eggs
into the well and gradually stir flour towards the
centre. Mix well.

Add salt and thick coconut milk and blend. Strain
if there are lumps. Test the consistency of the
batter by making one pancake first. Add a little
more water or flour if the batter is too thick or
too thin.

Heat the frying pan (preferably non-stick) and
brush with oil. When the pan is hot, pour in
batter through a Roti Jala mould, rotating it to
form a lacy pattern. Cook till set and stack on a
plate, putting pieces of screwpine leaf between
the pancakes.

Note: Roti Jala can be made hours in advance and
heated in the oven just before serving. It is eaten
with Dry Curry Chicken (p.22).

Sambal Timun

Preparation: 10 minutes
Cooking: 12 minutes

2 cucumbers
8 shallots, sliced thinly
¼ pineapple, cut into ½ cm (¼ in) wedges
2 teaspoons dried shrimp paste, roasted
6 red chillies
½ teaspoon salt
4 tablespoons vinegar
juice of 8 limes
2 teaspoons black shrimp paste
60 g (2 oz) dried prawns, pounded
5 teaspoons sugar

Quarter cucumbers lengthwise and remove soft
centre. Cut at a slant into ½ cm (¼ in) pieces.

Mix cucumbers, shallots and pineapple in a
bowl.

Pound dried shrimp paste, then add chillies and
salt and pound coarsely. Stir in vinegar, lime
juice, black shrimp paste and dried prawns.

Finally, add sugar and mix well. Refrigerate for
1-2 hours. Serve cold.

Chinese

Spare Ribs Cooked in Red Sauce

Preparation: 15 minutes
Cooking: 35 minutes

600 g (1⅓ lb) spare ribs
8 tablespoons sweet red sauce *or* barbecue sauce
1 tablespoon light soy sauce
4 tablespoons oil
6 cloves garlic, chopped
1 tablespoon black soy sauce
½ teaspoon pepper
2 teaspoons Tabasco sauce
300 ml (½ pint) water
½ teaspoon salt
3 onions, each cut into 6 wedges
2 green chillies, seeded and cut into long strips
1 sprig Chinese parsley *or* 2 stalks spring onion, cut
    into 2½ cm (1 in) lengths

Season spare ribs with 1 tablespoon sweet red sauce and light soy sauce. Set aside.

Heat oil in a wok and brown garlic. Add seasoned spare ribs and stir-fry for 3 minutes till fragrant.

Add black soy sauce, pepper, Tabasco and stir-fry for 15 minutes, adding water a little at a time till used up.

Stir in remaining sweet red sauce and salt and cook covered for another 2 minutes, then uncover and stir-fry for 8 minutes. If spare ribs are still not tender, add more water and cook longer.

Cook till sauce is thick, add onions and green chillies and remove to a serving dish.

Serve garnished with either Chinese parsley or spring onion.

Hokkien Special Braised Pork

Preparation: 15 minutes
Marinating: 30 minutes
Cooking: 1½ hours

600 g (1⅓ lb) pork (shoulder or trotter meat), cut
    into 2½ cm (1 in) cubes
2 tablespoons black soy sauce
3 tablespoons light soy sauce
4 tablespoons sugar
1 teaspoon pepper
4 tablespoons oil
12 cloves garlic, peeled and bashed
15-20 dried Chinese mushrooms, soaked in boiling
    water 15-20 minutes
10-15 cooked chestnuts, skin removed
extra sugar
extra light soy sauce

Marinate meat in black soy sauce, light soy sauce, sugar and pepper for 30 minutes.

Rub pepper onto the meat and set aside.

Heat oil in a wok and fry garlic for 1 minute over low heat. Add meat and stir-fry over moderate heat for a few minutes before adding Chinese mushrooms.

Add 120 ml (4 fl oz) water and, simmer, stirring frequently, till sauce is thick, then simmer till meat is tender, adding ½ cup water every now and then as it evaporates.

Add boiled chestnuts and black soy sauce. Season to taste with sugar and light soy sauce.

Serve with hot rice.

Note: This dish is a must in Hokkien homes. It tastes better if prepared a day before serving.

Pork with Sweet and Sour Sauce

Preparation: 25 minutes
Marinating: 20 minutes
Cooking: 15 minutes

600 g (1⅓ lb) pork tenderloin, pork chop *or* meat
    from front leg (*cheng twee*)
2 tablespoons light soy sauce
1 teaspoon black soy sauce
¾ teaspoon pepper
½ teaspoon bicarbonate of soda
2 tablespoons plain white flour
6 tablespoons tapioca flour
oil for deep-frying
2 eggs, beaten slightly
2 stalks Chinese celery, cut into 1 cm (½ in) lengths
2 stalks spring onion, cut into 1 cm (½ in) lengths

Sweet and Sour Sauce
2 onions
1 large cucumber
3 tomatoes
2 red chillies
1 tablespoon tapioca flour
350 ml (12 fl oz) water
1 tablespoon tomato sauce
2 teaspoons chilli sauce
2 tablespoons Chinese plum sauce *or* plum jam
1 tablespoon vinegar
2 tablespoons sugar
½ teaspoon salt
4 tablespoons oil
2 cloves garlic, chopped finely

Cut meat into 2½ × 1 cm (1 × ½ in) pieces. Marinate for 20 minutes with light soy sauce, black soy sauce, pepper, and bicarbonate of soda. Sift plain white flour and tapioca flour together into a bowl.

Heat oil in a wok for deep-frying. Dip meat in beaten eggs, then coat with mixed flour. Deep-fry in hot oil till meat turns golden brown. Remove and drain.

Put meat in a serving plate and pour hot sauce over it. Serve immediately, garnished with celery and spring onion.

Sweet and Sour Sauce
Slice onions into ½ cm (¼ in) thick rings. Cut cucumber into quarters lengthwise, then slice away the central pulp. Cut each length at a slant into 1 cm (½ in) pieces. Cut each tomato into 6 wedges. Halve chillies lengthwise, remove seeds and cut each half into 4-5 long strips.

Mix tapioca flour, water, tomato sauce, chilli sauce, plum sauce (or jam), vinegar, sugar and salt in a bowl.

Heat oil in a wok and fry chopped garlic, onions, cucumber, tomatoes and chillies for about 2 minutes. Pour in the sauce mixture and simmer for about 1 minute till gravy thickens.

Char Siew (Red Pork Roast)

Preparation: 10 minutes
Marinating: 1 hour
Roasting: 1 hour
Oven setting: 225°C, 425°F, Gas Regulo 9

600 g (1⅓ lb) pork (front trotter meat)
2 tablespoons light soy sauce
1 teaspoon black soy sauce
1 teaspoon salt
½ teaspoon red colouring powder diluted with 2
    tablespoons water
4 tablespoons thick syrup
3 tablespoons oil

Marinate meat in a mixture of all ingredients listed above, except oil, for at least one hour.

Cut meat into two long pieces and place in a roasting pan.

Brush oil on both sides of meat. Pour half of the marinade into the pan.

Roast for 45 minutes in a preheated oven, then remove and turn meat over. Pour remaining marinade over meat and roast for another 15 minutes at the same temperature.

Slice thinly and serve with Dried Noodles (p.107).

Crispy Pork Chops

Preparation: 10 minutes
Marinating: 30 minutes
Cooking: 12 minutes

900 g (2 lb) pork chops (8 or 9 pairs joined at one end)
1 teaspoon salt
3 tablespoons sugar
¾ teaspoon pepper
3 teaspoons black soy sauce
3 teaspoons light soy sauce
3 egg yolks and 2 egg whites, beaten together
280 g (10 oz) self-raising flour
20 or more cream crackers, pounded
oil for deep-frying
4 potatoes, cut into 3 mm (⅛ in) thick slices
4-5 tomatoes, halved crosswise
3 onions, chopped
8-9 round slices pineapple, 1 cm (½ in) thick
½ cup cooked green peas

Sauce
18 tablespoons tomato ketchup
½ teaspoon salt
2 teaspoons tapioca flour mixed with ¼ cup water
2 teaspoons sugar

Separate the chops into pieces. Marinate with salt, sugar, pepper, black soy sauce and light soy sauce for at least 30 minutes.

Mix flour and pounded biscuits. Dip pork chops in beaten eggs, coat with flour and biscuit crumb mixture. Dip once again in beaten eggs and give another coating of flour and biscuit crumbs.

Deep-fry chops in hot oil till golden brown. Drain in a sieve.

Filter the oil used for deep-frying and use to fry potato slices, tomato halves, chopped onions and pineapple rings separately.

Remove all but 2 tablespoons oil and add sauce ingredients. Bring to a boil, then add fried pineapple rings, chopped onion and cooked green peas. Turn off heat at once.

Spread pairs of pork chops on an oval serving plate and arrange potato slices and tomato halves around them. Carefully place one pineapple ring, with a little sauce, peas and chopped onion on each pair of pork chops. Serve immediately.

Pork with Bamboo Shoots and Mushrooms in Soy Sauce

Preparation: 15 minutes
Cooking: 25 minutes

6 dried Chinese mushrooms
120 ml (4 fl oz) boiling water
8 shallots
2 cloves garlic
8 tablespoons oil
1 tin (about 500 g/18 oz) winter bamboo shoot, shredded
300 g (10 oz) shoulder pork, sliced into 2½ cm (1 in) pieces about ½ cm (¼ in) thick
1 teaspoon sugar
¾ tin (about 170 g or 6 oz) mushroom sauce
120 ml (4 fl oz) water
2-3 teaspoons hot chilli sauce
1 onion, diced

Soak Chinese mushrooms in boiling water for 20 minutes (save 4 tbs of water after soaking), then cut into 1 cm (½ in) cubes. Keep mushroom water. Pound shallots and garlic.

Heat oil in a wok till it is smoking hot. Fry pounded shallots and garlic till soft, then add bamboo shoots and mushrooms. Cook for 5 minutes, then add 4 tablespoons mushroom water. Simmer till dry.

Add sliced pork and sugar and stir-fry for 4 minutes. Pour in half of the mushroom sauce and 120 ml (4 fl oz) water and simmer for 5 minutes. Add hot chilli sauce, remaining mushroom sauce and diced onion. Stir-fry till bamboo shoots are tender.

Ginger Beef with Cauliflower and Mange Tout

Preparation: 12 minutes
Marinating: 30 minutes
Cooking: 16 minutes

225 g (8 oz) beef tenderloin
1 tablespoon light soy sauce
1 teaspoon sugar
1 teaspoon tapioca flour
3 tablespoons water
1 tablespoon Chinese rice wine
½ teaspoon pepper
2 teaspoons oyster sauce
20 mange touts
7 tablespoons oil
225 g (8 oz) cauliflower, cut into bite-size pieces
1 teaspoon light soy sauce
10 slices ginger
½ carrot, cut into ½ cm (¼ in) thick slices
¼ teaspoon salt
120 ml (4 fl oz) water
225 g (8 oz) capsicum, cut into 1 cm (½ in) pieces
2 medium-sized tomatoes, quartered
1 onion, quartered

Slice tenderloin thinly and marinate for 30 minutes in light soy sauce, sugar, tapioca flour blended with 3 tablespoons water, rice wine, pepper and oyster sauce. String mange tout.

Heat 2 tablespoons of the oil in a wok and fry cauliflower for about 2 minutes. Sprinkle water as you fry to prevent it from looking shrivelled. Add light soy sauce and stir-fry till cauliflower is tender. Remove to a dish.

Next, fry ginger till crisp, then remove to a dish. Fry sliced carrot, adding 120 ml (4 fl oz) water and salt. Cook till tender.

In a clean wok, heat 1 tablespoon oil and fry capsicum. Remove to a dish.

Pour remaining oil into the wok and fry sea-soned beef for 2 minutes. Add mange tout, tomatoes, onion and cooked vegetables. Stir-fry briskly for 2 minutes and serve immediately.

Tenderloin in Oyster Sauce

Preparation: 7 minutes
Marinating: 30 minutes
Cooking: 5 minutes

900 g (2 lb) beef tenderloin, sliced thinly
1 tablespoon light soy sauce
2 tablespoons cornflour *or* tapioca flour
1 egg, beaten
¾ teaspoon sugar
½ teaspoon pepper
1 teaspoon ginger juice
1 teaspoon chilli sauce (more, if desired)
8 tablespoons oil
1 teaspoon chopped garlic
3-4 tablespoons oyster sauce
1½ teaspoons sugar
2 tablespoons Chinese rice wine *or* any red wine
7 stalks spring onion, chopped (use only the white portion)

Marinate beef for 30 minutes in a mixture of light soy sauce, cornflour (or tapioca flour), beaten egg, sugar, pepper, ginger juice and chilli sauce.

Heat oil in a wok and fry garlic for a few seconds. Add seasoned beef and stir constantly with a pair of wooden chopsticks to separate beef slices.

Add oyster sauce, sugar and rice wine (or red wine). Stir for half a minute, then add spring onion. Stir for another minute or two. Remove to a dish and serve immediately.

Chinese Style Fillet Steak

Preparation: 10 minutes
Marinating: 2 hours
Cooking: 12-15 minutes

900 g (2 lb) fillet steak
120 ml (4 fl oz) oil

Marinade

3 dessertspoons ginger juice
3 teaspoons Worcestershire sauce
2 dessertspoons light soy sauce
2 teaspoons HP sauce
2 tablespoons Chinese rice wine
3 dessertspoons lard or corn oil
1 teaspoon sesame oil
½ teaspoon mustard, blended with water to a paste
2 dessertspoons sago flour, tapioca flour *or* cornflour
¼ teaspoon pepper
½ teaspoon salt
2 teaspoons sugar
1 teaspoon bicarbonate of soda
2 dessertspoons cold water

Sauce
5 dessertspoons oxtail soup
6 dessertspoons tomato ketchup
1 dessertspoon Worcestershire sauce
1 dessertspoon HP sauce
½ teaspoon sesame oil
2 teaspoons sago flour, tapioca flour *or* cornflour
1½ teaspoons sugar
¼ teaspoon salt

Cut meat into thin slices and marinate in ingredients listed for at least 2 hours in the refrigerator. Turn slices of meat after 1 hour.

Heat 120 ml (4 fl oz) oil in frying pan and fry seasoned meat, taking care not to overcook.

Cook sauce and pour over steak just before serving. If desired, 2 or 3 eggs could be fried sunny side up and placed on meat.

Cantonese Tender Beef with Mixed Vegetables

Preparation: 12 minutes
Marinating: 30 minutes
Cooking: 8-10 minutes

340 g (12 oz) fillet steak, sliced thinly
1 tablespoon oyster sauce
2 tablespoons Chinese rice wine
1 teaspoon pepper
1 teaspoon sugar
¾ teaspoon sesame oil
1 teaspoon tapioca flour
1 tablespoon water
6 tablespoons lard
15 champignons, each halved
10 young corn cobs (tinned or frozen)
3 cloves garlic, chopped
2½ cm (1 in) piece ginger, sliced thinly
200 g (7 oz) capsicum, cut into 8 segments
2 red chillies, halved lengthwise, seeded, then cut
   into thin long strips
3 teaspoons light soy sauce
½ teaspoon pepper

Marinate beef for 30 minutes in a mixture of oyster sauce, rice wine, pepper, sugar, sesame oil, tapioca flour and water.

Heat 2 tablespoons lard in a wok and fry champignons and young corn together for 2 minutes. Push them to one side of the wok, add 1 tablespoon lard to the bottom of the wok and fry garlic for half a minute, then stir-fry ginger for another half a minute. Add capsicum and chillies and fry for another minute.

Mix all the vegetables together, add light soy sauce. Stir briskly and remove to a serving plate.

In a clean wok, heat remaining 3 tablespoons lard and fry seasoned beef for 2 minutes till just tender. Scatter meat evenly over fried vegetables, sprinkle pepper and serve immediately.

Crispy Five-Spice Chicken

Preparation: 10 minutes
Marinating: 30 minutes
Cooking: 17 minutes

1 chicken, about 1¼ kg (3 lb), cut into bite-size
    pieces
2 tablespoons light soy sauce
1 tablespoon Chinese rice wine *or* dry sherry
½ tablespoon salt
2 tablespoons sugar
1 teaspoon five-spice powder
1 tablespoon cornflour
oil for deep-frying
2 eggs, beaten lightly
8 tablespoons cornflour (more, if required)

Mix chicken pieces with light soy sauce, rice
wine, salt, sugar, five-spice powder, and cornflour. Leave in marinade for about 30 minutes.

Heat oil in a deep pan till smoking hot. Dip
marinated chicken pieces in beaten egg, then
coat evenly with cornflour. Deep-fry chicken till
golden brown in two separate batches.

Ginger Chicken Wings Cooked in Rough Salt

Preparation: 15 minutes
Marinating: 2 hours
Cooking: 20 minutes

12 large chicken wings, weighing about 900 g (2 lb)
12 stalks spring onion, chopped
2 tablespoons oyster sauce
2 tablespoons black soy sauce
2 tablespoons ginger wine
3 tablespoons ginger juice from a 10 cm (4 in) piece
    ginger
1 teaspoon sesame oil
2 tablespoons lard
2 tablespoons sugar
½ teaspoon salt
1-2 big pieces greaseproof paper
4½ kg (10 lb) rock salt

Marinate chicken wings in a marinade of chopped spring onion, oyster sauce, black soy sauce,
ginger wine, ginger juice, sesame oil, lard, sugar
and salt. Leave chicken in marinade for at least 2
hours, the longer the better.

Cut greaseproof paper according to the
measurements given in the diagram. Sun en-
velopes for 10 minutes, then pack chicken wings
into them. Seal down the side flaps.

Heat a wok and fry rough salt till hot. This takes
about 10-15 minutes over high heat. Keep
stirring the salt so that it warms evenly. Cover
paper-wrapped chicken in salt for 20 minutes.
Serve chicken wings hot in their wrappers.

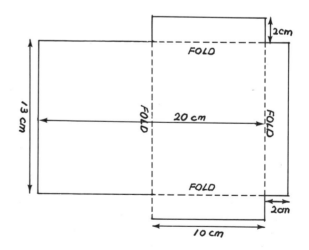

Paper-wrapped Chicken

Preparation: 15 minutes
Marinating: 2 hours
Cooking: 6 minutes

1½ kg (3⅓ lb) chicken
1 tablespoon light soy sauce
2 teaspoons black soy sauce
1 teaspoon brandy *or* 1 tablespoon rice wine
1 tablespoon lard oil
a few drops sesame oil
1 tablespoon oyster sauce
2 teaspoons sago flour
¼ teaspoon salt
¾ teaspoon pepper
2 sheets cellophane or greaseproof paper
oil for deep-frying

Cut chicken into small pieces and marinate for 2 hours in a mixture of all ingredients listed except oil for deep-frying.

Cut paper into 10 cm (4 in) squares. Wrap pieces of chicken in paper. Tuck loose ends in securely.

Deep-fry in two lots for 3 minutes each time. Drain and serve in wrappings.

Chicken with Pineapple

Preparation: 22 minutes
Cooking: 25 minutes

10 tablespoons tomato ketchup
4 teaspoons Tabasco sauce
1 tablespoon black soy sauce
1 tablespoon light soy sauce
3 tablespoons Chinese rice wine
2 tablespoons sugar
4 tablespoons oil
6 slices ginger, shredded
6 shallots, sliced thinly
900 g (2 lb) chicken, cut into bite-size pieces
250 ml (8 fl oz) water
3 tomatoes, each cut into 6 wedges
3 onions, each cut into 6 wedges
3 round pineapple slices, canned or fresh, each cut into 8 pieces
2 sprays Chinese parsley, chopped *or* 3 stalks spring onion cut into 2½ cm (1 in) lengths

Mix the following in a bowl: tomato ketchup, Tabasco sauce, black soy sauce, light soy sauce, rice wine and sugar.

Heat oil in a wok and stir-fry ginger and shallots for about 2 minutes till crisp, then add chicken. Stir continuously for 5-6 minutes.

Pour in prepared sauce mixture and continue stir-frying for 10 minutes, adding 250 ml (8 fl oz) water while cooking.

Add tomatoes, onions and pineapple slices. Fry for 3 minutes. When chicken is tender, add either Chinese parsley or spring onion and remove to a dish.

Cold Chicken with Peanut Butter Sauce

Preparation: 20 minutes
Cooking: 30 minutes

5.75 L (10½ pints) water, boiled
1 chicken, about 1½ kg (3⅓ lb)
2 tablespoons sugar
10 tablespoons water
340 g (12 oz) crunchy peanut butter
½ teaspoon sesame oil
¼ teaspoon salt
10 lettuce leaves
3-4 tomatoes, sliced

Bring 5.75 L (10½ pints) water to a boil in a deep pot. Plunge chicken into water and cover for 15-20 minutes.

Submerge cooked chicken in cold water for 5 minutes.

Skin and shred chicken. Refrigerate shredded meat for 30 minutes or more.

Dissolve sugar in 10 tablespoons water. Blend with peanut butter, sesame oil and salt.

Steam sauce for 6-8 minutes.

Cool sauce and mix with cold chicken. Place on a bed of lettuce and tomato slices and serve with Chinese pickles.

Chicken with Celery and Carrot

Preparation: 20 minutes
Marinating: 20 minutes
Cooking: 15 minutes

450 g (1 lb) chicken breastmeat
2 teaspoons light soy sauce
¾ teaspoon sugar
½ teaspoon salt
2 teaspoons red wine
2 teaspoons oyster sauce
1 teaspoon cornflour *or* tapioca flour
225 g (8 oz) celery
420 ml (¾ pint) water
¼ teaspoon salt
1 big carrot
350 ml (12 fl oz) water
1 chicken bouillon cube
250 ml (8 fl oz) water
1 teaspoon cornflour *or* tapioca flour
5 tablespoons oil
4 cloves garlic, chopped
½ teaspoon salt
½ teaspoon sugar
1 tablespoon Chinese rice wine *or* red wine

Slice meat into 2½ × 1 cm (1 × ½ in) slices and marinate for 20 minutes in light soy sauce, sugar, salt, red wine, oyster sauce, and cornflour or tapioca flour.

Remove leaves and roots of celery and cut stalks into 1 cm (½ in) slices at a slant. Boil in 420 ml (¾ pint) water with ¼ teaspoon salt for 3 minutes. Drain.

Cut carrot int 2 mm (1/16 in) thick slices and use biscuit cutters to give the slices leaf or flower patterns. Boil in 350 ml (12 fl oz) water for 5 minutes. Drain.

Dissolve chicken bouillon cube in 250 ml (8 fl oz) water and blend with cornflour (or tapioca flour).

Heat 3 tablespoons of the oil in a wok and add half the garlic. When brown, add chicken and stir-fry for 7 minutes. Remove to a serving plate.

Add remaining oil to the wok and brown the rest of the garlic. Add celery and carrot, stir-fry for 1 minute, then add salt, sugar, rice wine (or. red wine) and the chicken bouillon and flour mixture. Bring to a boil and quickly pour over chicken in the serving plate. Serve hot.

Ginger Chicken

Preparation: 15 minutes
Marinating: 15 minutes
Cooking: 16 minutes

1 chicken weighing about 1¾ kg (4 lb), *or* 5 chicken
    thighs and drumsticks
1 tablespoon oyster sauce
2 tablespoons light soy sauce
1 tablespoon black soy sauce
3 tablespoons Chinese rice wine
4 teaspoons sugar
5 tablespoons oil
5 × 2½ cm (2 × 1 in) piece ginger, shredded
1 teaspoon sesame oil
1 teaspoon finely chopped garlic
120 ml (4 fl oz) water

Chop chicken into bite-size pieces and marinate in a mixture of oyster sauce, light soy sauce, black soy sauce, rice wine and sugar for 15 minutes.

Heat 5 tablespoons oil in a wok and stir-fry ginger for 1 minute. Drip sesame oil in along the side of the wok. Stir ginger quickly, add garlic and stir for another minute to brown lightly.

Put in chicken pieces and marinating sauce. Stir-fry chicken for 5 minutes to bring out the seasoning flavour, especially of sesame oil and wine. After 5 minutes, add water and cook covered for 3 minutes. Uncover and stir-fry till sauce is almost dry and chicken just cooked.

Note: If frozen thighs and drumsticks are used, thaw out first, then use a fork to prick the meat deeply on both sides of the bone to allow the sauce to soak through while cooking.

Peking Duck

Preparation: 45 minutes
Cooking: 1¼ hours

1 duck, about 1¾ kg (4 lb)
10 stalks spring onion
10 thin slices ginger
¼ teaspoon salt
½ teaspoon pepper
1 teaspoon sugar
10 cloves garlic, bashed
10 cummin seeds, pounded
15 fennel seeds
4 star anise
2 tablespoons light soy sauce
¼ teaspoon five-spice powder
oil for deep-frying

Sauce
2 tablespoons preserved soy beans
2 teaspoons black soy sauce
1 teaspoon sesame oil
1 tablespoon water
3 tablespoons sugar

Pickled Vegetables
2 cucumbers
¼ teaspoon salt
1 small carrot
2 red chillies
3 tablespoons white vinegar
3 tablespoons sugar
1 teaspoon salt

Crush 5 stalks spring onion and stuff into duck with 5 slices ginger.

Rub both inside and outside of duck with salt and pepper and sugar.

Place duck in a shallow heatproof dish and spread remaining spring onion and ginger, together with garlic, cummin seeds, fennel seeds and star anise around duck.

Steam duck for an hour or till tender. Cool and drain well, then rub with light soy sauce and five-spice powder.

Heat oil in a wok till smoking hot. Turn off heat, wait a few seconds then slide duck into hot oil.

Turn on heat again and ladle hot oil over duck. Fry evenly till brown. Turn off heat if oil gets too hot.

Cut into bite-size pieces and serve with sauce and pickled vegetables in separate dishes.

Sauce
Blend all sauce ingredients together till smooth, then steam mixture for 10 minutes.

Pickled Vegetables
Quarter cucumbers lengthwise, remove soft centre and cut into strips or thin slices. Rub in salt.

Cut carrot into 3 lengthwise, then slice thinly. Cut chillies into long strips. Discard seeds.

Season these vegetables in white vinegar, sugar and salt a day before serving.

Oyster Prawns

Preparation: 10 minutes
Cooking: 8 minutes

600 g (1⅓ lb) large prawns (use the type with thin black transparent shells)
10 tablespoons oil
4 cloves garlic, chopped
4 tablespoons oyster sauce
3 tablespoons Chinese rice wine
3 teaspoons sugar
½ teaspoon pepper
4 tablespoons water
2 stalks spring onion, chopped (use only the green part)
1 French loaf

Fry prawns in 5 tablespoons hot oil in a wok till they turn red. Remove and drain.

Heat remaining 5 tablespoons oil in a wok and brown garlic. Add oyster sauce, Chinese rice wine, sugar, pepper and water. As soon as the mixture starts to simmer, add prawns and stir-fry quickly till prawns are cooked.

Garnish with spring onion and serve with chunky slices of French loaf.

Ginger Beef with Cauliflower and Mange Tout (p.39)

Crispy Pork Chops (p.38)

Crystal Prawns with Asparagus (p. 49)

48 Cold Dish. Clockwise from top: Century Eggs, White Cut Chicken (from Hainanese Chicken Rice, p.128), Golden Quail's Eggs (p.57), "Kai Guen" (p.57), Asparagus rolled in Ham, and Chinese Restaurant Style Pickles (p.138). Centre, Cold Prawns in Aspic (p.56)

Crystal Prawns with Asparagus

Preparation: 15 minutes
Marinating: 30 minutes
Cooking: 8 minutes

600 g (1⅓ lb) large prawns
¾ teaspoon bicarbonate of soda
⅓ teaspoon salt
1 teaspoon sugar
2 egg whites, beaten
1 tin (about 425 g or 15 oz) asparagus
oil for deep-frying
1 chicken bouillon cube
120 ml (4 fl oz) boiling water
4 teaspoons oyster sauce
1 tablespoon Chinese rice wine
½ teaspoon sugar
½ teaspoon salt
3 teaspoons cornflour or tapioca flour
4 tablespoons water

Shell and devein prawns, leaving tails behind. Marinate prawns in a mixture of bicarbonate of soda, salt, sugar and egg white.

Arrange asparagus in a circle on a serving plate, with the tips on the outside.

Heat oil in a wok and deep-fry prawns for 3 minutes or till cooked. Remove, drain and pile in the centre of the plate, so that prawns are encircled by asparagus.

Add chicken bouillon cube to boiling water and mix in oyster sauce, Chinese rice wine, sugar and salt. Bring to a boil, simmer for 3 minutes, then add cornflour or tapioca flour blended with 4 tablespoons water to thicken the sauce. Stir briskly, cook for 2 more minutes till quite thick and pour sauce over prawns and asparagus. Serve at once.

Crispy Prawn Fritters

Preparation: 10 minutes
Cooking: 15-18 minutes

600 g (1⅓ lb) large prawns (there should be about 12)
4 tablespoons self-raising flour
10 tablespoons rice flour
1 teaspoon baking powder
½ teaspoon sugar
¼ teaspoon salt
250 ml (8 fl oz) water
½ teaspoon Tabasco sauce
oil for deep-frying
2 cucumbers, peeled and sliced thinly
2 tomatoes, sliced thinly

Hot Chilli Dip
4 tablespoons garlic-flavoured chilli sauce
juice of 1 lemon or 5 limes, *or* 1 teaspoon white vinegar
2 tablespoons sugar
2 tablespoons Chinese plum sauce or apricot jam
pinch of salt

Peel off shells of prawns, leaving tails behind. Devein the prawns.

Sift self-raising flour, rice flour and baking powder into a large bowl. Mix thoroughly with sugar and salt. Make a well in the centre and gradually pour in 250 ml (8 fl oz) water. Work continuously till water and flour are well blended. If there are tiny lumps, sieve. Add Tabasco sauce to batter and mix well.

Heat oil in a wok. Dip prawns in thick batter and deep-fry till golden brown. Drain away excess oil with absorbent paper or place prawns on a wire rack for a few minutes.

Place prawns on a serving plate and decorate the edge with alternating slices of cucumber and tomato. Serve with Hot Chilli Dip.

Hot Chilli Dip
Mix the ingredients for the chilli dip and serve in a separate bowl with Crispy Prawn Fritters.

Prawns with Toasted Almonds

Preparation: 7 minutes
Marinating: 15 minutes
Cooking: 10 minutes

20 toasted almonds, halved
600 g (1⅓ lb) large prawns
2 teaspoons oyster sauce
½ teaspoon Worcestershire sauce
2 tablespoons Chinese rice wine
¼ teaspoon sesame oil
½ teaspoon pepper
1 teaspoon sugar
9 tablespoons tomato ketchup
1 teaspoon tapioca flour
6 tablespoons water
1 tablespoon sugar
5 tablespoons oil
1 teaspoon chopped garlic
2 stalks spring onion, chopped
2 tablespoons cooked green peas

If untoasted almonds are used, scald in boiling water and allow to soak for 15 minutes. Peel off skin and toast in the oven for 30 minutes till crisp. Almonds should be toasted a day earlier and stored in a clean airtight bottle.

Cut off feelers of prawns and marinate in oyster sauce, Worcestershire sauce, rice wine, sesame oil, pepper and sugar for 15 minutes.

Mix tomato ketchup, tapioca flour, water and sugar in a bowl.

Heat oil in a wok. When smoking hot, add garlic and stir-fry till light brown. Fry seasoned prawns for 3 minutes, then pour in the prepared sauce in the bowl. Stir for a few minutes, then scoop up the prawns with sauce onto a serving plate.

Garnish with spring onion and green peas. Sprinkle toasted almonds over and serve immediately.

Cuttlefish in Soy Sauce

Preparation: 8 minutes
Cooking: 9 minutes

450 g (1 lb) fairly big cuttlefish, about 10 cm (4 in) long
8 tablespoons oil
3 cloves garlic, chopped
2 onions, cut into ½ cm (¼ in) thick rings
1½-2 tablespoons black soy sauce
½ teaspoon salt
1½ teaspoons sugar
2 tomatoes, each cut into 6 wedges
¾ teaspoon pepper

Remove head and tentacles from the body of the cuttlefish. Remove ink sac and the transparent bone. Wash thoroughly and cut into 2½ cm (1 in) rings. Drain in a colander.

Heat a wok till smoking hot, add oil and fry garlic for a few seconds, quickly stir-fry onions for half a minute, then add cuttlefish.

After 3 minutes, add seasoning of black soy sauce, salt and sugar. Cook covered for 1 minute, then uncover and add tomato wedges. Stir-fry for 2 more minutes and quickly remove to a dish. Over-cooking toughens cuttlefish.

Sprinkle with pepper and serve with rice.

Crabmeat in Milk

Preparation: 25 minutes
Cooking: 8 minutes

3 big crabs weighing a total of 1¼ kg (3 lb) *or* 450 g
    (1 lb) cooked crabmeat
2.25 L (4 pints) water
300 ml (½ pint) fresh milk
2 tablespoons cornflour
2 egg whites
7 tablespoons oil
4 cloves garlic, chopped
300 g (10 oz) small prawns, shelled
60 g (2 oz) ham, chopped
100 g (3⅓ oz) green peas, scalded for 2 minutes in
    boiling water
salt and pepper to taste

If using live crabs, clean them thoroughly
(p.169). Boil crabs in 2.25 L (4 pints) water for
about 20 minutes, making sure that water is at
least 5 cm (2 in) above the crabs. Drain, cool,
then crack claws and legs with a pestle or the
back of a chopper. Remove meat.

Mix 3 tablespoons of the fresh milk with
cornflour, then blend with egg whites, crabmeat
and the rest of the milk.

Heat oil in a frying pan, fry garlic till brown then
stir-fry prawns for about 2 minutes. Quickly add
ham and crabmeat blended in milk with the
other ingredients. Stir briskly to break up the
crabmeat and add the green peas. Season. Serve
immediately.

Fu Yong Hai (Crabmeat Omelette)

Preparation: 20 minutes
Cooking: 5 minutes

225 g (8 oz) flaked crabmeat (sold in packets) or
    225 g (8 oz) crabmeat obtained from 3 medium-
    sized crabs weighing 700 g (1½ lb)
7 eggs
½ teaspoon salt
¾ teaspoon pepper
½ teaspoon sesame oil
3 teaspoons light soy sauce
9 tablespoons oil, preferably lard
a few lettuce leaves
2 stalks spring onion, chopped (use only the white
    portion)

If preparing the crabmeat, kill crabs and boil for
25 minutes. Crack shell and extract crabmeat
(see p.169 for method).

Beat eggs with salt, pepper, sesame oil and light
soy sauce. Mix seasoned eggs and cooked
crabmeat.

Heat oil in a flat frying pan, pour in egg and
crabmeat mixture and stir-fry for 3 minutes,
taking care not to overcook the omelette which
then becomes tough. Break up the omelette with
a spatula or a pair of chopsticks.

Put omelette on a plate lined with lettuce leaves
and sprinkle spring onion on top.

Sweet Sour Fish

Preparation: 30 minutes
Cooking: 20 minutes

1 Grouper or Sea Bass about 1¾ kg (4 lb)
¾ teaspoon salt
1 teaspoon pepper
340 g (12 oz) sago flour
120 g (4 oz) plain flour
2 eggs beaten
oil for deep-frying
3 stalks spring onion, cut into 2½ cm (1 in) lengths

Sweet Sour Sauce
1 cucumber
3 big onions
2 red chillies
4 tablespoons vinegar
3 tablespoons sugar
3 tablespoons oil
1 teaspoon chopped garlic
3 tomatoes
8 slices pickled ginger, shredded
8 round slices tinned pineapple, each cut into 6
   wedges
150 ml (¼ pint) tomato ketchup
60 ml (2 fl oz) syrup (from the tin of pineapple)
2 tablespoons sago flour or tapioca flour
300 ml (½ pint) water

Make 3 or 4 deep diagonal slashes on both sides of fish after seasoning with salt and pepper.

Sift sago flour and plain flour. Coat fish with beaten eggs then dredge them thoroughly with flour, pressing some into the cuts made.

Deep-fry fish on both sides till crisp. Remove to an oval serving dish, pour sauce on top and garnish with spring onion.

Sweet Sour Sauce
Halve cucumber lengthwise, remove soft centre and cut at a slant into 1 cm (½ in) slices. Quarter onions and cut chillies into long thin strips.

Pickle cucumber, onions and chillies in vinegar and sugar for at least 30 minutes.

Heat oil in a wok and brown garlic. Add pickled vegetables, tomatoes, pickled ginger and pineapple. Stir-fry for 2 minutes.

Pour in tomato ketchup, syrup and flour mixed with 300 ml (½ pint) water. Stir till thick.

Steamed Mushrooms and Chicken Wings

Preparation: 10 minutes
Marinating: 30 minutes
Cooking: 1 hour

20 dried Chinese Mushrooms
350 ml (12 fl oz) boiling water
450 g (1 lb) chicken wings
1 teaspoon salt
⅓ teaspoon pepper
½ teaspoon sesame oil
2 tablespoons Chinese rice wine
6 slices ginger, shredded
boiling water for steaming pot

Cut off mushroom stalks and soak in boiling water. Leave to soak overnight. Retain water.

Cut each chicken wing into 2 pieces and marinate in salt, pepper, sesame oil, rice wine and ginger.

Fill a Chinese porcelain steaming pot with seasoned chicken wings and mushrooms, add mushroom stock and sufficient boiling water to half-fill the pot. Place the pot in a steamer and steam for 1 hour. Place the pot on a plate when serving.

Fried French Beans and Cauliflower

Preparation: 12 minutes
Cooking: 16-20 minutes

7 tablespoons oil
300 g (10 oz) cauliflower, cut into bite-size pieces
1 medium-sized carrot, cut into ½ cm (¼ in) thick
  slices
120 ml (4 fl oz) water
4 cloves garlic, chopped
20 French beans, each sliced into 3 pieces at a slant
3 tablespoons water
225 g (8 oz) pork fillet, sliced thinly across the grain
1 teaspoon salt
1 teaspoon light soy sauce
½ teaspoon sugar
300 g (10 oz) medium-sized prawns, shelled
3-4 tomatoes, each cut into 6 wedges
2 onions, quartered

Heat 2 tablespoons oil in a wok and stir-fry cauliflower and carrot for 1 minute. Add 120 ml (4 fl oz) water and simmer for about 3 minutes till vegetables are cooked. Remove to a dish.

Add remaining oil to the wok and brown garlic. Add French beans and sprinkle in 3 tablespoons water while frying.

After 2 minutes, add pork, salt, soy sauce and sugar. Stir-fry for 5 minutes before adding prawns, tomatoes and onions.

Stir-fry for 1 minute, add cooked cauliflower and carrot, stir well for another minute and serve hot.

Stuffed Vegetable Marrow

Preparation: 15 minutes
Cooking: 40 minutes

340 g (12 oz) vegetable marrow
6-8 large dried Chinese mushrooms, soaked
some toothpicks
½ teaspoon pepper
2 stalks spring onion, chopped

Stuffing
225 g (8 oz) minced pork
¼ teaspoon pepper
½ teaspoon salt
1 teaspoon light soy sauce
½ teaspoon sugar
3 teaspoons tapioca flour
1 egg, beaten
2 tablespoons breadcrumbs

Sauce
1 chicken bouillon cube
 250 ml (8 fl oz) warm water
1 tablespoon light soy sauce
2 teaspoons sugar
¼ teaspoon salt
1 teaspoon tapioca flour
2 tablespoons lard
2 cloves garlic, chopped finely

Scrape vegetable marrow. Cut each marrow into half crosswise, then cut about 2½ cm (1 in) off each rounded end. Scoop out pulp and seeds from centre.

Stand marrows on a flat plate and fill with meat stuffing. Invert a Chinese mushroom over each opening and stick to the marrow with two toothpicks. Steam for about 15-20 minutes till marrows are cooked and tender.

When sauce is ready, pour over marrows and garnish with pepper and spring onion.

Stuffing
Mix minced meat with pepper, salt, light soy sauce and sugar in a large bowl. Use your hand to knead meat for 1 minute, then scoop up the meat and throw it down into the bowl with some force. Repeat this about 5 or 6 times. Add tapioca flour, beaten egg and breadcrumbs. Knead, scoop up and throw a few more times till ingredients are well mixed.

Sauce
In a bowl, dissolve bouillon cube in 120 ml (4 fl oz) warm water, then add remaining water, light soy sauce, sugar and salt.

Blend tapioca flour with a little of the bouillon mixture in a cup and pour in the contents of the bowl. Stir briskly for 1 minute and turn off heat when sauce thickens.

Beansprouts and Mushrooms

Preparation: 18 minutes
Cooking: 12 minutes

4 dried Chinese mushrooms
6 tablespoons oil
½ chicken bouillon cube
250 ml (8 fl oz) warm water
2 cloves garlic, chopped
600 g (1⅓ lb) beansprouts, cut off two ends
200 g (6⅔ oz) roast pork, shredded
2 red chillies, halved lengthwise, seeded and cut into
    thin strips
½ teaspoon salt
¾ teaspoon sugar
¼ teaspoon pepper
½ teaspoon sesame oil
1 tablespoon Chinese rice wine

Soak mushrooms in boiling water for 20 minutes. Squeeze out water and slice into 2 mm slices.

Heat 2 tablespoons oil in a wok, fry shredded mushrooms for a minute, then add half a chicken bouillon cube dissolved in warm water. Simmer over low heat for 10 minutes or longer till dry. Remove to a dish.

Heat remaining oil, brown garlic, then add beansprouts, mushrooms, roast pork and chillies with seasoning of salt, sugar, pepper, sesame oil and rice wine. Stir-fry for 2 minutes, taking care not to overcook beansprouts. This is best served immediately.

Soybean Sprouts with Prawns

Preparation: 12 minutes
Cooking: 6 minutes

4 tablespoons oil
3 cloves garlic, chopped
150 g (5 oz) minced pork
600 g (1⅓ lb) soybean sprouts, roots cut off (only
    available in Chinese Supermarkets)
½ teaspoon salt
2 tablespoons light soy sauce
300 g (10 oz) small prawns, shelled
2 tablespoons water

Heat oil in a wok and brown garlic. Add minced pork, stir-fry for 1 minute, then add soybean sprouts and stir-fry for another 2 minutes.

Add salt, and light soy sauce. After 1 minute, push contents of the wok to one side and add prawns to the bottom of the wok. Cover prawns with soybean sprouts and other ingredients.

Cook covered for 2 minutes. If too dry, sprinkle 2 tablespoons of water over the vegetable, while they are cooking.

Bittergourd with Preserved Soy Beans

Preparation: 12 minutes
Cooking: 13 minutes

300 g (10 oz) bittergourd
¼ teaspoon salt
3 tablespoons oil
2 cloves garlic, chopped
1 teaspoon preserved soy beans, pounded
½ teaspoon sugar
½ teaspoon pepper
225 g (8 oz) fillet steak, shredded
225 g (8 oz) small prawns, shelled
1 red chilli, halved lengthwise and seeded
2 tablespoons water

Halve bittergourd lengthwise and remove seeds. Cut into 2 mm slices at a slant. Run salt into bittergourd slices.

Heat oil in a wok and brown garlic, then add preserved soy beans and stir for 1½ minutes before adding bittergourd, sugar, and pepper.

After stir-frying for 8 minutes, add meat and prawns. Stir-fry for another 3½ minutes, sprinkling in water if bittergourd gets too dry.

Cucumber with Minced Pork

Preparation: 8 minutes
Cooking: 10 minutes

3 cucumbers
4 tablespoons oil
3 cloves garlic, chopped
200 g (6⅔ oz) minced pork
4 tablespoons water
2 tablespoons light soy sauce
½ teaspoon salt
200 g (6⅔ oz) small prawns, shelled
½ teaspoon pepper

Slice 2½ cm (1 in) off both ends of each cucumber. Rub the cut ends together to bring up the sap.

Quarter each cucumber lengthwise and cut off the soft centres. Cut cucumber quarters at a slant into 5 cm (2 in) lengths.

Heat oil in a wok, brown garlic, then add minced pork and cucumber. Stir-fry for 5 minutes till cucumber is half-cooked.

Add water, light soy sauce and salt. Cook covered for 2 minutes, then remove cover and stir-fry till cucumber is soft. Add prawns and cook for another 2 minutes.

Sprinkle with pepper just before serving.

Tender Long Beans

Preparation: 13 minutes
Cooking: 10 minutes

2 tablespoons light soy sauce
½ teaspoon salt
½ teaspoon pepper
1 teaspoon sugar
6 tablespoons oil
2 shallots, pounded
2 cloves garlic, pounded
200 g (6⅔ oz) dried prawns, pounded
225 g (8 oz) minced beef or pork
20 long beans, cut into 5 cm (2 in) lengths
½ teaspoon ground chilli
250 ml (8 fl oz) water

Mix the soy sauce, salt, pepper and sugar in a cup.

Heat oil in a wok and fry pounded shallots and garlic together for 2 minutes. Add dried prawns, stir-fry for 1 minute, then add minced beef or pork, long beans and ground chilli. Stir-fry for 3 minutes, pour in water and cook uncovered.

After 2 minutes, remove cover, stir for 2 more minutes, then add mixed seasoning ingredients. Stir and simmer till long beans are dry and tender.

Fried Spinach

Preparation: 14 minutes
Cooking: 6 minutes

600 g (1⅓ lb) spinach
4 tablespoons lard
2 cloves garlic, chopped
250 ml (8 fl oz) water
½ teaspoon salt
300 g (10 oz) small prawns, shelled

Pluck the leaves from the stalks. Peel off transparent skin of stalks and cut into 2½ cm (1 in) lengths. Discard tough portions of stalk near the roots.

Wash leaves and stalks separately and drain in 2 colanders.

Heat lard in a wok till smoking hot. Brown garlic, then add stalks. Stir-fry for half a minute, then add water to cook stalks. When dry, add salt and prawns. Cook for another 2 minutes, then add leaves. Stir constantly for 2 minutes to cook leaves till soft.

Fried Chye Sim

Preparation: 15 minutes
Marinating: 15 minutes
Cooking: 8 minutes

600 g (1⅓ lb) mustard greens (*chye sim*)
15 medium-sized prawns
150 g (5 oz) pork tenderloin or meat from front leg
1 teaspoon light soy sauce
1 teaspoon oyster sauce
½ teaspoon sugar
½ teaspoon pepper
½ teaspoon tapioca flour
1 cm (½ in) piece ginger
6 tablespoons oil
2 cloves garlic, chopped
120 ml (4 fl oz) water
⅓ teaspoon salt
½ teaspoon tapioca flour
4 tablespoons water

Cut vegetable into 5 cm (2 in) lengths. Separate stalks from leaves. Shell and devein prawns, leaving tails.

Slice meat thinly and season for 15 minutes with light soy sauce, oyster sauce, sugar, pepper and ½ teaspoon tapioca flour.

Smash ginger lightly with the side of a cleaver.

Heat 3 tablespoons oil in a wok. Fry ginger for ½ minute, then brown garlic. Add vegetable stalks and stir-fry for 1 minute. Add 120 ml (4 fl oz) water and simmer for 1 minute before adding leaves and salt. When stalks are tender and leaves cooked, remove to a serving dish.

In a clean wok, heat remaining 3 tablespoons oil and fry seasoned meat for 2 minutes. Add prawns. When meat and prawns are cooked, add tapioca flour blended with 4 tablespoons water. Cook for ½ minute till thick. Pour this sauce over the cooked vegetable and serve.

Cold Prawns in Aspic

Preparation: 30 minutes
Cooking: 15 minutes

6 large prawns
2 tomatoes
1 tablespoon green peas
12 asparagus spears
2½ teaspoons gelatin
4 tablespoons cold water
300 ml (½ pint) hot water
1 chicken bouillon cube

Steam prawns for 10-12 minutes until red, then peel and halve lengthwise.

Cut tomatoes into 1 cm (½ in) thick rings. Cook green peas in boiling water and drain.

Cut asparagus into 4 cm (1½ in) pieces, leaving the rest to be used as a garnish.

Mix gelatin with cold water to a thin paste. Then, while stirring, pour in hot water. Add chicken bouillon cube. Set aside to cool slightly.

Place peas grouped together at the bottom of a noodle bowl. Arrange prawns, tomato half-rings and asparagus decoratively in a complete circle around the side of the bowl.

Spoon gelatin into bowl to cover this layer, taking care not to "float" or dislodge the ingredients.

Repeat with another circle of prawns, tomato and asparagus, followed by gelatin till top of bowl is reached.

Arrange remaining tomato and cut asparagus in gelatin in centre of bowl.

Place bowl on a saucer and refrigerate for 45 minutes. When set, tilt the bowl and gently ease out aspic mould.

Use as a centrepiece of a Chinese *lam poon* (cold dish) surrounded by garnishes and other cold dish items.

"Kai Guen" (Fried "Chicken" Rolls)

Preparation: 15 minutes
Marinating: 30 minutes
Cooking: 25 minutes

14 thin slices pork chop
1 tablespoon Chinese rice wine
1 teaspoon sugar
1 tablespoon light soy sauce
2 teaspoons black soy sauce
1 teaspoon oyster sauce
½ teaspoon sesame oil
1 teaspoon pepper
225 g (8 oz) pig's liver
150 g (5 oz) cooked bamboo shoots
4 Chinese sausages
3 tablespoons flour
2 tablespoons water
oil for deep-frying

Score pork slices lightly with the back of a cleaver. Marinate in wine, sugar, light soy sauce, black soy sauce, oyster sauce, sesame oil and pepper for 30 minutes.

Steam liver for 10 minutes. When cool, cut into thin 2½ × 1 cm (1 × ½ in) pieces. Cut bamboo shoots and Chinese sausages the same size.

Blend flour with water to form a thick paste.

Spread pork slices on a tray and place a piece of liver, sausage and bamboo shoot on each slice of pork. Roll the meat and seal with flour paste.

Heat oil in a frying pan and deep-fry rolls till light golden. Drain dry on a wire sieve.

Serve rolls alone, garnished with cucumber slices and tomato wedges or as part of a cold dish.

Note: "Kai Guen" literally means "Chicken Rolls" but invariably pork and not chicken is used.

Golden Quail's Eggs

Preparation: 10 minutes
Cooking: 15 minutes

20 quail's eggs
1 kg (2¼ lb) prawns, shelled
¾ teaspoon salt
dash of pepper
2 teaspoons sago flour *or* tapioca flour
4 egg yolks, beaten
85 g (3 oz) breadcrumbs
oil for deep-frying

Sauce
5 tablespoons tomato ketchup
1 teaspoon Worcestershire sauce
1 teaspoon sugar

Boil and shell eggs.

Mince prawns with salt and pepper, then mix with flour.

Wrap minced prawns around eggs. Coat with beaten egg yolk and roll in breadcrumbs.

Deep-fry in hot oil and serve with tomato ketchup mixed with Worcestershire sauce and sugar.

Spiced Pigeon

Preparation: 5 minutes
Marinating: 30 minutes
Cooking: 8 minutes

1 pigeon
2 tablespoons light soy sauce
½ teaspoon sesame oil
1 tablespoon Chinese rice wine
2 tablespoons honey
1 teaspoon lemon juice
½ teaspoon salt
½ teaspoon ground star anise
oil for deep-frying
pepper
salt

Clean pigeon and marinate for 30 minutes in light soy sauce, sesame oil, rice wine, honey and lemon juice.

Rub salt and ground star anise on the inside of the pigeon.

Heat oil in a wok till smoking hot. Deep-fry pigeon till golden brown.

Tear pigeon into large pieces and serve alone or as part of a cold dish. Serve with pepper and salt.

Nonya (Straits Chinese)

Babi Tulang Masak Kiamchye
(Pork Ribs and Kiamchye Soup)

Preparation: 12 minutes
Cooking: 35 minutes

450 g (1 lb) pork ribs
450 g (1 lb) *kiamchye*
1 cm (½ in) piece ginger
3.75 L (6¾ pints) water
2 onions, quartered
3 preserved sour plums
3 tomatoes, quartered
½ teaspoon sugar
½ teaspoon salt, if necessary
dash of pepper

Chop pork ribs into bite-size pieces.

Cut *kiamchye* into 2½ cm (1 in) squares. Soak in water for 30 minutes, then squeeze dry.

Bash ginger lightly with the side of a cleaver, taking care to keep the piece intact.

Bring water to a boil, then add pork ribs and ginger. Simmer uncovered for 20 minutes. Add *kiamchye*, bring to a boil again and cook uncovered for 10 minutes.

Put in onions, preserved sour plums and tomatoes. Continue boiling for 5 minutes. Add sugar and salt, if necessary. Leave to cook for another 5 minutes, then serve with a dash of pepper.

Nonya Satay Babi Choo Chok

Preparation: 1 hour
Marinating: 2 hours
Cooking: 25 minutes

900 g (2 lb) pork tenderloin
450 g (1 lb) belly pork
1½ tablespoons ground coriander
2 tablespoons ground turmeric
5 tablespoons sugar
¾ tablespoon salt
oil for basting

Cut both types of meat thinly into 2½ cm (1 in) square slices.

Marinate for at least 2 hours in a mixture of ground coriander, ground turmeric, sugar and salt.

Thread pieces of tenderloin and belly pork alternately onto satay sticks. When ready to serve, grill over charcoal or place satay on grilling trays with sticks covered by aluminium foil.

Grill meat for 10 minutes, basting frequently with oil.

Serve with Nonya Satay Sauce (p.142), onion and cucumber wedges, and Ketupat (p.100).

Hati Babi Bungkus (Liver and Pork Balls)

Preparation: 20 minutes
Cooking: 30 minutes

450 g (1 lb) pig's liver
3 tablespoons oil
10 shallots, chopped finely
5 teaspoons coriander, roasted and ground finely
8 teaspoons sugar
½ teaspoon salt
2 teaspoons light soy sauce
3 teaspoons black soy sauce
½ teaspoon pepper
2 teaspoons tapioca flour
450 g (1 lb) minced pork
2 pieces pig's caul (*pang say yew*)
oil for deep-frying

Plunge liver into boiling water, remove at once and dice.

Heat oil in a wok and brown shallots. Add ground coriander, sugar, salt, light soy sauce and black soy sauce. Mix well, add cooked liver and stir-fry for 2 minutes.

When mixture cools, add pepper, tapioca flour and minced meat. Knead and shape into marble-sized balls.

Smooth out caul on working surface and wrap each meatball by rolling in the net, taking care not to use parts of caul which have holes. Cut away wrapped meatball from main caul.

Steam meatballs for 20 minutes, then cool.

When ready to serve, deep-fry over low heat and serve with Kuakchye Pickle (p.137).

Babi Tempra

Preparation: 7 minutes
Cooking: 12 minutes

450 g (1 lb) pork (from belly or front trotter)
4 tablespoons cooking oil
8 shallots, sliced
2 big onions, sliced
3 tablespoons juice of limes or lemon
5 teaspoons sugar
¼ teaspoon salt
3 tablespoons black soy sauce
3 red chillies, sliced

Cut pork into thin 2½ cm (1 in) slices.

Heat oil in a wok till hot. Stir-fry shallots till fragrant, then add onions.

After 1 minute, put in pork, lime or lemon juice, sugar and salt. Continue stir-frying, sprinkling with a little water now and then to prevent burning and to help cook meat.

When meat is cooked, add black soy sauce and chillies. Stir and remove to a dish.

Babi Pong Tay (Braised Pork in Preserved Soy Beans)

Preparation: 20 minutes
Marinating: 30 minutes
Pressure cooking: 20 minutes
Cooking: 1½ hours

1¼ kg (2½ lb) front trotter, with skin and some fat
4 tablespoons black soy sauce
120 ml (4 fl oz) light soy sauce
¾ teaspoon pepper
½ teaspoon salt
4 teaspoons sugar
30 shallots
10 cloves garlic
3 teaspoons preserved soy beans
10 dried Chinese mushrooms, soaked in boiling
   water for 20 minutes
6 tablespoons oil
200 g (6⅔ oz) bamboo shoots, sliced in wedges,
   ½ cm (¼ in) thick at the thicker end
1.5 L (2½ pints) water, or more

Clean pork and cut into bite-size pieces. Season with black soy sauce, light soy sauce, pepper, salt and sugar for at least 30 minutes.

Pound shallots, garlic and soy beans.

Drain mushrooms and keep the liquid.

Heat oil in a wok and fry shallots, garlic and preserved soy beans. Add mushrooms, mushroom water, bamboo shoots and seasoned pork. Slimmer for 8 minutes with 420 ml (¾ pint) water, stirring all the while.

Put meat in a pressure cooker, add 1 L (1¾ pints) water, or enough to cover the meat. Cook for 20 minutes in the pressure cooker till meat is quite tender.

Release heat by placing pressure cooker under running tap. When lid can be opened, simmer till sauce is quite thick.

If a pressure cooker is not available, pour contents of wok into a deep saucepan, add sufficient water to cover meat and simmer gently, covered, till meat is tender.

Chicken Curry with Peranakan Rempah

Preparation: 20 minutes
Cooking: 40 minutes

1 coconut, grated
900 ml (1½ pints) water
7 tablespoons oil
1¾ kg (4 lb) chicken, cut into bite-size pieces
2 teaspoons salt
1 tablespoon light soy sauce
4 potatoes, halved
2 tomatoes, quartered

Rempah
2½ cm (1 in) piece turmeric
4 candlenuts
8 slices galingale *or* green root ginger
2 stalks lemon grass
15 dried chillies, seeded, *or* 1 teaspoon ground chilli
5 red chillies, seeded
2 cloves garlic
30 shallots
1 tablespoon dried shrimp paste
4 tablespoons meat curry powder (p.143)

Mix coconut with 120 ml (4 fl oz) water. Squeeze and strain to obtain thick coconut milk. Add 750 ml (1¼ pints) water to residue. Squeeze and strain to obtain thin coconut milk.

Heat an Indian earthenware pot till hot. Add oil and fry *rempah* till fragrant.

Add chicken and 250 ml (8 fl oz) thin coconut milk. Simmer, stirring in an upward motion to prevent milk curdling. Cook over low heat for 20 minutes, adding thin coconut milk slowly till finished.

Stir in salt, and light soy sauce. After 10 minutes, add potatoes and tomatoes.

When potatoes are cooked, add thick coconut milk. Boil till red oil floats to the top.

Note: This curry tastes better if left overnight. When heating the next day, add 4 tablespoons water, bring to a boil and simmer for 5 minutes.

Ayam Buah Keluak
(Chicken Curry with Indonesian Black Nuts)

Preparation: 1 1/2 hours
Cooking: 1 1/4 hours

35 Indonesian black nuts
1.5 L (2 1/2 pints) water
5 tablespoons tamarind
250 ml (8 fl oz) water
3/4 coconut, grated
1 1/2 teaspoons salt
5 tablespoons oil
300 g (10 oz) minced pork
5 teaspoons sugar
450 g (1 lb) pork ribs, chopped into bite-size pieces
2 tablespoons light soy sauce
1 chicken, weighing about 1 3/4 kg (4 lb), cut into bite-size pieces

Rempah
4 cm (1 1/2 in) piece turmeric *or* 1 1/2 teaspoons ground turmeric
3 cloves garlic
2 stalks lemon grass
8 slices galingale *or* green root ginger
30 dried chillies, half of them seeded if a milder curry is preferred
7 candlenuts
1 1/2 teaspoons dried shrimp paste
6 red chillies, each quartered crosswise
35 shallots

Soak nuts 3 days in advance in sufficient water to cover.

Pound or blend all *rempah* ingredients except shallots. Blend shallots last for only half a minute so they remain coarse.

Add 250 ml (8 fl oz) of the 1.5 L (2 1/2 pints) water to tamarind. Squeeze with fingers and strain to obtain juice. Pour remaining 1.2 L (2 pints) water through the sieve gradually, squeezing tamarind pulp as you pour. Discard pulp and seeds.

Add 250 ml (8 fl oz) water to grated coconut, squeeze and strain to obtain milk. Add 1/4 teaspoon salt to milk and refrigerate.

Drain soaked nuts and scrub well to clean. Crack the smooth surface at the broadest part of the nut with a pestle, placing nut in the mortar, or chip off the smooth portions with a chopper, taking care not to take off part of your fingers in the process. Dig out the meat or kernel with cocktail fork or any clean small instrument, discarding any hard kernels that have a musty stale smell.

Heat oil in an earthen pot and fry *rempah* for 2 minutes till fragrant.

Remove a fifth of the *rempah*. Pound oily soft black kernels, then mix this with *rempah*. Add minced pork, 2 teaspoons sugar and 1/4 teaspoon salt. Mix well and stuff mixture into the shells.

Add pork ribs, 250 ml (8 fl oz) tamarind juice, remaining salt and sugar, and light soy sauce to remaining *rempah* in the earthen pot. Stir-fry for 5 minutes. Add chicken pieces and continue simmering for 5 more minutes.

Add 420 ml (3/4 pint) tamarind juice and allow to simmer for 10 minutes. Add stuffed nuts.

After 5 minutes, add remaining tamarind juice and simmer for 10 minutes, until gravy is reduced by half. Stir now and then.

When pork ribs are tender, add coconut milk from the refrigerator, bring to a boil and simmer for 5 minutes, or until red oil floats to the top.

Note: There are 5 ways of preparing *Buah Keluak:*

1 (As in this recipe) With pork ribs and chicken. Pounded kernels mixed with minced pork, *rempah* And seasoning, and pressed back into shell. Cooked with tamarind juice and coconut milk.
2 Similar to first variation, but minced pork is omitted.
3 With pork ribs. Shells stuffed with pounded kernels, minced pork and prawns, *rempah* and seasoning. Cooked with tamarind juice.
4 *Buah keluak* meat is fried with minced pork and prawns or crabmeat, *rempah* and seasoning for some minutes. The mixture is not stuffed back into shells. This is an appetiser which goes beautifully with hot rice or with bread as a sandwich paste. It can also be wrapped in banana leaves, folded like Otak-Otak see (p.70) and either grilled or steamed.
5 The kernels cooked with fish (Herring/*Ikan Parang* or Spanish Mackerel/*Ikan Tenggiri*), *rempah*, seasoning and tamarind juice.

Ayam Tempra

Preparation: 12 minutes
Cooking: 30 minutes

5 tablespoons oil
2 onions, sliced thinly
20 shallots, sliced
3-4 red chillies, each sliced into 4 long strips
900 g (2 lb) chicken, cut into bite-size pieces
2½ tablespoons sugar
½ teaspoon salt
4 tablespoons black soy sauce
4 tablespoons juice of lime
420 ml (¾ pint) water

Heat oil in a wok and fry onions, shallots and chillies for 1 minute, until soft. Then add chicken and stir-fry for about 10 minutes.

Add all other ingredients, bring to a boil and simmer till chicken is tender and sauce is thick.

Ayam Sioh (Tamarind Chicken)

Preparation: 10 minutes
Marinating: 10 hours
Cooking: 45 minutes

1 chicken, about 1½ kg (3⅓ lb)
4 tablespoons tamarind
420 ml (¾ pint) water
1 tablespoon vinegar
15 shallots, pounded
2 cloves garlic, pounded
3½ tablespoons coriander, roasted, ground and
   sifted
9 tablespoons sugar
1½ tablespoons salt
2 tablespoons black soy sauce
sufficient water to cover chicken
120 ml (4 fl oz) oil
1 cucumber, cut into wedges

Quarter chicken. Mix tamarind and 420 ml (¾ pint) water. Squeeze and strain to obtain juice.

Marinate chicken for 10 hours in a mixture of tamarind juice, vinegar, shallots, garlic, coriander, sugar, salt and black soy sauce. Make sure the chicken is well coated with mixture of ingredients.

Bring sufficient water to cook chicken to a boil in a deep pot. Submerge chicken with seasoning and simmer till tender.

Remove chicken and let it dry a little on a rack. In the meantime, continue cooking gravy in pot till quite thick.

Heat oil in a wok and fry chicken till golden brown. Cut into small pieces and pour thick gravy over it.

Serve Ayam Sioh with cucumber wedges.

Itek Chin (Braised Duck)

Preparation: 10 minutes
Cooking: 1 hour

1 duck, about 2 kg (4½ lb)
1½ tablespoons preserved soy beans
4 cloves garlic
10 shallots
3 red chillies
8 tablespoons oil
2-3 tablespoons coriander, roasted and ground finely
120 ml (4 fl oz) water
1½ tablespoons sugar
2 tablespoons black soy sauce
2½ cm (1 in) piece ginger, bashed
1 teaspoon pepper
salt to taste

Cut duck into bite-size pieces. Pound together preserved soy beans, garlic, shallots and chillies.

Heat oil in a wok and fry pounded ingredients till fragrant, then add ground coriander.

Add duck and fry for a few minutes before adding water. Allow to simmer, then add remaining ingredients.

Continue simmering till duck is tender. Add more water if gravy becomes too thick and duck is still not tender.

Assam Putih (Seafood in Tamarind)

Preparation: 6 minutes
Cooking: 8 minutes

8 large prawns, weighing approximately 300 g (10 oz) *or* small fish, e.g. Sprats *or* Whitings *or* 8 medium-sized cuttlefish
3 red chillies
4 green chillies
2½ tablespoons tamarind
600 ml (1 pint) water
1 teaspoon dried shrimp paste
2 teaspoons sugar
1 teaspoon salt
3-4 pieces dried tamarind
10 shallots, diced
2 stalks lemon grass, bruised

Shell prawns or clean and wash fish. If using cuttlefish, remove the ink sac.

Slit chillies halfway lengthwise from the tip, leaving stems intact. Mix tamarind and water. Squeeze and strain to obtain juice.

Mix dried shrimp paste with sugar, salt, dried tamarind and tamarind juice. Put in a pan together with shallots, lemon grass and chillies.

Bring to a boil over moderate heat and cook for about 5 minutes.

Add prawns, fish or cuttlefish and boil for another 3 minutes. Do not overcook.

Ikan Goreng Assam (Fried Tamarind Fish)

Preparation: 5 minutes
Marinating: 15 minutes
Cooking: 6 minutes

900 g (2 lb) Mackerel
4 tablespoons tamarind
5 tablespoons water
¾ teaspoon sugar
¾ teaspoon salt
½ teaspoon pepper
350 ml (12 fl oz) oil
1 cucumber, cut in wedges

Cut fish into 1 cm (½ in) thick slices. Combine all other ingredients except oil and leave fish to marinate in the mixture for at least 15 minutes.

Heat oil in a wok. Shake off as much of the marinade as possible from fish slices and fry 4 pieces at a time in hot oil. Cook for 3 minutes on one side, then turn fish and fry for another 3 minutes.

Serve with cucumber wedges.

Ikan Garam Assam

Preparation: 12 minutes
Cooking: 15 minutes

750 ml (1¼ pints) water
4 tablespoons tamarind
6 tablespoons oil
8 small sour starfruit, halved lengthwise (*or* juice of one lemon)
1 stalk lemon grass, bruised
4 teaspoons sugar
2 teaspoons salt
600 g (1⅓ lb) fish (preferably Grey Mullet) *or* prawns

Rempah
2½ cm (1 in) piece turmeric
1 stalk lemon grass
8 slices galingale *or* green root ginger
5 candlenuts
6 red chillies
20 shallots
2 ½ × ½ cm (1 × ¼ in) piece dried shrimp paste

Add water to tamarind. Squeeze and strain to obtain juice.

Heat oil in an earthen pot and fry *rempah* till fragrant. Add starfruit (or lemon juice), 1 cup tamarind juice and bruised lemon grass.

Stir-fry for 3 minutes, then add the second cup of tamarind juice. After another 3 minutes, add the third cup of tamarind juice, sugar, salt and fish or prawns. Cook till fish and prawns are done.

Ikan Kuah Ladah (Fish in Hot Gravy)

Preparation: 25 minutes
Cooking: 17 minutes

600 g (1⅓ lb) Mackerel *or* White Pomfret *or* Ray
   Fish
3 green aubergines
1 red chilli
1 green chilli
3 tablespoon tamarind
1.2 L (2 pints) water
4 tablespoons oil
2 pieces dried tamarind
2 teaspoons sugar
1 teaspoon salt

Rempah
2½ cm (1 in) piece turmeric *or* teaspoon ground
   turmeric
2 cloves garlic
20 shallots
2 teaspoons dried shrimp paste
8 slices galingale
13-20 white peppercorns
2 stalks lemon grass

Clean fish and cut into 5 × 2½ cm (2 × 1 in)
pieces. Halve aubergines lengthwise and cut into
5 cm (2 in) pieces. Make a cut about 1 cm (½ in)
deep down the middle of each piece.

Slit both chillies halfway down and remove
seeds. Blend tamarind and water. Squeeze and
strain to obtain juice.

Heat oil and fry *rempah*. Sprinkle on about 1-2
teaspoons of the tamarind juice. Stir-fry *rempah*
for a few minutes.

Add 120 ml (4 fl oz) tamarind juice, dried
tamarind pieces, aubergines and chillies. Simmer for about 5 minutes, then add remaining
tamarind juice, sugar and salt.

Stir, add fish and bring to a boil. Simmer for 7
minutes, or until fish is cooked.

Sambal Lengkong

Preparation: 30 minutes
Cooking: 2 hours

1¾ kg (4 lb) Carp or Grey Mullet
1½ coconuts, grated
420 ml (¾ pint) water
juice of 4 limes
2½ teaspoons salt
6 tablespoons sugar

Rempah
20 dried chillies
6 red chillies
4 green chillies
10 bird chillies
2½ cm (1 in) piece turmeric
1 tablespoon dried shrimp paste
15 shallots
10 candlenuts
2 stalks lemon grass
6 slices galingale *or* green root ginger

Cut fish into 15 cm (6 in) pieces.

Mix coconut with water. Squeeze and strain to
obtain 750 ml (1¼ pints) coconut milk.

Stir *rempah*, lime juice, salt and sugar into
coconut milk. Bring to a boil. Add fish and
simmer till cooked.

Remove fish and flake off flesh. Meanwhile boil
gravy down to half the original quantity.

Add fish to reduced gravy and cook for 1½
hours, stirring constantly, till fish is dry and
crisp.

Cool on greaseproof paper and pack in airtight
tins or bottles.

Ayam Buah Keluak (p.61)

Otak-Otak Bakar (p.70)

Popiah Goreng (p.77)

Masak Nanas Pedas (p.69)

Masak Nanas Pedas

Preparation: 15 minutes
Cooking: 18 minutes

600 g (1⅓ lb) mackerel or white pomfret
8 large prawns
½ pineapple
3½ tablespoons tamarind
900 ml (1½ pints) water
3 pieces dried tamarind
1-1½ teaspoons salt
2 tablespoons sugar
2 stalks lemon grass, crushed
2 bay leaves

Rempah
2½ cm (1 in) piece turmeric
1 stalk lemon grass
2½ cm (1 in) piece galingale or green root ginger
5 candlenuts
1 tablespoon dried shrimp paste
6 red chillies (pounded coarsely)
10 shallots (pounded coarsely)
1 clove garlic

Leave white pomfret or mackerel whole. Cut feelers off prawns, leave shells on.

Halve pineapple crosswise. Cut pineapple parallel to curved outer edge all round into ½ cm (¼ in) thick slices. Cut till core is reached. Discard core.

Mix tamarind with water. Squeeze and strain to obtain juice.

Mix *rempah* with tamarind juice, dried tamarind, salt, sugar and crushed lemon grass in a pot.

Let gravy boil for 10 minutes before adding pineapple. Add bay leaves. After 5 minutes, add fish and prawns together.

Simmer for 3 minutes only so as not to overcook seafood.

Ikan Masak Assam Pekat

Preparation: 7 minutes
Cooking: 15 minutes

3 mackerel 225-350 g (½-¾ lb) each
4 tablespoons tamarind
750 ml (1¼ pints) water
4 red chillies
3 green chillies
3 tablespoons oil
1¾ teaspoons salt
5 tablespoons sugar
3 small tomatoes, quartered
2 stalks lemon grass, bruised

Rempah
15 shallots
4 candlenuts
4 cm (1½ in) piece turmeric
1 tablespoon dried shrimp paste

Leave mackerel whole.

Mix tamarind with water. Squeeze and strain to obtain juice.

Slit chillies lengthwise up to 1 cm (½ in) from stem.

Heat oil in a wok and fry *rempah* till fragrant. Add 350 ml (12 fl oz) tamarind juice.

Bring to a boil, simmer for 5 minutes, then add salt, sugar, chillies, tomatoes and lemon grass.

Cook for another 5 minutes before adding remaining tamarind juice and fish.

Simmer till fish is cooked and gravy is thick.

Otak-Otak Bakar

Preparation: 40 minutes
Cooking: Over charcoal, 6 minutes
Under an electric grill, 8-10 minutes
Wrapped in aluminium foil, 4 minutes

20-25 banana leaves or aluminium foil
1¾ kg (4 lb) Haddock *or* 1¼ kg (2½ lb) fish paste
½ teaspoon salt
3 coconuts, grated
300 ml (½ pint) water
½ white coconut, grated
2 bay leaves
4 lime leaves, sliced thinly
2 turmeric leaves, shredded
1 teaspoon salt
2 teaspoons sugar
6 eggs, beaten
3 tablespoons tapioca or sago flour
4 tablespoons water

Rempah
3 tablespoons coriander
5 cm (2 in) piece turmeric or 1½ teaspoons ground
   turmeric
2 tablespoons dried shrimp paste
10 slices galingale *or* green root ginger
3 stalks lemon grass
10 candlenuts *or* blanched almonds
35 shallots
20 dried chillies, half of them seeded

Wash banana leaves and submerge in boiling water for 1 minute to soften. Cut each leaf into 23 × 28 cm (9 × 11 in) pieces.

Fillet fish and slice diagonally into 1 cm (½ in) wide pieces. Season with salt.

If fish paste is used, pat into 8 × 4 × ½ cm (3 × 1½ × ¼ in) rectangular cakes and soak in salt water for 30 minutes to firm the paste. Drain dry when about to use.

Mix grated coconut with water. Squeeze and strain to obtain thick coconut milk. Discard residue.

Stir-fry white grated coconut in a dry pan till golden brown. Pound till fine.

Pound all *rempah* ingredients except coriander. Fry coriander seeds in a dry pan till fragrant. Pound or grind, then sift to obtain fine powder. Mix this with pounded *rempah* ingredients.

Mix *rempah* with fried coconut, coconut milk, bay leaves, lime and turmeric leaves, salt, sugar and beaten eggs. Mix flour with water and add to *rempah* mixture. Blend well.

Place about 4 slices of fish or one prepared fish cake on a piece of banana leaf and spread 3 tablespoons *rempah* mixture on top. Fold in the top and bottom edges of the leaf, then the sides.

Grill under an electric grill in 2 lots, cooking each side about 4-5 minutes, or cook over charcoal, allowing 3 minutes for each side. Take care not to burn banana leaves.

This goes beautifully with Nasi Lemak (p.100) or plain white rice and can also be served on top of toasted bread and butter.

Udang Goreng Assam (Fried Tamarind Prawns)

Preparation: 5 minutes
Marinating: 10 minutes
Cooking: 3-5 minutes

600 g (1⅓ lb) medium- or large-sized prawns
2 tablespoons tamarind
4 tablespoons water
1 teaspoon salt
½ teaspoon pepper
½ teaspoon sugar
175 ml (6 fl oz) oil or more
1 cucumber, cut in wedges

Trim off sharp ends of feelers and legs of prawns, but leave shells on. Blend tamarind with water. Squeeze and strain to obtain a thick paste.

Marinate prawns with salt, pepper, sugar and tamarind paste for 10 minutes.

Fry prawns in hot oil over moderate heat for 2-3 minutes till shells are crisp. Serve with cucumber wedges.

Sambal Udang Kering with Crispy Shallots

Preparation: 15 minutes
Cooking: 40 minutes

450 g (1 lb) dried prawns
5 limes
420 ml (¾ pint) oil
6 tablespoons icing sugar
5 cloves garlic, sliced
600 g (1⅓ lb) shallots, sliced thinly

Rempah
15 red chillies, seeded
1 teaspoon dried shrimp paste
10 shallots
3 fragrant lime leaves *or* 2 stalks lemon grass

Begin preparation a day in advance. Soak dried prawns in water for 30 minutes. Rinse and drain dry. Pound prawns finely and squeeze in juice of limes. Sun till dry.

Heat 6 tablespoons oil in a wok till smoking hot then fry *rempah* for a few minutes over low heat.

Remove *rempah* from wok and strain the oil. Rub this chilli-flavoured oil into dried prawns with your fingers.

Heat 4 tablespoons oil and fry dried prawns till dry and crisp. Remove wok from heat and blend in icing sugar. Place wok back on heat and stir-fry for a minute, taking care not to over-fry the dried prawns which should have a sandy and crispy texture. Remove to a dish.

Heat the remaining oil in the same wok and fry garlic till crisp. Remove garlic from the wok and fry shallots in the same oil till golden brown.

Place both shallots and garlic on a piece of greaseproof paper. When cool, mix with dried prawns. An hour later, when the mixture is at room temperature, pack in airtight bottles.

Sambal Udang Kering goes well with toasted bread and Nasi Lemak (p.100).

Sambal Udang Kering with Coconut Milk

Preparation: 10 minutes
Cooking: 1 hour

½ coconut, grated
120 ml (4 fl oz) water
1 tablespoon tamarind
5 tablespoons water
420 ml (¾ pint) oil
600 g (1⅓ lb) dried prawns, ground finely
5 lime leaves (optional)
4 tablespoons sugar

Rempah
20 dried chillies
4 red chillies
10 bird chillies
½ tablespoon dried shrimp paste
20 shallots
6 candlenuts *or* 10 blanched almonds
2 stalks lemon grass
4 thin slices galingale *or* green root ginger
4 cm (1½ in) piece turmeric
10 peppercorns

Mix grated coconut with 120 ml (4 fl oz) water. Squeeze and strain to obtain milk. Mix tamarind with 5 tablespoons water. Squeeze and strain for juice.

Heat oil in a wok and stir-fry *rempah* till fragrant. Pour coconut milk slowly into simmering *rempah*, stirring constantly.

Add ground dried prawns, lime leaves, if used, and sugar. Simmer over moderate heat, stirring briskly, till mixture is crisp. This will take about an hour.

Sambal Udang Kering can be served with Lontong (p.100), used as a sandwich filling, or taken with Nasi Lemak (p.100).

Fried Cuttlefish with Rempah

Preparation: 12 minutes
Marinating: 15 minutes
Cooking: 8-10 minutes

900 g (2 lb) cuttlefish
4 tablespoons tamarind
200 ml (⅓ pint) water
5 tablespoons oil
2 teaspoons coarse salt
5 teaspoons sugar
3 round slices pineapple, each cut into 8 segments
2 onions, quartered

Rempah
10 dried chillies *or* ½ teaspoon ground chilli
3 red chillies
20 black peppercorns *or* ¾ teaspoon ground pepper
15 shallots
3 cloves garlic
2½ cm (1 in) piece turmeric *or* ¾ teaspoon ground turmeric

Slit cuttlefish down the centre and remove ink sac. Clean and halve each cuttlefish. Remove thin dotted membrane covering the cuttlefish. Make shallow criss-cross cuts over cuttlefish and cut each half into 3-5 triangular pieces. Mix cuttlefish with pounded *rempah* ingredients and leave to marinate for 15 minutes, then scrape off *rempah*.

Mix tamarind with water. Squeeze and strain to obtain juice.

Heat oil in an earthen pot. Fry *rempah* for about 1 minute till fragrant. Add tamarind juice, salt and sugar. Simmer for 1 minute, then add pineapple and onion. Cook for 2 minutes.

Add cuttlefish and cook covered for another 2 minutes. Remove cover and stir-fry for just 1 more minute to cook cuttlefish. Do not overcook or cuttlefish will be tough.

Cuttlefish Sambal with Meat and Prawn Stuffing

Preparation: 25 minutes
Cooking: 15 minutes

10 medium-sized cuttlefish
225 g (8 oz) minced beef or pork
180 g (6 oz) minced prawn
⅓ teaspoon salt
½ teaspoon pepper
3 tablespoons tamarind
120 ml (4 fl oz) water
¼ coconut, grated
5 tablespoons water
4 tablespoons oil
1 teaspoon sugar
salt to taste
250 ml (8 fl oz) water

Rempah
10 shallots
8 dried chillies
4 red chillies, seeded
4 candlenuts *or* 6 blanched almonds
2½ × ½ cm (1 × ¼ in) piece dried shrimp paste
¼ teaspoon ground turmeric

Wash cuttlefish thoroughly to remove ink.

Mince beef or pork with prawns, salt and pepper. Stuff cuttlefish with minced meat. Secure ends with toothpicks.

Mix tamarind and 120 ml (4 fl oz) water. Squeeze and strain to obtain juice.

Mix coconut and 5 tablespoons water. Squeeze and strain to obtain coconut milk.

Heat oil in a wok and fry *rempah* till fragrant. Add tamarind juice, coconut milk, sugar and salt to taste, and water.

When mixture boils, add stuffed cuttlefish. Simmer over low heat for 10 minutes to cook stuffing. Turn off heat when gravy is quite thick.

Serve immediately with hot rice.

Assam Sotong Goreng

Preparation: 8 minutes
Marinating: 30 minutes
Cooking: 7 minutes

10 medium-sized cuttlefish
4 tablespoons tamarind
175 ml (6 fl oz) water
½ teaspoon salt
120 ml (4 fl oz) oil
1 cucumber, cut into wedges

Clean cuttlefish.

Mix tamarind and water. Squeeze and remove seeds. Marinate cuttlefish in tamarind juice and salt for 30 minutes, then drain away liquid.

Heat oil in a wok till hot. Fry cuttlefish till oil is black. Stir-fry till dry.

Serve with cucumber.

Chilli Kepeting (Chilli Crabs)

Preparation: 20 minutes
Cooking: 14 minutes

2 kg (4½ lb) blue crabs *or* any crabs available
175 ml (6 fl oz) oil
3 cloves garlic, chopped
2 thick slices ginger
2 tablespoons preserved soy beans, pounded
1 tablespoon sugar
18 tablespoons tomato ketchup
5 tablespoons garlic-flavoured chilli sauce
175 ml (6 fl oz) water
2 eggs, beaten
1 tablespoon tapioca flour or sago flour, blended with 175 ml (6 fl oz) water

Cut each crab into 4 or 6 pieces.

Heat oil in a wok and brown garlic. Add ginger and preserved soy beans.

After a minute, add crabs with sugar, tomato ketchup and chilli sauce. Fry well, adding ¾ cup water to cook crabs.

Cook covered for a few minutes, then stir and cover once again till crabs are cooked. Add flour and water mixture. Turn off heat when gravy is thick.

Kacang Panjang with Rempah Titek Lepas (Spicy Long Bean Soup)

Preparation: 7 minutes
Cooking: 15 minutes

1.2 L (2 pints) water
2 teaspoons salt
100 g (3⅓ oz) dried prawns, pounded
300 g (10 oz) long beans, cut into 2½ cm (1 in) lengths
200 g (6⅔ oz) small prawns, shelled

Rempah
3 candlenuts
2 teaspoons dried shrimp paste
6 shallots
2 red chillies (pound this coarsely)

Bring water to a boil and add *rempah*, salt, and dried prawns. Simmer for 5 minutes, then add long beans and continue boiling for 5 minutes till long beans are tender.

Add fresh prawns and cook for just 2 minutes.

This soup is very refreshing on a hot day.

Labu Air Masak Sambal Blacan
(Long Bottle Gourd Fried with Shrimp Paste)

Preparation: 10 minutes
Cooking: 12 minutes

300 g (10 oz) long bottle gourd
30 g (1 oz) dried prawns
3 tablespoons oil
250 ml (8 fl oz) water
2 eggs, beaten
200 g (6⅔ oz) small prawns, shelled
dash of pepper

Rempah
1 tablespoon dried shrimp paste
3 red chillies
5 shallots
10 peppercorns *or* ½ teaspoon ground pepper

Cut gourd into wedges, thicker edge about 1 cm (½ in) thick.

Pound dried prawns coarsely.

Heat oil in a wok and fry *rempah* and dried prawns till fragrant. Pour in water and bring to a boil then add gourd. Cook covered for 8 minutes.

Uncover and stir-fry till gourd is soft. Add beaten eggs, stirring briskly to mix, and fresh prawns. Continue to boil for 4 minutes.

Serve with a dash of pepper.

Terung Masak Lemak

Preparation: 15 minutes
Cooking: 20 minutes

3 aubergines
¾ coconut, grated
750 ml (1¼ pints) water
4 tablespoons oil
¾ teaspoon salt
300 g (10 oz) medium-sized prawns, shelled
juice of 2 limes

Rempah
10 dried chillies *or* 1 teaspoon ground chilli
3 red chillies, seeded
10 shallots
1 clove garlic

Cut each aubergine crosswise into 3 pieces, then halve each piece.

Mix coconut with 4 tablespoons water. Squeeze and strain to obtain 4 tablespoons thick coconut milk. Add 750 ml (1¼ pints) water to residue for thin coconut milk.

Heat oil in an earthen pot and fry *rempah* over medium heat fill fragrant. Take care not to burn it.

Add 350 ml (12 fl oz) thin coconut milk and let it boil for 5 minutes. Then add aubergine and stir gravy with an upward movement to prevent milk from curdling.

After 5 minutes, add remaining thin coconut milk and salt. Boil for 5 more minutes, then add prawns and thick coconut milk. Cook for another 3 minutes, stirring constantly.

Add lime juice just before serving.

Jantung Pisang (Banana Flower Salad with Prawns)

Preparation: 20 minutes
Cooking: 5 minutes

2 large banana flowers
1½ cucumbers
6 small sour starfruit *or* juice of half lemon
1½ coconuts, grated
salt to taste
1 tablespoon Sambal Blacan (p.139)
1 tablespoon juice of limes
sugar to taste
600 g (1⅓ lb) small prawns, boiled and shelled
12 shallots, sliced and deep-fried till crisp

Halve banana flowers lengthwise. Remove skin and soft centre of cucumber and shred. Slice starfruit thinly (if used).

Place banana flowers, cucumber and starfruit (or lemon juice) in a salad bowl.

Squeeze and strain coconut to obtain thick coconut milk.

Simmer coconut milk, add salt to taste and cook over low heat for a few minutes, stirring constantly.

Stir in Sambal Blacan mixed with lime juice and sugar. Mix well and pour over ingredients in salad bowl.

Garnish with prawns and crispy shallots. Serve chilled.

Kangkung Masak Lemak Udang
(Fried Water Convolvulus with Prawns)

Preparation: 15 minutes
Cooking: 12 minutes

900 g (2 lb) water convolvulus (available in Chinese
   Supermarkets only)
1.2 L (2 pints) water
1½ coconuts, grated
5 tablespoons oil
60 g (2 oz) dried prawns, pounded coarsely
225 g (8 oz) small prawns, shelled
½ teaspoon salt
¼ teaspoon baking powder (optional)

Rempah
4 red chillies
5 shallots
3 candlenuts *or* 5 blanched almonds
1 teaspoon dried shrimp paste

Pluck off tender water convolvulus leaves and
pluck stems into 4 cm (1½ in) lengths.

Add 250 ml (8 fl oz) water to grated coconut and
squeeze and strain to obtain thick coconut milk.
Add remaining water to residue to obtain thin
coconut milk.

Heat oil in a wok and stir-fry dried prawns and
rempah together till fragrant.

Add water convolvulus, fresh prawns and thin
coconut milk. Stir-fry for about 3 minutes then
add thick coconut milk, salt and baking powder,
if used (to keep leaves green).

Simmer till water convolvulus is just cooked
(about 5 minutes).

Sambal Kimchiam
(Coconut Cream Salad with Lily Flowers)

Preparation: 20 minutes
Cooking: 22 minutes

200g (6⅔ oz) dried lily flowers
1.6 L (2¾ pints) water
300 g (10 oz) medium-sized prawns
8 small sour starfruit *or* juice of one lemon
1 cucumber
2 red chillies
3 coconuts, grated
6 tablespoons water
½ teaspoon salt
3 teaspoons sugar

Rempah
3 red chillies
1 tablespoon dried shrimp paste, roasted
5 shallots
juice of 5 limes

Soak lily flowers in water for 1 hour. Strain, then
boil uncovered for 10 minutes in 3 cups water
until water dries up. Squeeze dry.

Bring 1 L (1¾ pints) water to a boil and put in
prawns with shells still on. Cook for 2 minutes,
then remove shells. Halve prawns lengthwise.

Cut starfruit into ½ cm (¼ in) thick rings, (if
used).

Quarter cucumber lengthwise. Cut away central
pulp and seeds. Slice at a slant into pieces 2 mm
thick.

Halve chillies lengthwise, remove seeds and cut
each chilli into 10 long thin strips.

Mix grated coconut with 6 tablespoons water.
Squeeze and strain to obtain thick coconut milk.
Bring coconut milk and salt to a boil over low
heat, then remove from heat immediately.

Pound *rempah* ingredients and mix with lily
flowers and sugar. Mix half the coconut milk
with lily flowers and place on a small flat dish.
Garnish with starfruit, cucumber and prawns.
Top with remaining coconut milk and decorate
with chilli strips.

Refrigerate and serve salad cold.

Rebong Masak Lemak (Bamboo Shoots in Coconut Milk)

Preparation: 30 minutes
Cooking: 1 hour

1 coconut, grated
1.5 L (2½ pints) water
4 tablespoons oil
90 g (3 oz) dried prawns, ground finely
900 g (2 lb) pork ribs, chopped into bite-size pieces
¾ teaspoon salt
2 tablespoons light soy sauce
600 g (1⅓ lb) canned bamboo shoots, cut into thin
   ½ cm (¼ in) wedges
450 g (1 lb) small prawns, shelled

Rempah
20 peppercorns
2½ cm (1 in) piece turmeric *or* 1 teaspoon ground
   turmeric
2 tablespoons coriander, roasted
20 dried chillies
5 red chillies
5 candlenuts
1 stalk lemon grass
4 slices galingale *or* green root ginger
1 tablespoon dried shrimp paste

Mix grated coconut with 250 ml (8 fl oz) water. Squeeze and strain to obtain thick coconut milk. Add remaining 1.2 L (2 pints) water to residue. Squeeze and strain to obtain thin coconut milk.

Heat oil in a pot and fry *rempah* till fragrant, then add dried prawns.

After ½ minute, add pork ribs and 250 ml (8 fl oz) thin coconut milk. Cook covered for 5 minutes over moderate heat, then uncover and stir for a minute.

Add salt, light soy sauce and bamboo shoots with another cup thin coconut milk.

Simmer over low heat till almost dry, then pour remaining thin coconut milk into pot. Simmer for another 25 minutes, stirring every now and then.

When meat is tender, add thick coconut milk and small prawns. Stir continuously over low heat for 5 minutes.

Serve with hot rice.

Belimbing and Prawn Sambal

Preparation: 7 minutes
Cooking: 8-10 minutes

2 coconuts, grated
2 tablespoons water
pinch of salt
3 tablespoons oil
15 small sour starfruit, cut into 1 cm (½ in) rings
600 g (1⅓ lb) medium-sized prawns, shelled and
   deveined
sugar to taste
salt to taste

Rempah
1 tablespoon dried shrimp paste, toasted
5 chillies
10 shallots
1 clove garlic

Mix coconut with water. Squeeze and strain to obtain thick coconut milk.

Heat oil in a wok and fry *rempah* till fragrant.

Add starfruit, prawns and part of the coconut milk. Stir upwards over low heat to prevent milk curdling.

Add remaining coconut milk and simmer till gravy is milky white. Season to taste.

Kiamchye Goreng (Fried Kiamchye)

Preparation: 10 minutes
Cooking: 12 minutes

225 g (8 oz) *kiamchye*
100 g (3⅓ oz) belly pork
2 firm soybean cakes
1-2 red chillies
4 tablespoons oil
2 cloves garlic, chopped finely
1 teaspoon black soy sauce
2 teaspoons sugar
dash of pepper

Soak *kiamchye* in water for 1 hour to remove excess salt. Squeeze dry and shred finely.

Slice belly pork into pieces ½ cm (¼ in) thick.

Quarter soybean cakes, then divide into 8, and finally into 16 pieces.

Slice chillies lengthwise into very thin strips.

Heat oil in a wok and fry soybean pieces for 3 minutes till quite crisp. Remove to a dish.

In the same oil, brown garlic and fry *kiamchye* for about 3 minutes until vegetable is quite dry. Add belly pork and fry for another 3 minutes.

Add black soy sauce, sugar, chillies and fried soybean pieces. Keep stirring till vegetable dries.

Sprinkle with pepper before serving.

Popiah Goreng (Spring Rolls)

Preparation: 25 minutes
Cooking: 1½ hours

700 g (1½ lb) spring roll skins
1 tablespoon tapioca flour blended with water to make a thick paste
oil for deep-frying

Filling
300 g (10 oz) cooked bamboo shoots
2.25 L (4 pints) water
10 cloves garlic
2 tablespoons preserved soy beans
60 g (2 oz) dried prawns, soaked in cold water for 5 minutes
120 ml (4 fl oz) oil
420 ml (¾ pt) water
2 teaspoons sugar
3 teaspoons light soy sauce
1 teaspoon black soy sauce
½ teaspoon pepper
2½ kg (5½ lb) yam bean, peeled and shredded
420 ml (8 fl oz) water
300 g (10 oz) minced pork
450 g (1 lb) belly pork, boiled and shredded finely

Boil cooked bamboo shoots in 2.25 L (4 pints) water for 45 minutes, then drain and shred.

Pound the garlic, then add preserved soy beans and crush. Pound dried prawns separately.

Heat wok till hot, put in 120 ml (4 fl oz) oil and fry pounded ingredients for 2 minutes. Add bamboo shoots and 250 ml (8 fl oz) water. Simmer for 10 minutes, adding another 250 ml (8 fl oz) water till bamboo shoots are tender.

Add sugar, light soy sauce, black soy sauce, pepper and yam bean. Stir-fry the mixture for 10 minutes, adding 420 ml (¾ pint) water gradually, till yam bean is cooked. This will take another 15 minutes.

Mix in minced pork and belly pork and stir-fry for 8 minutes till meat is cooked.

To Assemble Popiah
For big popiah, use 1 sheet spring roll skin. If you want cocktail popiah, cut each skin into quarters.

Place some of the filling on the lower half of the sheet. Fold bottom edge, then fold in the right and left edges. Roll away from you and seal the end with the flour paste. Fry immediately or freeze in a plastic box. Thaw for 30 minutes to deep-fry.

To Cook Popiah
Half-fill a deep wok with oil and heat. Fry popiah till crisp and golden brown. Remove from oil and drain.

If cooking large popiah, cut each into 4 pieces and serve immediately with Vinegar Chilli Sauce (p.141) and thick sweet black sauce (*tim cheong*) or barbecue sauce.

Tauhu Masak Titek (Beancurd Pepper Soup)

Preparation: 5 minutes
Cooking: 10 minutes

225 g (8 oz) salt fish bones
2 pieces soft soybean cakes
60 g (2 oz) dried prawns
3 tablespoons oil
1.2 L (2 pints) water
1 teaspoon light soy sauce
½ teaspoon salt
225 g (8 oz) fresh prawns, shelled
2-3 stalks spring onion, finely chopped

Rempah
20-30 peppercorns
3 candlenuts *or* 5 blanched almonds
10 shallots
1 tablespoon dried shrimp paste
2-3 red chillies

Cut salt fish bones into 8 pieces and soak in water for 30 minutes to remove excess salt.

Cut each soft soybean cake into 8 pieces and pound dried prawns.

Heat oil in a wok and fry salt fish bones for a minute, then remove to a dish. Add dried prawns to the same oil, then the *rempah*. Stir-fry till fragrant.

Put back the salt fish bones and pour in water. Bring to a boil and simmer for 5 minutes. Add light soy sauce and salt.

After 3 minutes, gently slide soft soybean pieces and fresh prawns into boiling soup and cook for another minute.

Serve piping hot, garnished with spring onion.

Chap Chye

Preparation: 20 minutes
Cooking: 45 minutes

90 g (3 oz) lily flowers
250 ml (8 fl oz) oil
10 dried yellow soybean pieces (*tee taukee, taupoay*), each cut into 3 × 4½ cm (1¼ × 1¾ in) pieces
12 cloves garlic, pounded
36 shallots, pounded
2½-3 tablespoons preserved soy beans, pounded
60 g (2 oz) dried prawns, pounded coarsely
2.25 L (4 pints) water
10 dried Chinese mushrooms, soaked in boiling water for 15-20 minutes
30 g (1 oz) dried soybean sticks (*taukee*), cut into 5 cm (2 in) lengths and soaked in water to soften
300 g (10 oz) streaky pork, cut into thin long strips
450 g (1 lb) cabbage, cut into 5 cm (2 in) square pieces
60 g (2 oz) transparent noodles, soaked in water to soften

Cut off hard ends of lily flowers. Knot into pairs then soak in water to soften.

Heat oil in a wok and fry dried yellow soybean pieces for about 1 minute over moderate heat. Remove to a dish.

In the same oil, stir-fry pounded garlic for 1 minute till fragrant, then add pounded shallots and stir for 2 minutes. Put in preserved soy beans, stir, then add dried prawns.

After stir-frying for 1 minute pour in 250-420 ml (8-16 fl oz) water. Bring to a boil and add mushrooms and tied lily flowers. Simmer for a few minutes, then add fried *tee taukee* and *taukee*.

Leave to simmer for a few more minutes before adding streaky pork and remaining water.

In the last 10 minutes of cooking, put in cabbage. Add transparent noodles at the last minute.

Note: Chap Chye is usually eaten with rice and Sambal Blacan (p.139) or a Chin Char Loke dip (p.141). It keeps well for 2-3 days and tastes much better if kept at least overnight before serving.

Indian and Sri Lankan

Malabar Mutton Curry

Preparation: 15 minutes
Cooking: 40 minutes

1⅓ kg (3 lb) mutton
3 teaspoons salt
1½ coconuts, grated
1.2 L (2 pints) water
175 ml (6 fl oz) oil
1 teaspoon mustard seeds
30 shallots, sliced
10 slices ginger, shredded
5 cm (2 in) cinnamon stick
1 star anise, broken into segments, one segment
  pounded
5 cloves
8 cardamoms, bruised
6 stalks curry leaves *or* 6 bay leaves
2 tablespoons poppy seeds
5 potatoes, quartered
3 big onions, each cut into 6 wedges
3 tomatoes, quartered
juice of ¾ lemon

Rempah
5 tablespoons ground coriander
3-4 tablespoons ground chilli
1½ tablespoons ground turmeric
1 teaspoon black pepper
2 tablespoons ground fennel
1 tablespoon ground cummin

Cut mutton into 2½ cm (1 in) cubes and season
with salt.

Mix coconut with 250 ml (8 fl oz) water. Squeeze
and strain to obtain thick coconut milk. Add
remaining water to residue. Squeeze and strain
to obtain thin coconut milk.

Heat oil in a wok. When smoking hot, throw in
mustard seeds. Add shallots and ginger when
mustard seeds pop, then stir in *rempah*, cinnamon, star anise, cloves, cardamoms and curry or
bay leaves.

Stir-fry till fragrant, add mutton and 250 ml (8 fl
oz) thin coconut milk. Stir occasionally, adding
thin coconut milk a little at a time. If mutton is
still not tender when thin coconut is used up,
add water.

When mutton is tender, add poppy seeds,
potatoes, onions, and tomatoes with thick coconut milk. Finally, add lemon juice.

Serve with Nasi Kunyit (p.98), Mango Chutney
(p.92), Cucumber Salad with Coconut Milk
(p.90), fried cashew nuts, prawn crackers and
sliced bananas.

Minced Meatballs

Preparation: 10 minutes
Cooking: 15 minutes

225 g (8 oz) minced mutton, beef or pork
2 big onions, chopped
1½ tablespoons plain flour
2 tablespoons cooked rice, mashed
1 teaspoon ground chilli
1¼ tablespoons ground coriander
¾ teaspoon ground turmeric
1½ teaspoons pepper
salt to taste
2 sprigs coriander *or* mint leaves, chopped
oil for deep-frying

Combine all ingredients except oil. Roll with
palms of hands into small 4 cm (1½ in) balls.

Heat oil in a wok over moderate heat and fry
meatballs 6 or 7 at a time till golden brown.

Mutton Curry for Paratha

Preparation: 20 minutes
Cooking: 30 minutes

120 g (4 oz) ghee
15 shallots, sliced
2½ cm (1 in) piece ginger, sliced thinly
4 cloves garlic, sliced
2½ cm (1 in) cinnamon stick, broken into 2 pieces
4-5 cardamoms, bruised
450 g (1 lb) mutton, cut into 2½ cm (1 in) cubes
250 ml (8 fl oz) water
5 tomatoes, each cut into 6 wedges
120 ml (4 fl oz) yoghurt
10 cashew nuts or almonds, ground
3 big onions, diced

Rempah
½ teaspoon ground chilli
1 teaspoon ground coriander
½ teaspoon ground cummin
½ teaspoon ground fennel
½ teaspoon pepper
½ teaspoon ground turmeric

Heat ghee in a wok and fry sliced shallots, then ginger and garlic. Add cinnamon, cardamoms and mutton.

Sprinkle *rempah* over mutton, stir and add tomatoes and yoghurt. Stir-fry for a few minutes then add 4 tablespoons water.

Keep adding water as curry dries till mutton is tender, then add ground cashew nuts or almonds and diced onions. Cook till gravy is thick.

Mutton Curry with Dorothy's Curry Powder

Preparation: 15 minutes
Cooking: 1½ hours

¾ coconut, grated
750 ml (1¼ pints) water
225 g (8 oz) meat curry powder (p.143)
2 tablespoons water
175 ml (6 fl oz) oil
20 shallots, sliced
4 cloves garlic, sliced thinly
2½ cm (1 in) cinnamon stick
4 segments star anise
6 cardamoms, bashed lightly
6 cloves
1 teaspoon mustard seeds
1 tablespoon poppy seeds, ground
1½ kg (3⅓ lb) mutton, cut into bite-size pieces
5 stalks curry leaves
2 potatoes, diced
2 big onions, diced

Mix coconut with 120 ml (4 fl oz) water. Squeeze and strain to obtain thick coconut milk. Add remaining 600 ml (1 pint) water to residue. Squeeze and strain to obtain thin coconut milk.

Blend curry powder with water to make a thick paste.

Heat oil in a wok till smoking hot and fry shallots and garlic till soft. Add cinnamon stick, star anise, cardamoms, cloves, mustard seeds, ground poppy seeds, mutton, curry paste and curry leaves.

Stir-fry till meat is well-covered with spices, then add 250 ml (8 fl oz) thin coconut milk. Simmer adding thin coconut milk, a cup each time, till mutton is tender.

Put in diced potatoes and onions. When ingredients are cooked, add thick coconut milk. Simmer over low heat till curry is dry.

Note: If mutton is still not tender after all the thin coconut milk has been used, add water.

Keema

Preparation: 20 minutes
Cooking: 30 minutes

225 g (8 oz) minced mutton or beef
3 tablespoons meat curry powder (p.143)
salt to taste
3 tablespoons ghee *or* 5 tablespoons oil
2 big onions, sliced or diced
1 teaspoon cardamom seeds
5 cloves
2 segments star anise
1 cm (½ in) cinnamon stick
1 cm (½ in) piece ginger, pounded
2 cloves garlic, pounded
420 ml (¾ pint) water or thin coconut milk
2 big potatoes, cut into 2 cm (¾ in) cubes
2 big tomatoes, cut
into 2 cm (¾ in) cubes
60 g (2 oz) green peas
1 sprig coriander leaves, chopped
2 red chillies, seeded, cut into thin long strips

Mix minced mutton with curry powder and salt.

Heat oil in a wok. Add onions, fry till soft, then add cardamom seeds, cloves, star anise, cinnamon, ginger, garlic and minced meat.

Stir-fry till fragrant and dry. Add 120 ml (¼ pint) water or coconut milk. Simmer for 5 minutes and add potatoes and remaining liquid.

Cook covered for 2 minutes, then stir-fry till meat and potatoes are cooked. Add tomatoes and green peas and cook for a few more minutes.

Garnish with chopped coriander leaves and chilli strips. Serve with Paratha (p.92).

Pork Curry

Preparation: 13 minutes
Marinating: 30 minutes
Cooking: 35 minutes

1 coconut, grated
1 L (1¾ pints) water
1 kg (2¼ lb) pork (front trotter meat)
150 g (5 oz) meat curry powder (p.143)
1 teaspoon salt
5 tablespoons water
5 tablespoons oil
30 shallots, sliced
3 onions, sliced thinly
2 cloves garlic, sliced thinly
5 medium-sized potatoes, halved

Mix coconut and 4 tablespoons water. Squeeze and strain to obtain thick coconut milk. Add remaining water to residue. Squeeze and strain to obtain thin coconut milk.

Cut pork into bite-size pieces and season with 30 g (1 oz) curry powder and salt for 30 minutes. Blend remaining curry powder (add more if desired) with water to make a thick paste.

Heat oil in a wok and fry shallots, onions and garlic. Add curry paste and fry till fragrant before adding pork.

After stir-frying for 3 minutes, add 250 ml (8 fl oz) thin coconut milk. Simmer for 5 minutes, stirring now and then. Continue adding 250 ml (8 fl oz) thin coconut milk every 5 minutes till used up.

When meat is tender, add potatoes and cook till soft. Add thick coconut milk and simmer for 5 minutes, stirring constantly to prevent milk from curdling.

Serve with rice and side dishes of fried peanuts, sliced green bananas, Mango Chutney (p.92), fried salt fish, prawn crackers, salted duck's eggs, Cucumber Salad (p.90) and Vegetable Salad (p.90).

Chicken Curry with Dorothy's Curry Powder

Preparation: 20 minutes
Cooking: 45 minutes

2 kg (4½ lb) chicken
110 g (4 oz) meat curry powder (p.143), blended
   with a little water to a paste
1 teaspoon salt
1 coconut, grated
1.2 L (2 pints) water
120 ml (4 fl oz) oil
1 teaspoon mustard seeds
3 cloves garlic, pounded
30 shallots, pounded
2 stalks curry leaves
4 potatoes, quartered
4 tomatoes, quartered
2 big onions, cut into 6 wedges
salt to taste

Rempah
1 cm (½ in) cinnamon stick
1 segment star anise
5 cloves
1 tablespoon ground chilli
2 tablespoons ground coriander
1 teaspoon fennel
1 teaspoon cummin

Cut chicken into small pieces and season with salt.

Mix coconut and 120 ml (4 fl oz) water. Squeeze and strain to obtain thick coconut milk. Add remaining water to residue. Squeeze and strain to obtain thin coconut milk.

Heat oil in an earthen pot, fry mustard seeds till they pop, then add garlic and shallots. Fry till soft.

Add curry paste, chicken, *rempah* and curry leaves. Stir-fry till fragrant.

Pour in thin coconut milk in 3 portions, stirring chicken occasionally till tender.

When chicken is almost cooked, add potatoes, tomatoes and onions. Pour in thick coconut milk when curry is ready. Season to taste and simmer till red oil floats to the top.

Tomato Chicken

Preparation: 15 minutes
Marinating: 30 minutes
Cooking: 30 minutes

1¾ kg (4 lb) chicken, cut into 8-10 big pieces
1 teaspoon ground turmeric
2 tablespoons ground chilli
4 tablespoons ground coriander
½ teaspoon pepper
6-8 tablespoons tomato puree
750 ml (1¼ pints) water
9 tablespoons ghee
3 cloves garlic, sliced
25 shallots, sliced
2½ cm (1 in) piece ginger, shredded
2 onions, chopped
1½ teaspoons cardamom seeds
4 cloves
5 cm (2 in) cinnamon stick
8-10 tomatoes, diced
6-7 tablespoons plain yoghurt
salt to taste
1 tablespoon sugar
2 sprigs coriander leaves

Marinate chicken for 30 minutes with turmeric, chilli, coriander and pepper.

Mix tomato puree with 120 ml (4 fl oz) water.

Heat ghee in a wok over moderate heat and fry garlic and shallots till soft, then add ginger, onions, cardamom seeds, cloves and cinnamon.

After a few minutes, add chicken and stir-fry for 5 minutes, adding water a little at a time as gravy thickens.

Add tomatoes, tomato puree, yoghurt, salt and sugar. Simmer till chicken is cooked and tender.

Garnish with coriander leaves and serve with plain rice or Nasi Kunyit (p. 98).

Easy Chicken Curry

Preparation: 15 minutes
Cooking: 35 minutes

1¾ kg (4 lb) chicken
¾ coconut, grated
420 ml (¾ pint) water.
2 onions, each cut into 6 wedges
salt to taste
3 stalks curry leaves
4 segments star anise
5 cm (2 in) cinnamon stick
20 shallots, sliced
8 slices ginger, shredded
6 cloves garlic, sliced
2 stalks lemon grass, bruised

Rempah
20 dried chillies (half of them seeded) *or* 2
    tablespoons ground chilli
1 tablespoon fennel *or* 1 teaspoon ground fennel
4 cm (1½ in) piece turmeric *or* ¾ teaspoon ground
    turmeric
3 cloves
2 tablespoons ground coriander
1 teaspoon ground cummin

Cut chicken into bite-size pieces.

Mix coconut with 120 ml (4 fl oz) water. Squeeze and strain to obtain coconut milk.

Put *rempah* in an earthen pot with all other ingredients except chicken and curry leaves. Blend well then add chicken.

Stir thoroughly and simmer over moderate heat for 20 minutes, stirring now and then to prevent coconut milk curdling.

Cover, bring to a boil and simmer for 10 minutes. When chicken is tender and gravy quite thick, add curry leaves. (If drier curry is preferred, simmer longer, uncovered.)

Chicken Vindaloo

Preparation: 15 minutes
Marinating: 30 minutes
Cooking: 30 minutes

5 cm (2 in) piece ginger
120 ml (4 fl oz) white vinegar
900 g (2 lb) chicken, quartered
3 teaspoons ground turmeric
3 teaspoons ground cummin
1½ teaspoons mustard seeds, ground coarsely
20-25 dried chillies (half of them seeded), ground, *or*
    1 tablespoon ground chilli
1½ teaspoons salt
120 ml (4 fl oz) oil *or* ghee
25 shallots, pounded
6 cloves garlic, pounded
110 g (4 oz) sugar

Grind ginger with 2 teaspoons vinegar.

Marinate chicken for 30 minutes with ground turmeric, ground cummin, ground mustard, ground chilli, ground ginger and ½ teaspoon salt.

Heat oil or ghee and fry pounded shallots then garlic till soft. Add seasoned chicken, remaining vinegar and salt, and sugar.

Stir-fry for about 5 minutes, then add sufficient water to cover chicken. Simmer for 20 minutes, stirring now and then till chicken is cooked.

Duck Vindaloo

Preparation: 20 minutes
Marinating: 1 hour
Cooking: 1 hour

2 kg (4½ lb) duck, cut into 8 pieces
175 ml (6 fl oz) ghee
4 cloves garlic, pounded
20 shallots, pounded
4 tablespoons sugar
175 ml (6 fl oz) white vinegar
water to cook duck

Rempah
3 teaspoons ground turmeric

2 teaspoons ground cummin
2 teaspoons ground chilli *or* 20 dried chillies
2½ cm (1 in) piece ginger
2 tablespoons vinegar

Marinate duck in *rempah* for 1 hour.

Heat ghee in a wok and fry garlic and shallots till soft. Add duck and sugar.

Stir-fry for 10 minutes adding vinegar a little at a time. Add sufficient water to cook duck. Simmer till tender.

Duck Curry

Preparation: 15 minutes
Marinating: 30 minutes
Cooking: 1 hour

2 kg (4½ lb) duck
3 tablespoons meat curry powder (p.143)
2 teaspoons salt
1 coconut, grated
1.5 L (2½ pints) water
4 tablespoons ghee *or* oil
15 shallots, sliced thinly
3 cloves garlic, sliced thinly
2½ cm (1 in) piece ginger, shredded
5 tablespoons meat curry powder blended with
    water to a thick paste
1 tablespoon sugar
salt to taste
2 tablespoons vinegar
2 screwpine leaves, knotted together
2 onions, quartered

Cut duck into small pieces and marinate for 30 minutes with 3 tablespoons curry powder and 2 teaspoons salt.

Mix coconut and 250 ml (8 fl oz) water. Squeeze and strain to obtain thick coconut milk. Add 1.2 L (2 pints) water to residue. Squeeze and strain for thin coconut milk.

Heat oil in a pot. Fry shallots, garlic and ginger in that order till soft. Add curry paste, sugar, salt and vinegar with duck. Stir-fry for 10 minutes, adding 420 ml (¾ pint) thin coconut milk while frying.

Add screwpine leaves and cook covered for 5 minutes. Uncover, add remaining thin coconut milk and simmer for 20 minutes. If a more tender meat is preferred, add 420 ml (¾ pint) water and continue simmering till gravy is thick.

Add thick coconut milk and onions, simmer for a few more minutes.

Serve with hot rice.

Duck Padre

Preparation: 20 minutes
Cooking: 30 minutes

2 kg (4½ lb) duck
1 coconut, grated
1.6 L (2¾ pints) water
5 tablespoons oil *or* ghee
5 cm (2 in) cinnamon stick
1 teaspoon cardamom seeds
4 segments star anise
6 cloves
1-2 teaspoons sugar
1½ teaspoons salt
3 tablespoons vinegar
5 tablespoons wine *or* 1 tablespoon brandy

Rempah
2 tablespoons coriander, roasted
1 tablespoon fennel, roasted
2 teaspoons cummin, roasted
20 dried chillies
1 stalk lemon grass
20 shallots
3-4 cloves garlic
4 cm (1½ in) piece ginger

Cut duck into 4 cm (1½ in) pieces.

Mix coconut with 250 ml (8 fl oz) water. Squeeze and strain to obtain thick coconut milk. Add 1.25 L (2¼ pints) water to residue. Squeeze and strain to obtain thin coconut milk.

Mix thin coconut milk with *rempah* in a saucepan and bring to a boil. Simmer for 10 minutes over low heat.

Meanwhile, heat oil or ghee in a wok and fry ingredients in this order: cinnamon, cardamoms, star anise and cloves.

Add duck and stir-fry with sugar, salt and vinegar for about 5 minutes.

Pour in coconut milk gravy and boil till duck is tender. Add thick coconut milk and wine or brandy. Simmer for a few more minutes.

Malabar Fish Curry

Preparation: 15 minutes
Cooking: 20-30 minutes

Cod steaks *or* any fish in whole (i.e. Red Snappers *or* Lemon Soles) about 1 kg (2 lb)
2 teaspoons salt
25 shallots
2 cloves garlic
6 tablespoons tamarind
175 ml (6 fl oz) water
1-1½ coconuts, grated
1.25 L (2¼ pints) water
3-4 aubergines
6 tablespoons oil
1 teaspoon mustard seeds
4 cm (1½ in) piece ginger, shredded
6 stalks curry leaves
2½ cm (1 in) cinnamon stick
3 onions, quartered
3 tomatoes, quartered
salt to taste

Rempah
2-4 tablespoons ground chilli
5 tablespoons coriander, roasted *or* 3 tablespoons ground coriander
3 tablespoons ground cummin
1 tablespoon ground fennel
1 tablespoon ground turmeric
40 black peppercorns, ground *or* 1 tablespoon black pepper
10 white peppercorns, ground *or* ½ teaspoon white pepper
1 teaspoon cardamon seeds

Season fish with 2 teaspoons salt for 30 minutes. Rinse off salt just before cooking.

Pound shallots and garlic together.

Blend tamarind with 175 ml (6 fl oz) water. Squeeze and strain to obtain juice.

Blend grated coconut with 250 ml (8 fl oz) water. Squeeze and strain for thick coconut milk. Add remaining water to residue. Squeeze and strain for thin coconut milk.

Mix *rempah* ingredients with a quarter of the thick coconut milk.

Halve aubergines lengthwise. Quarter each half lengthwise.

Heat oil in a wok or an earthen pot and fry mustard seeds till they pop. Add shallots, garlic and ginger. Stir-fry till soft, then add curry leaves, cinnamon and *rempah*.

After about 2 minutes, when *rempah* is fragrant, add 250 ml (8 fl oz) thin coconut milk. When it boils, add aubergines and another 250 ml (8 fl oz) of thin coconut milk. Stir-fry for 5 minutes.

Add fish, onions, tomatoes, salt and tamarind juice. Keep adding thin coconut milk till used up. When aubergines and fish are almost cooked, add thick coconut milk. Simmer for 2-3 minutes and season to taste. Serve immediately with hot rice.

Fish Pudichi

Preparation: 20 minutes
Cooking: 20 minutes

450 g (1 lb) Tuna *or* Mackerel
¾ coconut, grated
420 ml (¾ pint) water
2 tablespoons oil
1 cm (½ in) cinnamon stick
2 cloves garlic, sliced
2 stalks curry leaves
salt to taste
juice of ¾ lemon

Rempah
15 dried chillies
½ teaspoon ground turmeric
10-15 shallots
1 cm (½ in) piece ginger
1 stalk lemon grass

Cut fish into 2-3 pieces.

Blend coconut and water. Squeeze and strain to obtain coconut milk. Mix coconut milk and *rempah*.

Heat oil in a wok and fry cinnamon and garlic till garlic is soft. Add curry leaves.

After half a minute, pour in coconut milk and *rempah* mixture. Bring to a boil and simmer for 10 minutes, stirring upward to prevent coconut milk curdling.

Add fish and seasoning. When fish is almost cooked, add lemon juice and simmer for another 2 minutes.

Fish Curry with Dorothy's Curry Powder

Preparation: 10 minutes
Cooking: 20 minutes

900 g (2 lb) Mackerel, Red Snapper *or* Cod
2¾ teaspoons salt
1¼ coconuts, grated
3.5 L (6¼ pints) water
5 tablespoons tamarind
175 ml (6 fl oz) water
3 aubergines
250 ml (8 fl oz) cooking oil
1½ teaspoons mustard seeds
30 shallots, sliced thinly
3 cloves garlic, sliced thinly
4 cm (1½ in) piece ginger, shredded
2½ cm (1 in) cinnamon stick
4 stalks curry leaves
1½ teaspoons cummin, roasted and ground
1 teaspoon fennel, roasted and ground
175 g (6 oz) fish curry powder (p.144)
3 tomatoes, halved
2 onions, quartered
6 small lady's fingers (*okra*)
3 green chillies, halved lengthwise
2 red chillies, halved lengthwise
1 tablespoon oil

Cut fish into 5-6 large pieces and season with ¾ teaspoon salt.

Squeeze and strain grated coconut to obtain thick coconut milk. Add 3.5 L (6¼ pints) water to residue. Squeeze and strain to obtain thin coconut milk.

Mix tamarind with 175 ml (6 fl oz) water. Squeeze and strain to obtain juice.

Cut each aubergine into 3 pieces crosswise, then halve each piece. Make a deep cut about halfway down each piece.

Heat oil in a wok or Indian earthenware pot and fry mustard seeds till they pop.

Stir-fry shallots and garlic, till soft then add ginger, cinnamon, curry leaves, cummin and fennel.

After stirring for ½ minute, add curry powder and stir-fry for at least 2 minutes.

Pour in 420 ml (¾ pint) thin coconut milk and simmer, stirring once in a while. After a few minutes add another 1 L (1¾ pints) thin coconut milk.

Put in aubergines and remaining thin coconut milk.

When aubergines are slightly cooked, add tomatoes, onions and fish.

Simmer, stirring for 8-10 minutes, then add tamarind juice and remaining 2 teaspoons salt.

When fish is nearly cooked, add lady's fingers, chillies and thick coconut milk. Cook for another 10 minutes. Keep stirring to prevent coconut milk curdling.

Serve with plain rice and *papadum* (a spicy Indian cracker).

Spicy Squid Curry

Preparation: 15 minutes
Cooking: 13 minutes

900 g (2 lb) squids
½ coconut, grated
420 ml (¾ pint) water
3 tablespoons ghee *or* oil
2 cloves garlic, sliced
2 onions, cut into 1 cm (½ in) rings
1 cm (½ in) piece ginger, shredded
¼ teaspoon fennel
2½ cm (1 in) cinnamon stick
2 stalks curry leaves
3 tablespoons fish curry powder (p.144)
¾ teaspoon ground turmeric
½ teaspoon ground chilli (optional)
3 tablespoons water
½ teaspoon sugar
salt to taste
juice of 4 limes *or* ¾ lemon

Clean squids, removing ink sac; cut into 2½ cm (1 in) pieces.

Mix coconut with 250 ml (8 fl oz) water. Squeeze and strain to obtain thick coconut milk. Add remaining water to residue. Squeeze and strain to obtain thin coconut milk.

Heat oil and fry garlic, then onions, till soft. Add ginger, fry for 1 minute, then add fennel, cinnamon and curry leaves.

After 1 minute, add squids. Mix curry powder, turmeric, chilli with water into a thick paste. Add to squids. Season to taste.

Pour in thin coconut milk and stir-fry for 5 minutes. Finally, add thick coconut milk and lime or lemon juice. Simmer for another 5 minutes.

Dry Crab Curry

Preparation: 15 minutes
Marinating: 15 minutes
Cooking: 25 minutes

3 big crabs, cut into bite-size pieces
⅓ coconut, grated
6 tablespoons oil
4 cloves garlic, sliced
14 shallots, sliced
2½ cm (1 in) piece ginger, shredded
6-8 tablespoons water
3 tomatoes, quartered
1 teaspoon sugar
1 teaspoon salt
4 tablespoons tomato ketchup
1 sprig coriander leaves

Rempah
2 teaspoons fennel
2 teaspoons cummin
30 white peppercorns
15 black peppercorns
1 tablespoon ground chilli
2 teaspoons ground turmeric

Season crabs in *rempah* for 15 minutes. Squeeze coconut in a muslin cloth to obtain thick coconut milk.

Heat oil in a wok and fry garlic, shallots then ginger till soft. Add seasoned crabs. Stir-fry for 5 minutes, adding water. Cover.

After some minutes, add tomatoes and season to taste. Sprinkle more water over crabs if too dry.

Pour in tomato ketchup. Stir-fry till crabs are cooked. Add coconut milk and simmer for just one more minute.

Garnish with coriander leaves and serve with hot rice.

Dry Lobster Curry

Preparation: 20 minutes
Marinating: 10 minutes
Cooking: 15 minutes

3 big lobsters, about 1¾ kg (4 lb)
salt to taste
1 coconut, grated
1 L (1¾ pints) water
12 tablespoons ghee *or* 10 tablespoons oil
2½ cm (1 in) piece ginger, shredded
15 shallots, sliced thinly lengthwise
2 cloves garlic, sliced thinly across
2 stalks curry leaves
2 onions, quartered
2 tomatoes, quartered
3 green chillies, quartered lengthwise

Rempah
2 tablespoons fennel
3 teaspoons cummin
2 teaspoons mustard seeds
40 black peppercorns
2 tablespoons ground chilli
2 teaspoons ground turmeric

Cut away feelers of lobsters. Steam till lobsters turn red, then marinate in *rempah* and salt for 10 minutes.

Blend coconut and 420 ml (¾ pint) water. Squeeze and strain to obtain coconut milk.

Heat ghee or oil in a wok. Fry ginger, shallots, then garlic for 3 minutes.

Add seasoned lobsters, curry leaves and remaining 420 ml (¾ pint) water. Cook covered for 3 minutes.

Remove cover and stir-fry, adding coconut milk a little at a time. Turn heat to low, add onions, tomatoes and chillies. Stir-fry till quite thick.

Serve with hot rice.

Murungakai (Drumstick) Curry

Preparation: 12 minutes
Cooking: 18 minutes

7 drumsticks (*murungakai*) (see page 171)
1 coconut, grated
420 ml (¾ pint) water
3 tablespoons tamarind
120 ml (4 fl oz) water
4 tablespoons ghee
10 shallots, sliced
2 cloves garlic, sliced
salt to taste
2 tablespoons vegetable curry powder (p.144),
    blended to a paste with a little water
3 red chillies, halved lengthwise
2 green chillies, halved lengthwise

Cut drumsticks into 7½ cm (3 in) lengths.

Blend coconut with 250 ml (8 fl oz) water. Squeeze and strain for thick coconut milk. Add 250 ml (8 fl oz) water to the residue. Squeeze and strain for thin coconut milk.

Mix tamarind and water. Squeeze and strain to obtain tamarind juice.

Heat ghee in a wok and fry shallots, garlic and drumsticks for a few minutes. Pour contents of wok into an earthen pot. Add salt, curry paste, thin coconut milk, tamarind juice and chillies.

Bring to a boil over medium heat, then simmer over low heat till cooked. Add thick coconut milk, season to taste and simmer for another 5 minutes. Remove from heat.

Note: If you wish to add prawns, put in with thick coconut milk (last step).

Dry Potato Curry with Prawns

Preparation: 15 minutes
Cooking: 25 minutes

450 g (1 lb) potatoes
3 teaspoons vegetable curry powder (p.144)
salt to taste
¼ coconut, grated
120 ml (4 fl oz) water
4 tablespoons ghee
2 onions, diced
225 g (8 oz) small prawns, peeled
1 stalk curry leaves

Boil potatoes in their jackets till cooked. Peel and cut into 2½ cm (1 in) cubes. Add curry powder and salt.

Blend coconut with water. Squeeze and strain to obtain thick coconut milk.

Heat ghee in a wok and fry onions slightly, then add prawns. Stir-fry for a minute before adding potatoes and curry leaves. After 2 minutes, add 4 tablespoons coconut milk. Stir-fry for a few more minutes, then add remaining coconut milk. Cook over low heat till quite dry.

Coconut Sambal

Preparation: 30 minutes
Cooking: 2 minutes

1 tablespoon tamarind
3-4 tablespoons water
6 shallots, sliced
3 green chillies, seeded and sliced
1 cm (½ in) piece ginger
1 clove garlic
3 stalks curry leaves
¾ white coconut, grated
1 tablespoon oil
1 teaspoon mustard seeds
3 dried chillies, each cut into 3 pieces

Blend tamarind with water. Squeeze and strain to obtain thick pulpy tamarind juice.

Grind shallots, green chillies, ginger, garlic and curry leaves together. Add tamarind juice and white grated coconut. Grind or blend to a paste.

Heat oil in a wok and throw in mustard seeds. When they pop, add dried chillies and stir-fry for a minute. Add mustard seeds and chillies to coconut sambal.

Sothi (Vegetables in Coconut Milk)

Preparation: 15 minutes
Cooking: 12-15 minutes

¼ cabbage, shredded *or* 10 lady's fingers (*okra*)
300 g (10 oz) prawns
½ coconut, grated
600 ml (1 pint) water
3 tablespoons cooking oil
1 teaspoon mustard seeds
10 shallots, sliced finely or pounded coarsely
3 red chillies, each cut lengthwise into 6 long strips
2 stalks curry leaves
¾ teaspoon ground turmeric
salt to taste
juice of 3 limes

If lady's fingers are used, wash and dry, then cut at a slant into 1 cm (½ in) thick pieces. Fry gently in a dry pan for a couple of minutes to congeal sticky juice.

Peel prawns and cut into ½ cm (¼ in) pieces.

Blend coconut with 120 ml (4 fl oz) water. Squeeze and strain to obtain thick coconut milk. Add 420 ml (¾ pint) water to residue. Squeeze and strain to obtain thin coconut milk.

Heat oil in a wok. When smoking hot, fry mustard seeds till they pop. Add shallots, fry till soft, then add chillies and curry leaves.

After stirring for a minute, add vegetable, ground turmeric, salt and thin coconut milk. When vegetable is soft, add prawns and thick coconut milk.

As soon as gravy begins to curdle, remove wok from heat and add lime juice.

Bittergourd Sambal with Fish

Preparation: 15 minutes
Cooking: 12 minutes

750 g (1⅔ lb) bittergourd
⅓ teaspoon turmeric
salt to taste
420 ml (¾ pint) oil
¼ coconut, grated
175 ml (6 fl oz) water
5 shallots, sliced
2 green chillies, quartered lengthwise
juice of ½ lime
Cod Fillet (cut into 2 in pieces)

Halve bittergourd lengthwise. Dig out seeds and cut at a slant into 3 mm slices. Rub in turmeric and salt.

Heat oil in a wok and deep-fry bittergourd till crisp. Drain and place in a dish.

Mix coconut milk with water. Squeeze and strain to obtain coconut milk.

Put coconut milk with shallots, green chillies and lime juice in a pot and bring to a boil. Add fish and cook for 3 minutes. Season to taste.

Pour gravy with fish over bittergourd.

Bittergourd with Turmeric

Preparation: 10 minutes
Cooking: 7 minutes

450 g (1 lb) bittergourd
¾ teaspoon ground turmeric
salt to taste
175 ml (6 fl oz) oil

Cut bittergourd into half across, then halve again. Dig out seeds. Cut at a slant into 3 mm thick rings. Rub in turmeric and salt.

Heat oil in a wok and fry bittergourd till quite crisp.

Serve as a side dish with rice and curry.

Brinjal Curry

Preparation: 15 minutes
Cooking: 20 minutes

450 g (1 lb) aubergines
½ teaspoon ground turmeric
½ teaspoon salt
4 tablespoons oil
½ coconut, grated
250 ml (8 fl oz) water

Rempah
2½ cm (1 in) slice fish (Mackerel)
10 dried chillies, roasted
10 shallots
2 cloves garlic
½ cm (¼ in) piece ginger
1 stalk lemon grass
1 teaspoon vinegar
salt to taste

Halve aubergines crosswise, then quarter each half lengthwise. Rub with turmeric and salt. Set aside for some minutes, then fry in oil.

Blend coconut with water. Squeeze and strain to obtain coconut milk.

Bring coconut milk to a boil with *rempah*. Simmer till gravy is very thick. Add cooked aubergines and simmer for a few more minutes.

Vegetable Salad

Preparation: 10 minutes

2 round slices pineapple, ½ cm (¼ in) thick
1 cucumber, sliced thinly
pinch of salt
1 onion, diced
juice of ½ lemon
1 teaspoon sugar
2-3 red chillies, seeded and sliced or chopped

Cut each pineapple slice into 8 pieces. Mix cucumber with salt, then add pineapple, onion, lemon juice, sugar and chillies.

Cucumber Salad with Coconut Milk

Preparation: 15 minutes

2 cucumbers
salt to taste
½ coconut, grated
4 tablespoons water
1 red chilli
2 green chillies
juice of 4 limes
1 onion, sliced into thin rings

Slice cucumbers thinly, sprinkle salt over slices and leave aside for a few minutes. Squeeze slightly to remove excess water.

Blend coconut with water. Squeeze and strain to obtain thick coconut milk.

Cut red and green chillies lengthwise into thin strips. Discard seeds.

Put cucumber slices and chilli strips in a deep dish with lime juice and onion rings. Pour coconut milk over the salad.

If salad is to be used later, add salt to coconut milk and refrigerate. This salad goes well with Indian curries.

Pineapple Putchree

Preparation: 10 minutes
Cooking: 15 minutes

1 pineapple
3 teaspoons ground turmeric
5 tablespoons oil
2 sticks cinnamon, each 2½ cm (1 in) long
1½ teaspoons cardamom seeds
4 segments star anise
8 cloves
2½ cm (1 in) piece ginger, sliced
2 onions, cut into thin rings
4 green chillies, halved lengthwise
4 red chillies, halved lengthwise
7 tablespoons granulated sugar
¼ teaspoon salt

Remove skin of pineapple. Quarter lengthwise and slice away hard core. Slice into 1 cm (½ in) thick wedges.

Mix pineapple wedges with ground turmeric and cook over medium heat for 5 minutes. Remove from heat and leave in a sieve to drain.

Heat oil in a wok and fry ingredients, adding in the order listed: cinnamon, cardamom seeds, star anise, cloves, ginger, onions. When fragrant, add pineapple, chillies, sugar and salt. Stir constantly for another 5 minutes over moderate heat.

Pineapple Pickle

Preparation: 15 minutes

1 almost ripe pineapple
1 onion
5 tablespoons vinegar
salt to taste
1 teaspoon sugar

Rempah
15 g (½ oz) mustard seeds
6-8 dried chillies
2 cloves garlic
2½ cm (1 in) piece ginger
¼ teaspoon ground turmeric

Cut pineapple and onion into ½ cm (¼ in) cubes.

Mix *rempah* with vinegar, salt and sugar. Add pineapple and onion and mix well.

Pineapple and Raisin Chutney

Preparation: 25 minutes
Cooking: 20 minutes

280 g (10 oz) sugar
1 tablespoon salt
4 tablespoons white vinegar
120 ml (4 fl oz) water
140 g (5 oz) 1 cm (½ in) pineapple cubes
175 g (6 oz) white raisins
120 ml (4 fl oz) Chinese plum sauce
2 onions, cut into 1 cm (½ in) cubes
4 green chillies, halved lengthwise, then sliced into 4
   pieces

Rempah
10 dried chillies, half of them seeded, or 1 teaspoon
   ground chilli
2½ cm (1 in) piece ginger
3 cloves garlic
4 red chillies (ground coarsely)

Put sugar, salt, vinegar, water and *rempah* into a deep enamel pot. Boil till sugar dissolves, stirring constantly to prevent burning.

Add pineapple cubes and raisins. Simmer, stirring constantly, till pineapple is cooked, then add Chinese plum sauce and finally onions and green chillies.

Mango Chutney

Preparation: 15 minutes
Cooking: 40 minutes

6 big green mangoes
4 tablespoons ghee *or* oil
15 shallots, sliced
6 dried chillies, each seeded and cut into 2 or 3
    sections
8 tablespoons demerara *or* brown sugar
½ teaspoon salt
750 ml (1¼ pints) water
120 g (4 oz) raisins, ground

Peel mangoes and halve lengthwise. Cut flesh from seeds.

Melt ghee in a pot and fry shallots and chillies. Add mangoes, sugar, salt and water. Stir in ground raisins.

Cook covered over low heat for about 30 minutes till mango is soft, stirring once in a while to prevent burning.

Uncover and stir continuously till chutney is thick.

Mango Chutney goes well with any hot curry.

Paratha

Preparation: 30 minutes
Cooking: 30 minutes

600 g (1⅓ lb) self-raising flour
120 ml (4 fl oz) fresh milk
120 ml (4 fl oz) water
1 teaspoon salt
1 teaspoon sugar
2 eggs, beaten
225 g (8 oz) ghee

Place flour in a heap on a smooth clean working surface. Make a well in the centre by pushing flour to the sides.

Pour milk, water, salt and sugar into this well. Work flour towards the centre, kneading well.

As you knead, add beaten eggs. Knead for at least 10 minutes till a smooth dough is obtained.

If dough is too dry, wet palms of hands and continue kneading. Pinch into 7 or 8 balls.

Cover balls of dough with a wet towel and leave to rise in a warm place overnight or for 12-15 hours.

Flatten each ball with the palm of your hand into a flat disc.

Roll out till thin and fold in 2 sides. Pull up to a narrow "rope" of dough and coil downwards into a round bun.

Flatten with a rolling pin or the palm of your hand into a 20 cm (8 in) pancake.

Sprinkle ghee generously on an iron griddle. Place a pancake on the griddle.

Sprinkle ghee on upper surface of Paratha while frying. Turn over and fry the other side. Both sides should be golden brown and crisp.

Note: For an illustration of method, see opposite.

Easy Thosai

Preparation: 15 minutes
Cooking: 30 minutes

175 g (6 oz) black gram dhal
350 g (12 oz) rice flour
salt to taste
420 ml (¾ pint) water
4 tablespoons ghee

Soak dhal in water for about 1 hour.

Put rice flour, dhal and salt in a blender. Add water and blend to a smooth paste.

Leave overnight or for 8-10 hours in a large pot to ferment. Refrigerate if not using for breakfast.

Grease an iron griddle with ghee. Pour a ladleful of batter onto griddle and spread by making circular movements with the back of the ladle.

When one side is cooked, spread ½ teaspoon ghee on upper surface and turn over.

Serve with Coconut Sambal (p.88).

Making Paratha

1 Pat ball of dough with fingers and palms to flatten.

2 Roll out long and thin.

▲
3 Fold in two sides.

4 Pull up to a thin "rope".
▼

5 Let "rope" come down in a coiling motion. Guide it with the other hand.
▼

▲
6 The finished coiled ball of dough, set aside till ready to roll out and cook on griddle.

Clockwise from top: Tomato Chicken (p.82) with Mango Chutney (p.92)
and Rasam (p. 117)

Clockwise: Dry Lobster Curry (p.87), Chapati (p.97), Dhal Vadai (p.97)
and Mutton Curry (p.80)

Clockwise: Malabar Fish Curry (p.85), Cucumber Salad with Coconut Milk (p.90), Papadum, and Pineapple Putchree (p.91)

Dhal Vadai

Preparation: 30 minutes
Cooking: 10 minutes

750 g (1⅔ lb) black gram
3 tablespoons rice flour
1 tablespoon plain flour
¾ teaspoon salt
1 teaspoon sugar
2 big onions, diced
2 teaspoons vegetable curry powder (p.144)
oil for deep-frying
8 green chillies

Soak dhal in boiling hot water for 2 hours, then drain. Grind or blend two-thirds of the dhal to a paste, leaving remainder as whole grains.

Mix paste and whole grain dhal with rice flour, plain flour, salt, sugar, onions and curry powder.

Shape into balls, then flatten to 5 cm (2 in) patties about 2½ cm (1 in) thick. Deep-fry patties in hot oil.

Serve with whole green chillies or Vinegar Chilli Sauce (p.141).

Chapati

Preparation: 45 minutes
Cooking: 20 minutes

350 g (12 oz) plain flour *or* thuvar dhal flour
   (commonly called "Chapati flour")
¼ teaspoon salt
1½ teaspoons melted ghee *or* butter (optional)
11 tablespoons water
extra flour for dusting board
extra ghee

Sift flour with salt into a deep bowl. Make a well in the centre. Add melted ghee or butter (if used) to well and push flour towards the centre. Rub with fingers. Add water gradually and mix by hand to a firm dough. If dough is too stiff sprinkle on a little water. Knead dough for 10-15 minutes.

Cover dough with a damp cloth and leave to rise for at least 2 hours, preferably overnight for a very light chapati.

Mould into 4 cm (1½ in) balls. Roll out to thin 15 cm (6 in) rounds on a lightly floured board.

Grease a hot griddle with a little ghee. Wipe away excess ghee. Fry chapati in the order rolled out, i.e., the first one rolled should be cooked first. Fry one side for half a minute then turn to brown the other side.

Press lightly around the edges of chapati with a folded dry tea towel to form air bubbles. When cooked, hold chapati with a pair of tongs and place for just a second or so directly on the grill. This causes chapati to puff up. Turn over, and wait another second or so, then transfer to a plate. Rub with a little ghee or butter to soften.

Rice and Noodles

Nasi Kunyit (Yellow Glutinous Rice)

Preparation: 10 minutes
Cooking: 40 minutes

600 g (1⅓ lb) glutinous rice
1½ tablespoons freshly ground turmeric
1 tablespoon lemon juice
1½ white coconuts, grated
120 ml (4 fl oz) water
1 banana leaf *or* Chinese leaf
4 screwpine leaves, knotted in pairs

Wash and drain rice. Add ground turmeric, lemon juice and water to a level 7 ½ cm (3 in) above rice. Leave for at least 8 hours. Drain off water just before cooking.

Mix grated coconut with 1 tablespoon water. Squeeze and strain to obtain thick coconut milk. Add remaining water to residue. Squeeze and strain to obtain thin coconut milk.

Line base of steamer with banana leaf or Chinese leaf, pricking holes through the leaf where steamer holes are to allow steam through.

Place rice on leaf and screwpine leaves on rice. Steam for 20 minutes over boiling water.

Scoop rice into a large bowl and pour in thin coconut milk. Stir, then cover and steam for another 10 minutes.

When rice is almost cooked, stir in thick coconut milk. Continue steaming till rice is cooked.

Note: In the Peranakan tradition, Nasi Kunyit is distributed with Chicken Curry (p.60) to friends and relatives when a baby is a month old. At home, it is served with Udang Goreng Assam (p.70) and Belimbing and Prawn Sambal (p.76).

Tomato Rice

Preparation: 20 minutes
Cooking: 30 minutes

1 kg (2 lb) Basmati rice
120 ml (4 fl oz) oil
4 cloves garlic, sliced
10 shallots, sliced
4-6 tablespoons ghee
4 segments star anise
5 cm (2 in) cinnamon stick
6 cardamoms, bruised
1 big onion, diced
4 cm (1½ in) piece ginger, chopped
250 ml (8 fl oz) canned tomato soup
3 tablespoons tomato purée
1 L (1¾ pints) water
⅓ teaspoon salt
1 teaspoon sugar
3 tablespoons yoghurt
2 tablespoons evaporated milk

Wash and drain rice.

Heat oil in a wok and fry garlic and shallots till crisp and golden. Set aside in a dish.

Heat ghee in a clean wok and fry star anise, cinnamon and cardamoms. Add onion and ginger, stir-fry for half a minute.

Add rice and stir-fry for 3 minutes. Transfer contents of wok to a pot or rice cooker.

Add tomato soup, tomato purée and water with seasoning to rice. Mix well and cook till dry.

Loosen rice grains and stir in yoghurt and milk. Cook for another 5 minutes. Garnish with deep-fried garlic and shallots just before serving.

Serve Tomato Rice with meat curry and a pickle or vegetable salad.

Nasi Briani

Preparation: 1¹/₂ hours
Cooking: 30 minutes

8 cloves garlic, sliced
5 cm (2 in) cinnamon stick, broken into small pieces
4 segments star anise
2 teaspoons poppy seeds
8 cardamoms
2 teaspoons ground fennel
450 g (1 lb) Basmati rice
¹/₂ teaspoon ground turmeric
6 tablespoons butter
6 slices ginger, shredded
20 shallots, sliced thinly
2¹/₂ cm (1 in) piece fresh turmeric, ground *or* 2
   teaspoons ground turmeric
350 ml (12 fl oz) yoghurt, more if preferred
1³/₄ teaspoons salt
1³/₄ kg (4 lb) chicken, quartered
1 tablespoon coriander, roasted, ground and
   wrapped in a muslin bag
120 ml (4 fl oz) cooking oil
90 g (3 oz) ghee
2¹/₂ cm (1 in) cinnamon stick
water to cook rice
20 cashew nuts, deep-fried
90 g (3 oz) raisins
20 shallots, sliced and deep-fried
4 cloves garlic, sliced and deep-fried

Pound garlic, cinnamon, star anise, poppy seeds, cardamoms and fennel together.

Wash rice and soak in water mixed with ground turmeric for 30 minutes. Drain thoroughly.

Heat butter and fry ginger, shallots and fresh turmeric till fragrant. Add 4 tablespoons yoghurt with ¹/₂ teaspoon salt.

Mix well, then add pounded ingredients, chicken, another 4 tablespoons yoghurt and ¹/₂ teaspoon salt. Also add coriander in muslin bag. Fry till chicken is cooked.

Heat oil and ghee in a wok and add cinnamon stick. After half a minute, add remaining yoghurt and salt. Stir well, then add rice.

Transfer well-mixed contents of wok to a deep pot. Add sufficient water to a level 2 cm (³/₄ in) above rice. Cover and cook for 30 minutes or till rice is tender.

Stir in half the fried cashew nuts, raisins, deep-fried shallots and garlic. Garnish rice with the remainder just before serving.

Thai Pulot with Mango

Preparation: 20 minutes
Cooking: 40 minutes

450 g (1 lb) glutinous rice
water
1¹/₂ coconuts, grated
120 ml (4 fl oz) water
2 teaspoons sugar
1 teaspoon salt
5-6 medium-sized Thai mangoes

Soak glutinous rice in water for at least 3 hours, then drain.

Put rice in top compartment of double boiler. Add cold water to reach 1 cm (¹/₂ in) above rice. Steam for 20 minutes till cooked but still grainy.

Blend coconut wiith 120 ml (4 fl oz) water. Squeeze and strain to obtain coconut milk.

Scoop 4 tablespoons coconut milk out and cook over very low heat, stirring constantly, till thick.

Dissolve sugar and salt in remaining coconut milk. Stir this into cooked hot rice with a pair of chopsticks. Set aside for 10 minutes.

Peel mangoes and slice lengthwise as near the seed as possible to get 2 thick large pieces from each mango. Cut mango pieces into ¹/₂ cm (¹/₄ in) slices.

Place mango to one side of each serving plate and scoop cooked rice next to mango. Spoon coconut milk over rice.

Nasi Lemak (Fragrant Coconut Milk Rice)

Preparation: 8 minutes
Cooking: 20 minutes

350 ml (12 fl oz) water
140 g (5 oz) grated coconut
600 g (1⅓ lb) long-grain Thai rice
½ teaspoon salt
2-3 fragrant screwpine leaves, knotted together

Add 120 ml (4 fl oz) water to grated coconut, squeeze and strain to obtain thick coconut milk. Add 250 ml (8 fl oz) water to the residue and squeeze to obtain thin coconut milk.

Wash rice till clean, then put in a rice cooker. Mix 175 ml (6 fl oz) thick coconut milk with the thin coconut milk. Pour over the rice so that milk level is 2 cm (¾ in) above the surface of the rice. Add salt and knotted screwpine leaves.

Cook rice for 14 minutes or until dry. Use a wooden ladle or a pair of chopsticks and quickly loosen the grains. Sprinkle remaining thick coconut milk over the rice and stir to distribute evenly.

Cover and dry rice over low heat until coconut milk is absorbed and rice is fragrant.

Serve Nasi Lemak with any two or three of the following: Ikan/Udang Goreng Assam (pp.63, 70), Kangkung Masak Lemak Udang (p.75), Sambal Udang (p.29), Sambal Blacan (p.139), Otak-Otak Bakar (p.70), and cut cucumbers.

Compressed Rice for Lontong/Ketupat – An Easy Method

Preparation: 10 minutes
Cooking: 20 minutes

680 g (1½ lb) rice
water
pinch of salt
2 screwpine leaves, tied into a knot

Add sufficient water to rice to a level 5 cm (2 in) above rice. Stir in salt and put in screwpine leaves.

Cook for 20 minutes over moderate heat till water is absorbed. Rice should be moist.

Mash with the back of a wooden spoon or blend in an electric blender till smooth.

Transfer rice to a 10 cm (4 in) square tin fitted with a flat lid slightly smaller than 10 cm (4 in) square.

Press lid firmly onto rice and place a mortar or some other heavy object on top.

Leave in the refrigerator for 6-8 hours, then remove weight and cut into rectangular slices ½ cm (¼ in) thick.

To serve Lontong
Place lontong in a deep plate, then pour Sayur Lodeh (p.31) over it. Serve with any of these Lontong side dishes: Tempe Goreng (p.32), Sambal Udang (p.29), Coconut Serondeng (p.32), Sambal Lengkong (p.64), Belimbing and Prawn Sambal (p.76), Ikan Masak Assam Pekat (p.69), Mutton Rendang (p.19) and Sambal Telur (p.24).

Ketupat
For ketupat, cut compressed rice into 2½ cm (1 in) cubes and serve with either Malay Satay (p.20) or Nonya Satay (p.58).

Fried Rice

Preparation: 10 minutes
Cooking: 12 minutes

2 eggs, beaten
2-2½ tablespoons light soy sauce
dash of pepper
175 ml (6 fl oz) oil
3 cloves garlic, chopped finely
4 shallots, sliced finely
225 g (8 oz) minced pork *or* Char Siew (Red Pork
   Roast) (p.37), diced finely
1 pair Chinese sausages, sliced
3-4 slices bacon, shredded
340 g (12 oz) small prawns, shelled
225 g (8 oz) crabmeat
60 g (2 oz) green peas
2 red chillies, sliced finely (optional)
½ teaspoon salt
110 g (¼ lb) cold cooked rice
2 stalks spring onion, sliced finely

Season beaten eggs with 1 teaspoon light soy sauce and pepper. Set aside. Heat oil in a wok till smoking hot and brown garlic and shallots. Add pork, Chinese sausages, bacon, prawns, crabmeat, green peas, chillies (if used) and salt.

Stir for a few seconds, then add rice and cook for about 5 minutes, stirring briskly to mix ingredients thoroughly. Season with more light soy sauce.

Move rice to side of wok, add beaten eggs to the bottom to form omelette; then break egg into little pieces with the spatula. Mix with rice and sprinkle with spring onion.

Kai Cheok (Chicken Porridge)

Preparation: 10 minutes
Cooking: 1 hour 10 minutes

450 g (1 lb) rice
3.5 L (6¼ pints) water
2 kg (4½ lb) chicken
sufficient boiling hot water to cover chicken
2 chicken bouillon cubes
1 teaspoon salt
150 ml (¼ pint) oil
15 shallots, sliced thinly crosswise
pepper
10 cm (4 in) piece young ginger, finely shredded
6-8 stalks spring onion, chopped
4 tablespoons light soy sauce

Boil rice in 3.5 L (6¼ pints) water in a deep pot over moderate heat. If it threatens to boil over, turn heat down. Cook 40 minutes or till grains are broken and porridge takes on a thick consistency. Add more water if necessary till the right consistency is reached.

Halve chicken and put in a pot with sufficient boiling hot water to cover chicken. Stir in chicken bouillon cubes and salt, and continue to cook on low heat for 30 minutes.

When chicken is cooked, remove and shred meat.

Heat oil in a wok and stir-fry shallots till golden brown. Scoop out crispy shallots and oil to a small bowl.

To serve Kai Cheok, scoop porridge into individual deep bowls. Add shredded meat and garnish with crispy shallots, a little oil, pepper, shredded ginger and spring onion. Serve with light soy sauce in a saucer.

Teochew Fish Porridge

Preparation: 15 minutes
Cooking: 40 minutes

900 g (2 lb) Mackerel *or* White Pomfret
½ teaspoon salt
175 ml (6 fl oz) oil
10 shallots, sliced thinly crosswise
225 g (8 oz) rice
2.75 L (5 pints) water
225 g (8 oz) dried prawns
4 teaspoons light soy sauce
pinch of salt
2 lettuce leaves, shredded coarsely
pepper
1½ teaspoons *tung chye*
4 stalks spring onion, chopped
2 tablespoons light soy sauce

Cut fish into thin slices and season with ½ teaspoon salt.

Heat 4 tablespoons oil in a wok and fry shallots till golden brown. Scoop out oil and crispy shallots to a small bowl.

Put rice and 2.75 L (5 pints) water in a deep pot. Cook for 30 minutes. Porridge should be watery with soft but whole rice grains.

Just before serving, put in fish, dried prawns, 4 teaspoons light soy sauce and a pinch of salt. Turn off heat.

To serve, put a few pieces of lettuce in individual serving bowls. Ladle porridge into bowl and garnish with pepper, ¼ teaspoon *tung chye*, crispy shallots with a little oil and spring onion.

Serve extra light soy sauce separately in a small saucer.

Chicken Macaroni

Preparation: 10 minutes
Cooking: 50 minutes

5.5 L (10 pints) water
450 g (1 lb) macaroni
½ teaspoon pepper *or* 12 peppercorns, ground
1 chicken, about 2 kg (4½ lb), halved
2 chicken bouillon cubes
2 tablespoons light soy sauce
2 teaspoons salt
1½ teapoons sugar
5 slices bread
420 ml (¾ pint) oil
15 shallots, sliced thinly crosswise
6 stalks spring onion, chopped
pepper

Bring 1.25 L (2¼ pints) water to a boil and cook macaroni for 10 minutes till centres are cooked.

Drain in a sieve and run cold water through macaroni to stop the cooking process.

Bring remaining 3.75 L (6¾ pints) water to a boil. Add pepper and chicken. Cook covered for 15 minutes.

Remove cooked chicken and plunge into cold water. Shred meat.

Throw chicken bones back into stock. Boil for 20 minutes or longer over moderate heat. Strain.

Dissolve chicken bouillon cubes in a little water and stir into stock with light soy sauce, salt and sugar.

Cut bread into small cubes. Heat oil in a wok and deep-fry bread cubes till golden brown. Scoop onto greaseproof paper.

Strain oil. Reheat 120 ml (4 fl oz) oil and stir-fry shallots till crisp. Remove oil and shallots to a bowl.

To serve, put a ladleful of macaroni in each serving bowl, top with chicken meat and pour boiling hot soup over this.

Garnish with fried bread cubes, crispy shallots, spring onion and pepper. Serve immediately.

Nonya Meesiam with Assam Gravy

Preparation: 20 minutes
Cooking: 45 minutes

600 g (1⅓ lb) rice vermicelli
½ coconut, grated
1.5 L (2½ pints) water
750 ml (1¼ pints) oil
9 tablespoons sugar
1 tablespoon salt
5 tablespoons light soy sauce
1¼ kg (2¾ lb) medium-sized prawns, shelled and
   deveined
juice of ½ lemon *or* 4 limes
4½ tablespoons tamarind
2 onions, chopped finely
90 g (3 oz) dried prawns, ground finely
6 tablespoons preserved soy beans
½ teaspoon salt
extra water to cook rice vermicelli
3 firm soybean cakes, diced
600 g (1⅓ lb) beansprouts, scalded for 1 minute in
   boiling water
10 stalks Chinese chives, cut into 1 cm (½ in)
   lengths
8 hardboiled eggs, sliced

Rempah
40 dried chillies
8 red chillies
30 shallots
2 cloves garlic

Soak rice vermicelli in cold water for 8 minutes
or till soft, then drain and set aside.

Mix coconut with 5 tablespoons water. Squeeze
and strain to obtain coconut milk.

Heat 175 ml (6 fl oz) oil in a wok and fry *rempah*
till fragrant. Add 3 tablespoons sugar, 1 tablespoon salt and 3 tablespoons light soy sauce with
fresh prawns.

Pour in coconut milk and simmer for 2 minutes.
Stir gently, then add lemon or lime juice.

Divide this sambal into 3 roughly equal portions:
(1) for cooking gravy – with no prawns; (2) for
cooking rice vermicelli – with a third of the
prawns; (3) for garnish – with remaining prawns.

Blend tamarind with 1 cup water. Squeeze and
strain to obtain juice.

Prepare assam gravy. Heat 120 ml (4 fl oz) oil in
a wok and fry diced onion for 1 minute. Put in
dried prawns, preserved soy beans and tamarind
juice.

Stir-fry for 2 minutes then add plain sambal
portion (no prawns) and 1.2 L (2 pints) water.
Bring to a boil and simmer for 10 minutes. Stir in
salt and 5 tablespoons sugar.

Heat 175 ml (6 fl oz) oil in a wok and put in
second sambal portion (with less prawns) and
rice vermicelli.

Sprinkle with a little water to keep rice vermicelli slightly damp. Stir constantly with a
spatula and a pair of chopsticks till cooked. Add
remaining 2 tablespoons light soy sauce and 1
tablespoon sugar.

In a clean wok heat remaining oil and fry diced
soybean cakes till light brown. Drain.

To serve, put rice vermicelli in individual plates,
top with beansprouts and pour a ladleful of
boiling gravy over this.

Garnish with fried diced soybean cakes. Chinese
chives, egg slices and a little of the third sambal
portion (with more prawns).

Serve immediately.

Thai Meesiam

Preparation: 15 minutes
Cooking: 25 minutes

450 g (1 lb) rice vermicelli
hot water to cover rice vermicelli
3-4 drops red colouring
175 ml (6 fl oz) oil
6 shallots, sliced thinly crosswise
3 firm soybean cakes, halved and sliced thinly
2 tablespoons light soy sauce
2½ tablespoons fish sauce (*nampla*)
300 g (10 oz) beansprouts
3 eggs
pinch of salt
2 tablespoons oil

1 coconut, grated
1 L (1¾ pints) water
60 g (2 oz) dried prawns, ground finely
225 g (8 oz) minced pork
450 g (1 lb) small prawns, shelled
2 tablespoons preserved soy beans, pounded
2 tablespoons sugar
3 red chillies, seeded and cut into long thin strips
2 sprigs coriander leaves, chopped
2 lemons, cut into 6 slices *or* 8 limes, halved
   crosswise
2 bunches lettuce, shredded
1 big onion, sliced into thin rings
15 red chillies, pounded *or* 2 tablespoons ground
   chilli

Rice Vermicelli

Soak rice vermicelli in hot water to which red colouring powder has been added. Drain after 4-5 minutes, taking care not to let rice vermicelli get too soft.

Heat oil in a wok and fry shallots till golden brown. Remove to a small dish.

In the same oil, fry soybean cake slices till light brown. Remove this to another dish.

In remaining oil, fry rice vermicelli with light soy sauce and 1½ tablespoons fish sauce for 6 minutes. Push rice vermicelli to side of wok and put beansprouts in the centre of wok for a minute or so till half-cooked. Remove.

Beat egg with salt. Pour 2 tablespoons oil in a clean wok.

Heat the wok. Pour egg into centre of wok and swirl it around to form a thin pancake. Cook for 1 minute.

Turn out onto a cutting board and cut into thin strips.

Mix coconut with 1 L (1¾ pints) water. Squeeze and strain to obtain coconut milk.

Bring coconut milk to a boil in a saucepan, then add ground dried prawns, pork, fresh prawns, pounded preserved soy beans and sugar.

Stir in remaining tablespoon fish sauce and cook for 8 minutes.

To serve, place rice vermicelli on a flat oval plate. Arrange egg strips on top, soybean cakes around the side. Garnish with sliced chilli and chopped coriander.

Serve gravy in a bowl. Arrange lemon slices or lime halves, shredded lettuce and onion rings on a flat plate. Serve ground chilli in a saucer.

Mee Sua with Kidneys

Preparation: 15 minutes
Cooking: 8-10 minutes

1 pair pig's kidneys
2 teaspoons salt (soaking)
3.75 L (6¾ pints) boiling hot water
1 tablespoon Chinese rice wine
12 small rolls fine rice vermicelli
3 tablespoons oil
2½ cm (1 in) piece ginger, shredded finely
3 cloves garlic, chopped
150 g (5 oz) pork fillet, sliced finely
½ teaspoon salt
1-2 tablespoons light soy sauce
150 g (5 oz) pig's liver, sliced finely
2 stalks spring onion, chopped
pepper

Clean kidneys by filling hole with water from a running tap. Halve lengthwise and cut out central white membrane. Soak them in boiling water with 2 teaspoons of salt for 2 minutes. Drain the water.

Make shallow criss-cross slits in smooth outer surface. Cut each kidney into 3 triangular pieces.

Soak kidneys in cold water for 15 minutes and drain. Scald in 1.2 L (2 pints) boiling hot water to get rid of the smell then drain again.

Add Chinese rice wine to kidney pieces and mix well. Leave to soak in wine till ready to serve.

Scald rice vermicelli in 1 L (1¾ pints) boiling hot water for ½ minute, then drain off excess water. Leave noodles a little moist to prevent them from sticking and forming lumps.

Heat oil in a wok and fry ginger and garlic till crisp.

Pour in remaining 6 L (2¾ pints) boiling hot water and add pork slices. When meat is half-cooked, stir in salt and light soy sauce.

Lastly, add liver and turn off heat at once so as not to overcook liver.

To serve, place a piece of kidney in each individual serving bowl. Scald with a little boiling hot soup.

Divide rice vermicelli into 6 portions and put one portion in each serving bowl.

Pour soup over vermicelli. Distribute slices of liver and meat evenly and garnish with chopped spring onion and pepper.

Hot Singapore Laksa Lemak

Preparation: 15 minutes
Cooking: 25 minutes

3-4 coconuts, grated
3.50 L (6¼ pints) water
1¼ kg (2⅔ lb) fresh thick rice vermicelli (*laksa meeboon*) or 2½ packets dried thick rice vermicelli
2.25 L (4 pints) boiling hot water
200 g (6⅔ oz) beansprouts
450 g (1 lb) medium-sized prawns
350 ml (12 fl oz) cooking oil
4 tablespoons coriander, roasted, ground and sifted
200 g (6⅔ oz) dried prawns, pounded finely
2 teaspoons salt
1 cucumber, peeled and shredded
36 cooked fishballs (available from Chinese supermarket)
3 fish cakes, sliced (available from Chinese supermarket)
30 red chillies, pounded
pepper

Rempah
3 cloves garlic
35 shallots
3 teaspoons dried shrimp paste
5 cm (2 in) piece turmeric
14 slices galingale
8 candlenuts
50 dried chillies, 20 of them seeded
3 stalks lemon grass

Mix coconut and 350 ml (12 fl oz) water. Squeeze and strain to obtain thick coconut milk. Add remaining 3.20 L (5¾ pints) water to residue. Squeeze and strain to obtain thin coconut milk.

Scald thick rice vermicelli in boiling water for 3 minutes. Remove to a colander to drain.

Scald beansprouts for 1 minute in the same boiling water. Remove to a dish. Cook prawns in boiling water for 2 minutes. Remove and shell when cool.

Heat oil in a wok and fry *rempah* and coriander for 2 minutes, then add dried prawns. Stir-fry till crisp.

Transfer contents of wok to a large saucepan. Pour in 420 ml (¾ pint) thin coconut milk. Bring to a boil. Simmer for 5 minutes, add another 1 L (1¾ pints) thin coconut milk and continue simmering for 5 more minutes. Pour in remaining thin coconut milk and boil for 10 minutes over moderate heat in uncovered saucepan.

Stir in salt. Continue simmering, stirring every now and then along the sides of the pot to prevent coconut milk from curdling.

When gravy is reduced to 2.25 L (4 pints), add thick coconut milk and boil, stirring constantly, till red oil floats on top.

To serve, divide thick rice vermicelli into 10-12 individual serving bowls. Pour gravy over this.

Garnish each bowl with beansprouts, shredded cucumber, 3 fishballs, prawns, slices of fish cake, ½-¾ teaspoon pounded chilli and a dash of pepper.

Note: When cooking dishes with thick coconut milk, never cover the saucepan after adding thick coconut milk as it tends to curdle along the sides.

Cantonese Fried Kway Teow (Fried Rice Noodles)

Preparation: 15 minutes
Cooking: 12 minutes

300 g (10 oz) pork ribs
1.75 L (3 pints) water
300 g (10 oz) medium-sized prawns
2 tablespoons oil
1½ kg (3⅓ lb) flat rice noodles (*kway teow*)
4 stalks mustard greens
300 g (10 oz) cuttlefish
1 tablespoon oil
5 cloves garlic, chopped
300 g (10 oz) pork fillet, sliced very thin

1 tablespoon light soy sauce
1 teaspoon tapioca flour
3 tablespoons water
¾ teaspoon pepper
12 stalks Chinese chives, cut into ½ cm (¼ in) lengths

Sauce
8 tablespoons lard oil
1 tablespoon light soy sauce
1 tablespoon tapioca flour
120 ml (4 fl oz) water

Yellow Noodles

Boil pork ribs in 1.25 L (2¼ pints) water for about 20 minutes. Discard ribs and keep stock.

Peel prawns and boil shells in 350 ml (12 fl oz) water for 5 minutes. Strain prawn stock.

Combine meat and prawn stocks. Boil till stock is reduced to 420 ml (¾ pint).

Heat wok till smoking hot, add 2 tablespoons oil and fry rice noodles till slightly burnt. Remove to a large oval serving dish.

Separate leaves and stalks of mustard greens. Cut stalks into 1 cm (½ in) lengths.

Clean cuttlefish, remove ink sac and bone, and cut into ½ cm (¼ in) rings.

Heat oil in a wok and brown garlic. Pour in 420 ml (¾ pint) stock, bring to a boil and simmer for 5 minutes.

Add sliced pork, light soy sauce and vegetable stalks. After 2 minutes, add leaves.

Blend tapioca flour with 3 tablespoons water and stir into stock.

Combine sauce ingredients, mix well, then add to stock. Put in cuttlefish, simmer for 1 minute, then pour contents of wok over rice noodles.

Sprinkle with pepper and Chinese chives. Serve with a small side dish of Pickled Green Chillies (p.135).

Hokkien Mee/Meehoon Soup

Preparation: 20 minutes
Cooking: 50 minutes

2.25 L (4 pints) water
4 pieces sugar-cane, each 5 cm (2 in) long, quartered
    lengthwise
120 g (4 oz) pork fat, cut into ½ cm (¼ in) cubes
25 shallots, sliced thinly crosswise
600 g (1⅓ lb) pork ribs
600 g (1⅓ lb) shoulder pork, with skin
1 teaspoon salt
90 g (3 oz) rock sugar, crushed
1 teaspoon pepper
3 tablespoons light soy sauce
2 teaspoons black soy sauce
30 g (1 oz) lard oil
750 g (1⅔ lb) medium-sized prawns
boiling hot water for prawns
900 g (2 lb) fresh yellow noodles *or* 300 g (10 oz)
    rice vermicelli
600 g (1⅓ lb) beansprouts
900 g (2 lb) water convolvulus, stalks cut into
    2½ cm (1 in) lengths
30 g (1 oz) dried prawns, ground
2 tablespoons oil
30 g (1oz) ground chilli
4-8 red chillies, sliced
8 tablespoons light soy sauce

Bring 2.25 L (4 pints) water to a boil with sugar-cane in a large saucepan.

While waiting for water to boil, fry pork fat in a hot wok till crisp and brown. Scoop brown fat to a dish, leaving oil behind. Turn down heat.

Stir-fry shallots in this oil till golden-brown. Scoop onto greaseproof paper and when cooled a little, keep in an airtight bottle.

In remaining oil, brown pork ribs for 1 minute. Put these in boiling water with shoulder pork, 1 teaspoon salt, rock sugar, pepper, light soy sauce and black soy sauce.

Simmer for 30 minutes. Remove shoulder pork. Cut away skin of shoulder pork and slice into thin 2½ × 1 cm (1 × ½ in) pieces.

Heat 30 g (1 oz) lard oil and fry fresh prawns slightly. Add sufficient boiling hot water to reach a level 5 cm (2 in) above prawns. Cook for 3 minutes.

Remove prawns from stock. Soak in cold water for 1 minute, then shell and halve lengthwise. Pour prawn stock into meat stock in saucepan.

Scald noodles or rice vermicelli for 1 minute in boiling stock. Remove to a sieve and run cold water through to stop cooking process.

Scald beansprouts and water convolvulus separately in stock for 1 minute.

In a non-stick pan, fry ground dried prawns with 1 tablespoon oil for 1 minute. Add ground chilli and stir-fry for another minute.

To serve, place beansprouts and water convolvulus at the bottom of individual noodle bowls. Pile noodles or rice vermicelli on top and ladle boiling hot soup over this.

Garnish each bowl with sliced pork, prawns and crispy shallots. Sprinkle with a little pepper.

In separate small saucers, serve sliced chilli, light soy sauce and chillied ground prawn.

Serve extra stock in separate soup bowls with more vegetable.

Mee Rebus Java

Preparation: 20 minutes
Cooking: 1 hour

450 g (1 lb) rump steak or brisket beef
sufficient water to cover beef
120 ml (4 fl oz) oil
600 g (1⅓ lb) sweet potatoes, steamed and mashed
2-3 tablespoons rice flour or plain white flour
3 tablespoons sugar
1 teaspoon salt
600 g (1⅓ lb) fresh yellow noodles
400 g (14 oz) beansprouts, roots removed
4-5 hardboiled eggs, cut in wedges
3 firm soybean cakes, diced and deep-fried
3 stalks coriander leaves, shredded
6 green chillies, sliced
10 shallots, sliced and fried
10 limes, halved crosswise

Rempah
2½ cm (1 in) piece fresh turmeric
15 dried chillies
4 candlenuts *or* blanched almonds
10 slices galingale *or* green root ginger
30 shallots
4 cloves garlic
6 teaspoons dried prawns
40 black peppercorns
4 tablespoons preserved soy beans

Put rump steak or brisket beef in a saucepan and cover with cold water. Bring to a boil and simmer till meat is tender. When meat is cool, shred or chop it. Put it back into stock and add sufficient boiling water to make 10 cups of liquid for gravy.

Heat oil in a wok and fry *rempah* till fragrant. Pour in the stock together with mashed sweet potatoes and bring to a boil. Allow to simmer for 10 minutes. Add flour mixed with a little water to thicken, then add sugar and salt. Leave aside and bring to a boil when required.

Scald noodles and beansprouts in boiling water. To serve, put some noodles into individual serving bowls, add beansprouts and pour hot gravy over each serving. Garnish with a few pieces of hardboiled egg, diced soybean, shredded coriander leaf, green chillies, fried shallot and lime.

Dried Noodles with Char Siew

Preparation: 5 minutes
Cooking: 5 minutes

1.75 L (3 pints) water
4 small rolls fresh *wonton mee or* 4 packets instant egg noodles
300 g (10 oz) Char Siew (p.37) (Barbecue Pork)
300 g (10 oz) mustard greens

Sauce
250 ml (8 fl oz) tomato ketchup
5 tablespoons chilli sauce
a few drops sesame oil
4 teaspoons lard oil
4 teaspoons light soy sauce

Bring water to a boil. Put in noodles, cook for 1 minute, then drain in a sieve and quickly run cold water from a tap through noodles.

Combine sauce ingredients and divide into 4 bowls. Put ¼ portion of noodles in each bowl. With a pair of chopsticks, toss noodles with sauce ingredients.

Scald vegetable in boiling water. Cut into 2½ cm (1 in) lengths and place over noodles. Top with slices of Char Siew. Serve hot.

Tasty Soups

Tauhu Masak Titek
(Nonya Beancurd and Pepper Soup)

Preparation: 10 minutes
Cooking: 15 minutes

2 soft soybean cakes
120 g (4 oz) fish bones *or* dried fish bones
3 tablespoons oil
60 g (2 oz) dried prawns, pounded
1.75 L (3 pints) water
1 teaspoon light soy sauce
3 stalks spring onion, chopped

Rempah
30 peppercorns
6 cashew nuts
15 shallots
1 tablespoon dried shrimp paste
2-3 red chillies (pounded coarsely)

Cut each soft soybean cake into 9 squares. Cut fish bones into small pieces and soak in water to get rid of excess salt. Dry fish bones.

Heat oil and fry fish bones slightly, then add dried prawns and *rempah*. Stir-fry till fragrant.

Pour in water. Simmer for 10 minutes, then add seasoning. Scoop out contents but leave stock.

Just before serving, put in soft soybean pieces and cook over low heat for 3 minutes. Garnish with spring onion and serve piping hot.

Wonton Soup

Preparation: 15 minutes
Cooking: 30 minutes

600 g (1⅓ lb) minced pork
½ teaspoon salt
3 tablespoons light soy sauce
1 teaspoon pepper
1 teaspoon sugar
900 g (2 lb) small prawns, shelled and minced
225 g (8 oz) crabmeat, shredded
2 eggs, beaten
1-2 teaspoons tapioca flour
60 wonton skins
450 g (1 lb) pork ribs
2.75 L (5 pints) water + extra
90 g (3 oz) dried young anchovies ("Silver Fish")
3 tablespoons light soy sauce
½ teaspoon pepper
3 stalks spring onion
dash of pepper

Mince pork with salt, light soy sauce, pepper and sugar. Add prawns and mince, then add crabmeat, beaten eggs and tapioca flour. Knead to mix well.

Place 1 teaspoon meat filling in the centre of each wonton skin. Bring corners together and twist to secure. Keep aside.

Bring to boil 420 ml (¾ pint) of water and put wonton into saucepan to cook for 5 minutes. Drain.

Boil pork ribs in 2.75 L (5 pints) water for 15 minutes. Add dried young anchovies and season soup with light soy sauce and pepper.

Boil for 5 minutes. Strain to get a clear soup.

Put clear soup to boil in saucepan and return the cooked wonton. Cook for 5 minutes.

Serve in a deep bowl garnished with spring onion and pepper.

Bawan Kepeting Soup
(Minced Crabmeat Ball Soup)

Preparation: 20 minutes
Cooking: 45 minutes

1¼ kg (2¾ lb) crabs
225 g (8 oz) bamboo shoots, shredded
3.25 L (5¾ pints) water
2¼ teaspoons salt
4 cloves garlic, chopped
6 tablespoons oil
450 g (1 lb) minced pork
1 egg
2 teaspoons tapioca flour *or* cornflour
⅔ teaspoon pepper
2 teaspoons light soy sauce
¼ teaspoon sugar
2 stalks spring onion, chopped

Steam crabs for 25 minutes. Crack shell, extract and shred meat.

Boil shredded bamboo shoots with 1 teaspoon salt in 1.25 L (2¼ pints) water for 30 minutes. Drain and squeeze dry.

Fry chopped garlic in hot oil for ½ minute till crisp. Turn off heat and scoop up. Use a third of the oil for meatballs, a third for garnishing soup and remainder for oiling hands when moulding meatballs.

Mix the following ingredients: minced pork, crabmeat, garlic oil, egg, tapioca flour or cornflour, ⅓ teaspoon pepper, ¼ teaspoon salt and 1 teaspoon light soy sauce.

Knead mixture, oil palms of hands and mould mixture into marble-sized balls. Set aside.

Boil remaining 1.75 L (3 pints) water in a pot and stir in remaining salt, light soy sauce and pepper together with sugar and bamboo shoots.

Boil for 5 minutes, then drop in meatballs and cook for another 5 minutes.

Garnish with spring onion and garlic oil.

Stuffed Sotong and Tunghoon Soup

Preparation: 15 minutes
Cooking: 10 minutes

2 shallots, sliced thinly crosswise
3 tablespoons oil
18 medium-sized cuttlefish
450 g (1 lb) minced pork
1 tablespoon light soy sauce
½ teaspoon salt
⅓ teaspoon pepper
1 teaspoon tapioca flour *or* cornflour
1.75 L (3 pints) water
½ teaspoon salt
1 tablespoon light soy sauce
60 g (2 oz) transparent noodles (*tunghoon*), soaked
    in water to soften
2 stalks spring onion
1 teaspoon *tung chye*
dash of pepper

Fry shallots in 3 tablespoons oil till crisp. Set aside crispy shallots and oil for garnishing.

Remove bone and ink sac of cuttlefish and clean.

Combine minced meat, light soy sauce, salt, pepper and tapioca flour or cornflour. Knead to mix thoroughly.

Stuff meat mixture into cavity of cuttlefish.

Meanwhile bring 1.75 L (3 pints) water to boil. When boiling, put in stuffed cuttlefish, ½ teaspoon salt and light soy sauce and boil for 7 minutes. Add transparent noodles and turn off heat immediately.

Garnish with crispy shallots, spring onion, *tung chye* and pepper.

Note: The soup may be prepared hours in advance. Bring to a boil when ready to serve, and only then add transparent noodles and garnishing.

Pong Tauhu Soup

Preparation: 30 minutes
Cooking: 1 hour

300 g (10 oz) bamboo shoots, shredded
4 L (7 pints) water
2 teaspoons salt
8 cloves garlic, chopped finely
9 tablespoons oil
300 g (10 oz) prawns
450 g (1 lb) minced pork
4 small firm soybean cakes
1 egg white
2 stalks spring onion, chopped
2 teaspoons tapioca flour
2 teaspoons light soy sauce
1 teaspoon black soy sauce
1 teaspoon pepper
1 tablespoon preserved soy beans, pounded
150 g (5 oz) belly pork
dash of pepper

Cook shredded bamboo shoots with 1 teaspoon salt in 4 L (7 pints) water for 25 minutes. Drain and squeeze dry.

Fry garlic in 6 tablespoons oil for ½ minute till crisp. Strain and keep only the oil.

Peel prawns and mince. Set aside. Heat 1 tablespoon oil and fry prawn shells slightly. Add 350 ml (12 fl oz) water and boil for 3 minutes. Strain for clear stock.

Combine meatball ingredients: minced pork, minced prawns, pounded soybean cakes, egg white, a third of the prepared garlic oil, half the chopped spring onion, tapioca flour, light soy sauce, black soy sauce, ½ teaspoon salt and 1 teaspoon pepper.

Knead well and mould into 2 cm (¾ in) balls. Oil hands with garlic oil to help mould meatballs.

Heat remaining 2 tablespoons oil and fry preserved soy beans.

Add remaining 1.75 L (3 pints) water and boil for 15 minutes. Drop in meatballs and stir in seasoning (½ teaspoon salt).

Add remaining 1.75 L (3 pints) water and boil for 15 minutes. Drop in meatballs and stir in seasoning (½ teaspoon salt).

Boil gently for 10 minutes till meatballs are cooked. (Cut one to check.)

Garnish with remaining garlic oil, spring onion and pepper.

Note: This rather elaborate Nonya soup is usually served only on festive days.

Duck in Kiamchye Soup

Preparation: 10 minutes
Cooking: 1 hour

900 g (2 lb) duck
340 g (12 oz) pork spare ribs
450 g (1 lb) *kiamchye*
6 sour plums
4 tomatoes, halved
6 slices ginger
2 onions, quartered
water to half-fill pot

Cut duck and spare ribs into bite-size pieces. Cut *kiamchye* into 5 cm (2 in) pieces, soak in water for a few minutes, then drain.

Place all the ingredients in a clay pot. About 2½ cm (1 in) of the pot should be submerged in water for steaming. Cover and steam for 1 hour. Do not uncover while steaming.

Sharksfin Soup with Crabmeat

Preparation: 30 minutes
Cooking: 1¼ hours

2 packets (160 g/5⅓ oz) dehydrated sharksfin
   hot water
750 g (1⅔ lb) shredded crabmeat *or* 3 crabs
900 g (2 lb) chicken
2.25 L (4 pints) water
2 chicken bouillon cubes
4 tablespoons water
2 tablespoons light soy sauce
2 teaspoons sugar
2 teaspoons brandy
½ teaspoon sesame oil
⅓ teaspoon pepper
2 teaspoons malt vinegar
2 tins (960 g/2 lb 2 oz) cream corn
2 egg yolks, beaten
8 tablespoons sweet potato flour
120 ml (4 fl oz) water

Soak sharksfin in hot water for 2 hours. Pick out and discard white lumps of cartilage.

If whole crabs are used, steam for 25 minutes, then crack the shell and extract meat. Shred crabmeat.

Cook chicken in 2.25 L (4 pints) water for 30 minutes for a rich stock. Dissolve chicken bouillon cubes in 4 tablespoons water and add to stock. Strain stock.

Put sharksfin in stock and boil for 10 minutes or till stock measures 1.25 L (2¼ pints). If there is too much stock, boil a little longer; if less stock, add boiling water.

Combine light soy sauce, sugar, brandy, sesame oil, pepper and malt vinegar in a bowl. Pour seasoning into boiling stock.

After 3 minutes, add two-thirds of the crabmeat, leaving remaining crabmeat for garnishing. Pour in cream corn and stir for 2 minutes.

Pour in beaten egg yolks to form long streaks in soup.

When egg strands have formed, add sweet potato flour blended with 120 ml (4 fl oz) water. Stir vigorously to mix thickening with soup.

When soup is thick, ladle into a soup bowl and garnish with remaining crabmeat.

Serve with malt vinegar and pepper.

Note: Sharksfin Soup is only served on special occasions.

Dom Yam Kung (Piping Hot Thai Soup)

Preparation: 15 minutes
Cooking: 10 minutes

700 g (1½ lb) large prawns *or* Mackerel/Cod fillets
4 stalks lemon grass
4 stalks spring onion
10-12 bird chillies
1.25 L (2¼ pints) water
8 lime leaves
120 ml (4 fl oz) lime juice
4 tablespoons fish sauce
6 mint leaves *or* 15 basil leaves
1 teaspoon chopped coriander leaves

Cut prawns into 3 pieces, leaving shell on. If fish is used, cut into bite-size pieces. (Remove head and tail if whole fish is used.)

Slice lemon grass and spring onion thinly. Lightly crush bird chillies.

Boil water in a saucepan. Add lemon grass and lime leaves. Boil for 5 minutes until aromatic.

Stir in lime juice and fish stock. Simmer for another 5 minutes. Add crushed bird chillies.

Pour stock into steamboat and fill funnel with live coals (if preferred). Alternatively, add prawns or fish, mint leaves, coriander leaves and spring onion to stock in the saucepan.

Let soup simmer, covered, for a few minutes. Serve immediately.

Winter Melon Soup

Preparation: 20 minutes
Cooking: 45 minutes

3 dried Chinese mushrooms
2-3 pairs chicken liver
1 big piece abalone, about 7½ × 10 cm (3 × 4 in)
5 water chestnuts, skinned
1 winter melon
225 g (8 oz) chicken breastmeat, cut into bite-size
　　pieces
10 button mushrooms, quartered
½ carrot, sliced into ½ cm (¼ in) rings
½ teaspoon salt
dash of pepper
1 tin (450 g/1 lb) abalone stock
1 tablespoon Chinese rice wine
60 g (2 oz) cooked green peas

Soak dried Chinese mushrooms for 20 minutes in boiling water. Drain and dice into 1 cm (½ in) pieces.

Cut each liver into 6 pieces. Cut abalone and water chestnuts into 1 cm (½ in) pieces.

Cut away top quarter of winter melon with a sharp knife. Carve designs on skin of larger portion. Scrape out flesh and discard seeds.

Slice off hard skin of top quarter of winter melon. Cut vegetable into small pieces.

Fill winter melon with chicken, button mushrooms, dried Chinese mushrooms, liver, carrot, water chestnuts, winter melon, salt, pepper, abalone stock and Chinese rice wine.

Stand melon in a deep bowl and place bowl on a steaming rack. Steam for 45 minutes.

Add green peas and abalone when soup is ready.

Thai Cabbage Soup

Preparation: 3 minutes
Cooking: 15 minutes

1 tablespoon butter
2 cloves garlic, bashed
1 L (1¾ pints) chicken stock
¼ teaspoon salt
1 tablespoon light soy sauce
½ teaspoon freshly ground pepper
½ teaspoon ground coriander
140 g (5 oz) shredded cabbage
2 stalks spring onion (white portion only), chopped
dash of pepper

Heat butter in a wok and fry garlic.

Add stock and seasoning (salt, light soy sauce, pepper and coriander). Simmer for 5 minutes. Transfer contents of wok to an enamel pot.

Add cabbage and boil for 8 minutes.

Garnish with spring onion and pepper just before serving.

Nasi Kunyit (p.98) with Belimbing and Prawn Sambal (p.76) and Chicken Curry with Peranakan Rempah (p.60)

113

Piping Hot Thai Soup (p.111)

Steamed Chicken and Longans in Yunan Pot (p.121)

Singapore East Coast Chilli Crabs (p.124)

Bird's Nest Soup with Crabmeat

Preparation: 10 minutes
Cooking: 2 hours

120 g (4 oz) bird's nest
hot water
900 g (2 lb) chicken
sufficient water to cover chicken
½ teaspoon salt
¼ teaspoon pepper
450 g (1 lb) crabs
2 stalks spring onion

Soak bird's nest in water overnight and when softened, clean. Simmer in hot water till cooked (approximately 30 minutes). Drain dry.

Stuff chicken with bird's nest. Place chicken in a porcelain pot and add sufficient water to cover. Stir in salt and pepper.

Place pot on a steaming rack in a deep wok with about 2½ cm (1 in) of the pot submerged in water. Cover and steam for 1½ hours.

Meanwhile, steam crabs for 25 minutes. Crack shell, extract and shred meat. Chop white portions of spring onion.

Serve Bird's Nest Soup garnished with crabmeat, and spring onion.

Rasam (Pepper Water)

Preparation: 7 minutes
Cooking: 15 minutes

2 tablespoons tamarind
300 ml (½ pint) water
¾ teaspoon coriander, roasted and ground coarsely
¼ teaspoon cummin
2 stalks curry leaves
⅓ teaspoon salt
1 teaspoon ghee *or* oil
¼ teaspoon mustard seeds
15 peppercorns, ground coarsely
1 clove garlic, sliced
5 shallots, sliced
3 dried chillies, broken into small pieces

Mix tamarind and water. Squeeze and strain to obtain juice. Stir in coriander. Bring to a boil and add cummin and curry leaves. Continue boiling for another 5 minutes. Add salt.

Heat oil in a frying pan and fry mustard seeds till they pop. Add peppercorns, garlic, shallots and dried chillies and fry for 1 minute.

Add fried ingredients to tamarind juice. Boil for another 3 minutes and remove from heat.

Claypot Specials

Beef and Asparagus in Yunan Pot

Preparation: 10 minutes
Cooking: 1 hour

1 tin (425 g/15 oz) asparagus
340 g (12 oz) beef (braising steak)
1 medium-sized carrot
water to fill Yunan pot
4 slices ginger, shredded
10-15 button mushrooms
1 tablespoon wine
salt to taste
¼ teaspoon pepper
4 tablespoons beef consommé

Cut asparagus into 2½ cm (1 in) pieces. Slice beef thinly to the same size. Slice button mushrooms.

Cut carrot into ½ cm (¼ in) rings and cut into patterns. Meanwhile, boil sufficient water to fill three-quarters of a Yunan pot.

Place all ingredients in the Yunan pot and pour boiling water over them.

Rest pot on a steaming rack in a wok. Make sure 7½ cm (3 in) of the pot is submerged. To prevent pot from slipping or breaking, place a clean towel between pot and steaming rack.

Cover and steam for 1 hour. When ready, place Yunan pot on a thick plate and serve.

Claypot Beef, Champignons and Spring Onions

Preparation: 14 minutes
Marinating: 15 minutes
Cooking: 12 minutes

600 g (1⅓ lb) fillet steak
1 tablespoon light soy sauce
2 teaspoons black soy sauce
1 teaspoon pepper
½ teaspoon sesame oil
2 tablespoons oyster sauce
1 teaspoon sugar
1 tablespoon tapioca flour *or* cornflour
3 tablespoons Chinese rice wine *or* dry sherry
6 tablespoons lard oil
2 cloves garlic, chopped
10 thin slices ginger
1 medium-sized carrot, sliced into thin rings
15 champignons, halved
10 stalks spring onion, cut into 2½ cm (1 in) lengths

Cut steak into 1 cm thick slices, then cut each slice into 3 pieces. Marinate in light soy sauce, black soy sauce, pepper, sesame oil, oyster sauce, sugar, flour and rice wine for 15 minutes.

Heat oil in a clay pot and brown garlic, then add sliced ginger and carrot and fry for 2 minutes.

Put in champignons. Stir-fry for another 2 minutes. Add steak.

After 2 more minutes, add spring onion. Cook covered for 1 minute.

Adjust taste by adding more light soy sauce, if desired.

Claypot Liver and Pork

Preparation: 8 minutes
Marinating: 15 minutes
Cooking: 12 minutes

300 g (10 oz) pig's liver, cut into thin 5 cm (2 in)
  slices
300 g (10 oz) pork fillet, cut into ½ cm (¼ in) thick
  slices
120 ml (4 fl oz) lard oil
1-2 teaspoons sesame oil
4 cloves garlic, chopped finely
2½ cm (1 in) piece young ginger, chopped finely
8 stalks spring onion, cut into 4 cm (1½ in) lengths
4 tablespoons Chinese rice wine
2 teaspoons brandy

Marinade for Liver
juice from 4 cm (1½ in) piece ginger
¾ teaspoon sugar
1½ teaspoons oyster sauce
1 tablespoon light soy sauce
2 teaspoons black soy sauce
¾ teaspoon pepper
2 tablespoons Chinese rice wine
1 teaspoon tapioca flour
2 tablespoons water

Marinade for Pork
1 teaspoon light soy sauce
1 teaspoon black soy sauce
½ teaspoon sugar
1 teaspoon oyster sauce
¼ teaspoon pepper
1 teaspoon Chinese rice wine
½ teaspoon tapioca flour

Mix marinade ingredients for liver and leave
liver to marinate for 15 minutes. Do the same
with pork.

Heat lard oil in a clay pot till smoking hot, then
add sesame oil.

Brown garlic, then ginger and add seasoned
pork. Cook for 5 minutes, uncovered, then add
liver and spring onion.

Mix wine and brandy and add to contents of pot.

Cover pot and cook for 2 minutes. Serve liver
and pork immediately in the same pot.

Soft Beancurd Soup in Yunan Pot

Preparation: 15 minutes
Cooking: 45 minutes

450 g (1 lb) minced pork
225 g (8 oz) crabmeat
¼ teaspoon pepper
⅓ teaspoon salt
4 tablespoons water
1 teaspoon tapioca flour *or* sago flour
8 water chestnuts, peeled and chopped finely
1 tin (340 g/12 oz) straw mushrooms
⅓ teaspoon salt
¾ teaspoon sesame oil
1 tablespoon light soy sauce
8 slices ginger, shredded
boiling water for soup
2 soft soybean cakes, cut into 4 cm (1½ in) squares

Mix and mince pork and crabmeat with pepper.
Dissolve ⅓ teaspoon salt in water and sprinkle
on meat while mincing.

Combine minced meat mixture with tapioca
flour or sago flour and chopped water chestnuts.
Shape into 2 cm (¾ in) balls.

Place meatballs at the bottom of a Yunan pot
with mushrooms, salt, sesame oil, light soy sauce
and ginger. Fill three-quarters of the pot with
boiling hot water.

Place Yunan pot on a steaming rack and make
sure 2½ cm (1 in) of the pot is submerged.

Put lid of Yunan pot in position, cover steamer
and steam for 45 minutes or till meat is cooked.

Add soft soybean pieces during the last 5
minutes of cooking time.

Three-Mushroom Chicken Soup in Yunan Pot

Preparation: 15 minutes
Cooking: 40 minutes

4 dried Chinese mushrooms
250 ml (8 fl oz) water
boiling hot water for soup and for soaking dried
  mushrooms
6 chicken thighs, each cut into 3 pieces
10 champignons
1 small carrot, diced
2 tablespoons light soy sauce
½ teaspoon sugar
4 tomatoes, halved
1 soft soybean cake, cut into 4 cm (1½ in) squares
2 stalks Chinese celery (use leaves only) *or* 2 stalks
  spring onion, chopped

Soak dried Chinese mushrooms in 250 ml (8 fl oz) of boiling water for 1 hour. Squeeze out excess mushroom liquid.

Half-fill Yunan pot with mushroom liquid and boiling hot water.

Put in chicken, mushrooms and diced carrot. Season with light soy sauce and sugar.

Cover Yunan pot and stand it on a steaming rack, making sure 2½ cm (1 in) of pot is submerged in steaming water.

Steam for 30 minutes. Put in tomatoes and soft soybean pieces. Steam for another 10 minutes.

Garnish with Chinese celery or spring onion just before serving.

Rice Wine Chicken in Clay Pot

Preparation: 5 minutes
Marinating: 30 minutes
Cooking: 15 minutes

1¾ kg (4 lb) chicken *or* 10 chicken thighs
3 tablespoons oyster sauce
2 tablespoons light soy sauce
1 teaspoon sugar
½ teaspoon pepper
1 tablespoon tapioca flour
120 ml (4 fl oz) oil
3 cloves garlic, chopped
2½ cm (1 in) piece ginger, shredded
1 medium-sized carrot, cut into 1 cm (½ in) rings
120 ml (4 fl oz) Chinese rice wine
6 stalks spring onion, white portions only
salt to taste

Debone chicken and slice meat. Marinate chicken in oyster sauce, light soy sauce, sugar, pepper and tapioca flour.

Heat oil in a clay pot and brown garlic and ginger. Add carrot and stir-fry for ½ minute.

Put in seasoned chicken and Chinese rice wine. Stir, then cook covered for 5 minutes.

When chicken is nearly cooked, throw in spring onion, season to taste and serve immediately in the pot.

Steamed Chicken and Longans in Yunan Pot

Preparation: 10 minutes
Cooking: 1 hour

1 kg (2¼ lb) chicken
20 dried longans
¾ teaspoon salt
2 tablespoons red *kokee* seeds
10 red Chinese dates, seeded
2 tablespoons Chinese rice wine
boiling water
3 slices ginger, shredded

Cut chicken into bite-size pieces. Crack shells of longans and remove seeds. Discard seeds and shells.

Put all ingredients in a Yunan pot and pour in boiling water to a level 2½ cm (1 in) from the top.

Place pot on a steaming rack and 2-3 small towels between pot and rack, making sure the central spout is not covered by towels. This will prevent pot from cracking. About 2½ cm (1 in) of the pot should be submerged in steaming water.

Cover and steam for 1 hour.

Place Yunan pot on a thick plate and serve garnished with shredded ginger.

Mixed Vegetables in Clay Pot

Preparation: 5 minutes
Cooking: 8 minutes

6 tablespoons oil
10 young corn cobs
20 straw mushrooms
2 tablespoons Chinese rice wine
4 tablespoons oyster sauce
1 tablespoon light soy sauce
2 teaspoons tapioca flour
5 tablespoons water
2 tomatoes, quartered
30 mange touts

Heat oil in a clay pot and add young corn cobs, mushrooms, Chinese rice wine, oyster sauce, light soy sauce, and tapioca flour mixed with water. Stir-fry for 5 minutes.

Add tomatoes and, after 1 minute, mange touts.

Cover pot and bring to serving table immediately. Serve with hot rice.

Claypot Corn Soup with a Difference

Preparation: 5 minutes
Cooking: 13 minutes

1½ tins (720 g/1⅔ lb) cream corn
1 tin (200 g/6⅔ oz) champignons, quartered
600 ml (1 pint) water
60 g (2 oz) white fungus
60 g (2 oz) cooked green peas
dash of pepper
pinch of salt
½ teaspoon sugar
½ chicken bouillon cube

Put cream corn and champignons in a clay pot. Add water and boil for 5 minutes.

Add white fungus, boil for 3 minutes, then add all other ingredients. Simmer in low heat for 5 minutes. Serve with rice or noodles.

Chinese New Year Waxed Duck Rice in Clay Pot

Preparation: 20 minutes
Marinating: 20 minutes
Cooking: 12-15 minutes

700 g (1½ lb) chicken, cut into bite-size pieces
1 tablespoon cornflour
½ teaspoon sesame oil
1 tablespoon light soy sauce
1 tablespoon lard
2 teaspoons black soy sauce
dash of pepper
200 g (6⅔ oz) belly pork
2 tablespoons black soy sauce
6 tablespoons oil
15 shallots, sliced thinly crosswise
1 kg (2 lb) rice
water to cook rice
2 thighs of waxed duck (wind-dried duck), cut into
   2½ cm (1 in) pieces
3 pairs Chinese sausages, cut at a slant into
   ½ cm (¼ in) slices
4 cm (1½ in) piece ginger, shredded
2 stalks spring onion, chopped
dash of pepper

Marinate chicken for 20 minutes in cornflour, sesame oil, light soy sauce, lard, black soy sauce and pepper.

Cut belly pork into thin slices and season in black soy sauce.

Heat oil and fry shallots till golden brown. Remove shallots to a dish.

Put rice in a clay pot and add water to a level 2 cm (¾ in) above rice.

When rice is half cooked, put chicken in pot and cover with rice.

After 5 minutes, or when rice is almost dry, place seasoned belly pork, waxed duck, sausages and shredded ginger on top of rice.

Allow rice to cook over very low heat until dry.

Garnish with crispy shallots, spring onion and pepper.

Claypot Sesame Chicken

Preparation: 15 minutes
Cooking: 25 minutes

1 chicken, about 1¼ kg (2¾ lb)
1 medium-sized carrot
5 tablespoons oil
1½ tablespoons sesame oil
5 cm (2 in) piece ginger, shredded
2 tablespoons light soy sauce
3 teaspoons black soy sauce
¼ teaspoon pepper
5 tablespoons Chinese rice wine
1 teaspoon sugar
420 ml (¾ pint) water
15-20 Chinese red dates
2 stalks spring onion, chopped

Cut chicken into 10 pieces. Quarter carrot crosswise and cut each quarter lengthwise into 6 pieces.

Heat oil in a clay pot, then trickle sesame oil along the side of the pot to bring out its full flavour.

Fry shredded ginger till crisp, then add chicken. Stir-fry over moderate heat for 5 minutes. Add seasoning (soy sauces, pepper, rice wine and sugar) and water.

Simmer for 10 minutes, add carrot and continue simmering till liquid is reduced by half. Throw in dates and simmer covered till chicken is tender and gravy thick.

Serve garnished with spring onion.

Sandy Pot Chestnut Rice

Preparation: 10 minutes
Marinating: 30 minutes
Cooking: 20 minutes

5 chicken thighs
2 teaspoons tapioca flour
¾ teaspoon pepper
1 tablespoon black soy sauce
2 chicken bouillon cubes dissolved in ½ cup hot
  water
1 teaspoon sesame oil
3 teaspoons oyster sauce
1½ teaspoons sugar
6 tablespoons oil
8 shallots, sliced thinly crosswise
3 slices bacon, chopped
4 stalks spring onion
2 pairs Chinese sausages
675 g (1½ lb) rice
5 tablespoons lard oil
water to cook rice
15 boiled chestnuts, chopped coarsely
2½ cm (1 in) piece ginger, shredded
dash of pepper

Marinate chicken for 30 minutes in tapioca flour, pepper, black soy sauce, chicken stock, sesame oil, oyster sauce and sugar.

Heat 6 tablespoons oil and fry shallots till golden brown. Remove shallots to a dish.

In the same oil, fry bacon till crisp.

Chop spring onion. Use only white portion and about 5 cm (2 in) of green portion.

Steam Chinese sausages for a few minutes, then cut into 1 cm (½ in) slices.

Fry rice in lard oil in a clay pot for 3 minutes. Add water to a level 2 cm (¾ in) above rice.

Cover pot and cook for 10 minutes over moderate heat. Uncover, stir rice and bury chicken and chestnuts in rice.

After 5 minutes, when rice should be quite dry, add shredded ginger and stir, making sure chicken pieces at the bottom change places with chicken pieces at the top.

Cover pot once more, lower heat and cook for a few more minutes till chicken is cooked and rice grainy.

Place sausages on top of rice and cover for 2 minutes.

Just before serving, garnish with crispy shallots, fried bacon, spring onion and pepper. Serve with any soup.

Hawker Favourites

Ponggol Fried Chilli Crabs

Preparation: 10 minutes
Cooking: 15 minutes

3 big crabs, about 1½ kg (3⅓ lb)
6 tablespoons oil
20 shallots, ground
3 cloves garlic, ground
2½ cm (1 in) piece ginger, ground
water for cooking crabs
1 tablespoon tomato ketchup
2 teaspoons sugar
60 g (2 oz) roasted ground peanuts

Rempah
5 red chillies
10 dried chillies
1 teaspoon dried shrimp paste
1 stalk lemon grasss
4 slices galingale *or* root ginger
4 candlenuts *or* 6 blanched almonds

Clean crabs and cut each into 4-6 pieces (see p. 169). Crack claws with a pestle.

Heat oil in a wok till very hot. Fry shallots, garlic and ginger for 2 minutes, then add *rempah* and stir-fry for another minute.

Add crabs and stir-fry, adding a little water every now and then, till crabs turn red.

Pour in tomato ketchup and sugar. Simmer for another 5 minutes, then toss with ground peanuts.

Note: Crab dishes in Singapore are popularly eaten with a French loaf.

Singapore East Coast Chilli Crabs

Preparation: 15 minutes
Cooking: 25 minutes

3 large crabs, about 1¾ kg (4 lb)
120 ml (4 fl oz) oil, preferably half corn oil and half lard
18 slices ginger, shredded
6 cloves garlic, chopped finely
2 tablespoons preserved soy beans, pounded

Seasoning Ingredients
2 tablespoons light soy sauce
4 tablespoons sugar
5 tablespoons garlic-flavoured chilli sauce
20 tablespoons tomato ketchup
350 ml (12 fl oz) water
2 eggs, beaten
¾ tablespoon tapioca flour blended with 6 tablespoons water
2 stalks spring onion (white portions only), chopped
2 sprigs coriander leaves *or* 5 stalks celery

Chop crabs into 6 pieces (see p. 169 for method). Chop each claw into 2 pieces.

Heat oil in a wok and fry ginger till half-cooked. Add garlic and stir-fry till crisp, then add preserved soy beans and stir-fry for 2 minutes.

Pour in seasoning ingredients and stir-fry for 2 minutes. Add crabs and stir briskly, then pour in 120 ml (4 fl oz) water and cook covered for 2 minutes.

Uncover and stir briskly once more, adding remaining water. After 5 minutes, add beaten eggs, stirring to mix with sauce.

When crabs are bright red, add flour paste.

Place in a shallow dish and garnish with spring onion and coriander leaves or celery. Serve with a French loaf.

Soup Kambing

Preparation: 20 minutes
Marinating: 30 minutes
Cooking: 1¹/₄ hours

1¼ kg (2¾ lb) mutton, cut into bite-size pieces
450 g (1 lb) mutton ribs
2½ tablespoons ginger juice
1 teaspoon ground turmeric
½ teaspoon salt
120 ml (4 fl oz) oil
15-20 shallots, sliced thinly lengthwise
5 cloves garlic, chopped
10 shallots, chopped
6.75 L (12 pints) water
4 screwpine leaves, knotted in pairs
3 tablespoons light soy sauce
3 tablespoons black soy sauce
½ teaspoon salt
1 teaspoon sugar
1 tablespoon rice flour mixed with 120 ml (4 fl oz) water
90 g (3 oz) ground cashew nuts *or* ground almonds
5 stalks celery, chopped, *or* 3 stalks spring onion, chopped
pepper

Rempah
4 tablespoons ground coriander
1 tablespoon ground fennel
1 tablespoon ground cummin
3 tablespoons ground poppy seeds

Spices tied in muslin
10 cardamoms, crushed
1 star anise, broken into segments, 2 segments crushed
10 cloves, ground coarsely
30 black peppercorns, ground coarsely
5 cm (2 in) cinnamon stick, broken into 3 or 4 pieces

Marinate mutton for 30 minutes in ginger juice, turmeric and salt.

Heat oil and fry sliced shallots till crisp and brown. Remove shallots and set aside for garnishing.

In the same oil, brown garlic. Set garlic aside for garnishing.

Again using the same oil, fry chopped shallots for ½ minute, then add *rempah* and seasoned mutton. Stir-fry for 5 minutes.

Transfer contents of wok to a deep pot. Add screwpine leaves, light soy sauce, black soy sauce, salt, sugar and spices tied in muslin.

Pour in 3.50 L (6 pints) water and bring to a boil. Cover and boil for about 30 minutes, then add remaining water. Cook for another 30 minutes, after which time mutton should be tender.

Add thickening of rice flour with water and ground cashew nuts or almonds and simmer uncovered for 5 minutes.

Adjust taste by adding more salt or water and ladle into soup bowls. Garnish with crispy shallots, garlic, chopped celery and pepper.

Serve with thick slices of French loaf.

Bahkut Teh

Preparation: 7 minutes
Cooking: 1¹/₄ hours

3.75 L (6¼ pints) water
900 g (2 lb) pork tenderloin and ribs
¾ teaspoon five-spice powder
1 star anise, 4 segments pounded finely
2½ cm (1 in) cinnamon stick, broken into 2 pieces
4 tablespoons light soy sauce
2 tablespoons black soy sauce
3 pieces sugar-cane, each 5 cm (2 in) long
12 cloves garlic, bashed slightly
30 g (1 oz) red *kokee* seeds
1 sprig coriander leaves, chopped
pepper

Bring water to a boil and add pork with all the other ingredients except coriander leaves and pepper.

Boil for 1 hour over moderate heat then cook for another 15 minutes over low heat till meat is tender. Stock should now be reduced to 1 L (1¾ pints).

Serve garnished with chopped coriander leaves and pepper.

Penang Laksa

Preparation: 30 minutes
Cooking: 45 minutes

1¼ kg (2¾ lb) thick rice vermicelli (*laksa meehoon*)
1¼ kg (2¾ lb) Tuna *or* Mackerel
4 tablespoons tamarind
1.25 L (2¼ pints) water
3 tablespoons sugar
¾ teaspoon salt
5 pieces dried tamarind
30 polygonum leaves, shredded
8-10 teaspoons black shrimp paste
5 pickled leeks, shredded
1 stalk wild ginger flower, sliced
2 cucumbers, peeled and shredded
½ pineapple, shredded
3 red chillies, sliced finely
30 mint leaves

Rempah
15 dried chillies
8 red chillies
3 stalks lemon grass
5 cm (2 in) piece galingale *or* root ginger
10 × 5 cm (4 × 2 in) piece dried shrimp paste
5 cm (2 in) piece turmeric
20 shallots

Scald thick rice vermicelli in boiling water for 1 minute. Drain in a colander.

Steam fish and shred fillet.

Mix tamarind with 1.25 L (2¼ pints) water. Squeeze and strain to obtain juice.

Mix *rempah* with tamarind juice in an enamel pot. Bring to a boil and simmer for 20 minutes, adding sugar, salt, dried tamarind pieces and polygonum leaves.

Put in shredded fish and simmer for another 5 minutes.

Divide thick rice vermicelli into 8-10 bowls. Pour gravy mixed with black prawn paste into bowls.

Garnish with a little of each of the following: leek, wild ginger flower, cucumber, pineapple, chilli and mint leaves.

Indian Mee Goreng

Preparation: 20 minutes
Cooking: 7 minutes

450 g (1 lb) fresh yellow noodles
100 g (3⅓ oz) mutton, cut into thin slices
½ teaspoon light soy sauce
½ teaspoon black soy sauce
dash of pepper
150 ml (¼ pint) oil
15 shallots, sliced thinly crosswise
1 big onion, sliced thinly lengthwise
3 stalks mustard greens, cut into 2½ cm (1 in) lengths
salt to taste
pepper to taste
2 tablespoons black soy sauce
1-2 teaspoons ground chilli
2 tablespoons water
300 g (10 oz) beansprouts
2-3 eggs
2 green chillies, cut into ½ cm (¼ in) rings
60 g (2 oz) mange touts
6 tablespoons tomato ketchup
2-3 tomatoes, cut into thin wedges
2 potatoes, boiled, halved and cut into ½ cm (¼ in) slices
4-5 stalks celery *or* spring onion, chopped

Wash noodles and drain in a colander. Season mutton in ½ teaspoon light soy sauce, ½ teaspoon black soy sauce and pepper.

Heat 5 tablespoons oil and fry shallots till golden brown. Keep oil and crispy shallots for garnishing.

Heat remaining oil in a wok and fry sliced onion for a few seconds, add vegetable and stir-fry, then add mutton with salt, pepper, 2 tablespoons black soy sauce and chilli.

Stir-fry for 1 minute, then add noodles. While frying noodles, sprinkle with a little water.

Put in beansprouts and crack in eggs. Stir briskly to coat noodles with egg.

Throw in chillies and mange touts with tomato ketchup, tomatoes and potatoes. Stir-fry for 1 minute or till *mee* (noodle) is dry.

Garnish with chopped celery or spring onion, pepper and fried shallots.

Fried Hokkien Meehoon Mee

Preparation: 20 minutes
Cooking: 10 minutes

2 L (2 qt) water
450 g (1 lb) streaky pork (*samchan*)
600 g (1⅓ lb) medium-sized prawns
4 big cuttlefish, ink sacs removed
250 ml (8 fl oz) lard oil
6 cloves garlic, chopped
3 eggs
600 g (1⅓ lb) fresh yellow noodles, washed and
    drained in a colander
150 g (5 oz) fresh rice vermicelli, washed and
    drained in a colander
600 g (1⅓ lb) beansprouts
8-10 stalks Chinese chives, cut into 2 cm (¾ in)
    lengths
8-10 dashes pepper
2-3 limes, halved crosswise
2 red chillies, sliced thinly
4 tablespoons light soy sauce

Seasoning:-
3 tablespoons light soy sauce
1 teaspoon sugar

Bring water to a boil and add seasoning and streaky pork.

Cook prawns in stock for 5-10 minutes. Remove and shell. Discard shells.

Scald cuttlefish in boiling stock for just a few seconds, then cut into ½ cm (¼ in) rings.

When stock has boiled for 30 minutes, remove meat, cool and shred. Boil a little longer if necessary to reduce stock to 420 ml (¾ pint).

Heat lard in a wok and brown garlic. Add shredded meat and stir-fry for a few seconds. Move to the side of the wok.

Beat eggs and fry lightly.

Throw in noodles and rice vermicelli and fry briskly for 1 minute.

Add half the stock. Stir and cover for 2 minutes.

Uncover, stir and add beansprouts and remaining stock.

Put in cuttlefish and prawns and lastly Chinese chives. Sprinkle pepper over contents of wok, stir and scoop out to a large oval dish.

Squeeze lime juice over noodles and rice vermicelli and serve with cut chillies and light soy sauce in a saucer.

Char Kway Teow (Teochew Fried Rice Noodles)

Preparation: 20 minutes
Cooking: 10 minutes

30 cockles *or* 300 g (10 oz) small prawns, shelled
    and trimmed
1 teaspoon salt (for prawns)
3 Chinese sausages
120 ml (4 fl oz) water
120-175 ml (4-6 fl oz) lard oil
1½ teaspoons chopped garlic
1¼ kg (2¾ lb) flat rice noodles
1 tablespoon black soy sauce
3 tablespoons light soy sauce
1-2 teaspoons chilli sauce
dash of pepper
extra water for frying rice noodles
2 eggs
450 g (1 lb) beansprouts
12 stalks Chinese chives, cut into 2½ cm (1 in)
    lengths

If cockles are used, pry open with the point of a knife.

If prawns are used, rinse under cold tap and rub with 1 teaspoon of salt.

Boil Chinese sausages in 120 ml (4 fl oz) water to soften. Cut a slant into ½ cm (¼ in) thick slices.

Heat oil in a wok and brown garlic. Add rice noodles and seasoning (soy sauces, chilli sauce and pepper). Stir-fry for 3 minutes, sprinkling with water as you fry.

Push noodles to one side and break in eggs. Scramble quickly with spatula then push in rice noodles and stir briskly to coat with egg.

Add sausages and prawns, if used, then beansprouts. Continue frying for 1 minute, taking care not to overcook beansprouts.

When rice noodles are dry, add Chinese chives and cockles. Stir just once or twice and serve immediately sprinkled with pepper.

Sotoh Ayam

Preparation: 45 minutes
Cooking: 1 hour

7 tablespoons oil
15 shallots, sliced thinly
5 cloves garlic, chopped
5.5 L (10 pints) water
3 tablespoons oil
5 × 2½ cm (2 × 1 in) piece galingale, sliced
2 star anise, broken into segments, 2 segments
    pounded finely
14 cloves
½ nutmeg, pounded *or* ¾ teaspoon ground nutmeg
25 peppercorns, coarsely ground *or* 1¼ teaspoons
    pepper
2 tablespoons sugar
2 tablespoons salt
1 chicken, about 2 kg (4½ lb), halved
2 chicken bouillon cubes
900 g (2 lb) beansprouts
1 kg (2 lb) Ketupat cubes (p.100)
2 stalks spring onion, chopped *or* 2 stalks celery,
    chopped
dash of pepper

Cutlets
225 g (8 oz) minced topside beef
700 g (1½ lb) potatoes, peeled, boiled and mashed
1¼ teaspoon salt
¾ teaspoon sugar
⅓ teaspoon pepper
¼ teaspoon grated nutmeg
420 ml (¾ pint) oil

Heat 4 tablespoons oil and fry shallots til crisp
and brown. Remove shallots. Brown garlic in the
same oil. Remove to a dish.

Bring water to a boil. Heat remaining 3 tablespoons oil and fry galingale, star anise and cloves.

When water boils, add fried spices together with
nutmeg, pepper, sugar and salt.

After 5 minutes, put in chicken halves and cook
over moderate heat for 15 minutes.

Remove chicken, plunge in cold water for a few
minutes, and separate meat from bones. Put
bones back into soup and shred meat.

Add chicken bouillon cubes to soup with a third
of the fried shallots. Continue boiling for 10
minutes then taste and add more salt or sugar as
desired. Remove bones.

Sometime while boiling soup, scald beansprouts
by putting in a wire basket and lowering basket
into soup for 1-2 minutes.

To serve, put 110 g (4 oz) Ketupat cubes in each
bowl. Top with shredded chicken and beansprouts and pour hot soup over this. Garnish
with fried shallots, fried garlic, chopped spring
onion or celery and pepper. Add a few pieces of
cutlet.

Cutlets
Knead cutlet ingredients together and mould
into patties. Fry in oil till cooked. Cut each cutlet
into 4-6 pieces.

Sri Lankan Thosai

Preparation: 20 minutes
Cooking: 30 minutes

450 g (1 lb) broken rice
175 g (6 oz) broken black gram
water
1 tablespoon ghee
6 shallots, chopped finely
3 dried chillies, cut into tiny pieces
6 stalks curry leaves (leaves only) shredded
⅓ teaspoon pepper
½ teaspoon ground cummin
½ teaspoon salt
sesame oil

Soak broken rice with just enough water to
cover for 6 hours.

Soak broken black gram for 6 hours in water.
Rub while washing so that black husk comes off.
Remove black husks.

Grind or blend rice and black gram together till
fine. Leave overnight. In the morning, batter
should be well risen. Add sufficient water to
batter to give a smooth and thick runny batter.

Heat ghee and fry shallots, dried chillies and
curry leaves for a few minutes. Add this with
pepper, ground cummin and salt to batter. Mix
well.

Heat an iron griddle and rub a little oil on its
surface.

Gently pour a ladleful of batter onto the centre
of the griddle and smooth it out into a big round
with the back of the ladle in a circular motion.

When one side is light brown, turn over and
cook the other side.

Serve with Coconut Sambal (p.88).

Hainanese Chicken Rice

Preparation: 25 minutes
Cooking: 35 minutes

Chicken
water for cooking chicken
1 chicken, about 2 kg (4½ lb)
7½ cm (3 in) piece ginger, sliced
1½ teaspoons salt
½ teaspoon sesame oil
4 tablespoons corn oil

Rice
1¼ kg (2¾ lb) rice
150 ml (¼ pint) lard oil
½ teaspoon salt
4 cloves garlic, bashed
2 chicken bouillon cubes, dissolved in 3 tablespoons
   hot water
chicken stock

Sauces and Garnishes
8-10 red chillies
⅓ teaspoon salt
6 tablespoons vinegar
1 teaspoon sugar
7½ cm (3 in) piece ginger, ground
pinch of salt
1 tablespoon oil
2 tablespoons black soy sauce
lettuce leaves
1-2 cucumbers, halved lengthwise and sliced at a
   slant
½ pineapple, sliced
4 tomatoes, sliced

Cooking Chicken
Bring water to a boil in a moderate-sized pot. Add chicken with ginger and salt. Cover pot.

Cook over moderate heat for 5 minutes, then turn off heat and let chicken continue cooking in hot water. At the end of 20-25 minutes, prick underside of wings or thighs to see if chicken is cooked.

Transfer chicken into a pot of cold water.

Hang up chicken and brush with sesame oil mixed with corn oil. Leave chicken to hang for 30 minutes before chopping.

Cooking Rice
Wash rice and allow to dry in a tray.

Fry rice in lard oil with salt, garlic and chicken bouillon stock. Stir till all the rice grains are coated with oil.

Pour in chicken stock (water used to boil chicken) to a level 2 cm (¾ in) above rice.

Cook rice over moderate heat till almost dry, then turn heat down to very low and cook till dry. Stir rice with a pair of chopsticks to separate grains.

Sauces
Pound chillies with ⅓ teaspoon salt, vinegar and sugar. Put in a saucer.

Mix ground ginger with a pinch of salt and oil in another saucer.

Put black soy sauce in a third saucer.

Cutting and Serving
Place garnishes decoratively on an oval plate.

Chop chicken and arrange on plate according to its anatomy:
(a) Chop neck into 4 pieces. Place at top centre of plate.
(b) Turn chicken to one side, slice off tail and place at bottom centre of plate.
(c) Halve chicken. Cut off wings at joints. Chop each wing into two and place at sides of plate.
(d) Cut off drumsticks and thighs at joints. Chop into 4 or more pieces. Place near bottom end of plate on either side.
(e) Remove breastmeat from breastbone. Flatten with the side of a chopper. Chop into neat pieces and place above wings.

Serve with sauces and rice in individual plates.

Murtabak

Preparation: 40 minutes
Cooking: 30 minutes

450 g (1 lb) plain flour
250 ml (8 fl oz) fresh milk
120 ml (4 fl oz) water
¾ teaspoon salt
8 eggs
3 big onions, chopped finely, seasoned with a little
  salt and ¼ teaspoon ground turmeric
225 g (8 oz) ghee
1 onion, sliced thinly lengthwise
½ cucumber, sliced
tomato sauce

Filling
5 tablespoons oil
450 g (1 lb) minced mutton or beef
1½ tablespoons ground coriander
¼ teaspoon ground fennel
¼ teaspoon ground cummin
¼ teaspoon pepper
¾ teaspoon salt
3 green chillies, cut into ½ cm (¼ in) rings

Heat oil and stir-fry all the other filling ingredients till cooked.

Prepare dough as described for Paratha (p.92) using flour, milk, water, salt and 2 eggs, (beaten).

Leave dough in a warm place overnight to rise. Divide risen dough into 6 balls.

Roll each ball of dough to a very thin skin-like rectangular layer.

Break an egg in the centre, use the palm of your hand to smear egg over "skin" then sprinkle mutton and 3 tablespoons or more chopped onion in the centre.

Fold in 4 sides, then fold again into half.

Sprinkle ghee generously on an iron griddle and fry Murtabak. Keep sprinkling ghee while frying.

Fry both sides till quite crisp and blotches of brown show in some places.

Serve Murtabak with a dish of onion and cucumber slices topped with tomato ketchup.

Indian Rojak

Preparation: 1½ hours
Cooking: 1 hour

Main Ingredients
(a) 8-10 firm soybean cakes
    200 g (6⅔ oz) small prawns
    oil for deep-frying
(b) 6-8 fermented soybean cakes
(c) 6-7 small crabs
(d) 4 potatoes
    1 teaspoon ground chilli
    ⅓ teaspoon salt
(e) 4 hardboiled eggs
(f) 6-8 firm soybean cakes
(g) 1 large piece soaked cuttlefish (*jee hoo*) (p.131)
    1 teaspoon ground chilli
    5 tablespoons oil
    ⅓ teaspoon salt
(h) hard fritters (p. 131)

Garnishes
450 g (1 lb) beansprouts, scalded for 1 minute in
boiling water
300 g (10 oz) yam bean, shredded
2 medium-sized cucumbers, shredded

Batter
1⅓ cups and 1 tablespoon plain flour
¼ teaspoon baking powder
½ teaspoon ground turmeric
1 teaspoon sugar
¼ teaspoon salt
120 ml (4 fl oz) water
1 egg, beaten

Sauce
900 g (2 lb) sweet potatoes
2.25 L (4 pints) water
1 tablespoon tamarind
5 tablespoons water
5 tablespoons oil
4 shallots, chopped
3 red chillies, seeded and ground
1½ teaspoons ground chilli
⅓ teaspoon salt
6 tablespoons granulated sugar
2 tablespoons or more roasted ground peanuts
a few drops black soy sauce
a few drops vinegar

Slice across each soybean cake, parallel to square surface, so that you have 2 thin squares. Halve each thin square diagonally. You should have 4 triangular pieces. Dip into batter and press 1-2 prawns onto each triangle. The batter will help prawns to stick. Deep-fry in oil.

Dip fermented soybean cakes in batter, then deep-fry and cut each into 4 pieces.

Dip crabs into batter and deep-fry for 5 minutes till golden brown.

Boil potatoes in their jackets, peel and rub in ground chilli and salt. Deep-fry and quarter each potato. Cut each egg into 4 with an egg slicer.

Halve firm soybean cakes diagonally and deep-fry in oil till light brown.

Slice cuttlefish into smaller pieces and marinate in ground chilli and salt. Fry in oil.

Batter
Mix dry ingredients in a bowl and add water slowly, mixing to a smooth paste. Leave for 1 hour.

To Prepare Hard Fritters

Preparation: 15 minutes
Cooking: 10 minutes

175 g (6 oz) plain flour
½ teaspoon baking powder
¾ teaspoon salt
½ teaspoon sugar
120 ml (4 fl oz) and 2 tablespoons water
1 big onion, chopped finely
1 green chilli, seeded and chopped finely
extra plain flour for dusting hands
oil for deep-frying

Mix flour, baking powder, salt and sugar in a bowl. Add water gradually, kneading as you add. Leave aside for 1 hour.

Just before frying, knead in chopped onion and chilli.

Shape into 7½ cm (3 in) long cylinders, about 2 cm (¾ in) in diameter at the middle and tapering to points at both ends. Dust hands with extra flour while moulding fritters as dough tends to be sticky.

Deep-fry fritters in oil till golden brown. Cut each into 4 pieces before serving.

Just before using batter, add egg and stir till smooth.

Sauce
Boil sweet potatoes, then blend in portions with 10 cups water.

Mix tamarind with 5 tablespoons water. Squeeze and strain for juice.

Heat oil in a clay pot and fry shallots with ground chilli. Add blended sweet potatoes and water mixture and stir.

After 3-5 minutes, add salt, sugar and tamarind juice.

Stir continuously over low heat for 3 minutes and adjust taste if desired. Add peanuts, black soy sauce and vinegar just before serving.

To Serve Rojak
Pile pieces of your favourite ingredients on a flat dish and top with garnishes. Dip into a bowl of Indian Rojak sauce as you eat.

To Prepare Soaked Cuttlefish
To prepare cuttlefish, soak dried cuttlefish overnight in a mixture of 3 tablespoons bicarbonate of soda and 1.6 L (2¾ pints) cold water. After 24 hours, drain, wash and soak in salt solution (2 tablespoons salt in 1.6 L/2¾ pints water) for another 8 hours

Penang Loh Bak

Preparation: 10 minutes
Cooking: 25 minutes .

300 g (10 oz) minced pork
450 g (1 lb) pork tenderloin (*koo loh yoke*), cut into
   7½ cm (3 in) long strips, about 2 cm (¾ in) thick
1 teaspoon five-spice powder
½ teaspoon pepper
3 tablespoons black soy sauce
¼ teaspoon salt
1½ teaspoons sugar
2 tablespoons tapioca flour
6 tablespoons sweet potato flour
250 ml (8 fl oz) water
120 ml (4 fl oz) oil
150 g (5oz) yam bean, chopped
2 big onions, chopped
2 big flat soybean skins
oil for deep-frying

Dorothy's Loh Bak Sauce
3 tablespoons black malt sauce
2 tablespoons Worcestershire sauce
3 tablespoons granulated sugar
2 red chillies, chopped
juice of ½ lemon
1 tablespoon light soy sauce
1 teaspoon mustard
1 tablespoon water

Hawker's Loh Bak Sauce
6 tablespoons black soy sauce
3 tablespoons sugar
¼ teaspoon five-spice powder
½ teaspoon tapioca flour
2 tablespoons water

Season minced pork and tenderloin in five-spice powder, pepper, black soy sauce, salt and sugar.

Add thickening (tapioca flour and sweet potato flour mixed with water).

Heat oil and fry yam bean till half-cooked. Add seasoned meat and thickening with chopped onions.

Stir-fry for a few minutes till meat is cooked.

Wipe soybean skins with a dry cloth to remove excess salt. Cut into 17½ × 10 cm (7 × 4 in) rectangular pieces.

Place a strip of tenderloin in the centre of each piece of soybean skin. Spread 1 tablespoon filling over tenderloin.

Wrap by folding into a cylinder and twisting both ends like a Christmas cracker.

Steam for 10 minutes. When cool, deep-fry in oil over moderate heat till light brown.

Cut into bite-size pieces and serve with sliced cucumber, Loh Bak Sauce and Vinegar Chilli Sauce (p.141).

Dorothy's Loh Bak Sauce
Blend all ingredients together or stir briskly for 2 minutes till sugar dissolves.

Hawker's Loh Bak Sauce
Mix all ingredients together and cook over low heat for 2 minutes till smooth. Cool before using.

Singapore Chinese Rojak

Preparation: 20 minutes
Cooking: 2 minutes

3 tablespoons tamarind
7 tablespoons water
5 tablespoons black shrimp paste
2 teaspoons Sambal Blacan (p.139)
juice of 5 limes
5 teaspoons red sugar
2 tablespoons palm sugar
1½ teaspoons black soy sauce
300 g (10oz) pineapple, cut into thin wedges
300 g (10oz) yam bean, cut into thin wedges
150 g (5oz) beansprouts, scalded for 1 minute in
    boiling water
3 medium-sized cucumbers, cut into wedges
300 g (10oz) water convolvulus, cut into 4 cm
    (1½ in) lengths and scalded for 1 minute in
    boiling water
1 wild ginger flower, sliced thinly
1 small green mango, sliced thinly
1-2 pieces dried soybean cakes, cut into thin ½ cm
    (¼ in) strips
1-2 tablespoons roasted ground peanuts

Mix tamarind and water. Squeeze and strain to obtain juice.

In a shallow earthenware bowl, mix black shrimp paste, Sambal Blacan, lime juice, red sugar, palm sugar and black soy sauce. Mix in tamarind juice a little at a time, tasting as you add. Add as much or as little as you wish.

Add all other ingredients listed, and toss the salad to mix with sauce.

Lastly, add ground peanuts and serve at once.

Pickles
and Dips

Penang Acar

Preparation: 2½ hours
Cooking: 1¼ hours

Vegetables
(a) 3 kg (6⅔ lb) cucumbers
    2 tablespoons salt
(b) 300 g (10 oz) cauliflower
(c) 450 g (1 lb) cabbage
    2 teaspoons salt
(d) 3 medium-sized carrots
(e) 560 g (1¼ lb) green papaya
    1 teaspoon salt
(f) 30 shallots
(g) 10 red chillies
(h) 10 green chillies

Vinegar Mixture A
1 L (1¾ pints) vinegar (only 900 ml/1½ pints)
    if vinegar is used)
750 ml (1¼ pints) water
6 tablespoons sugar
1 tablespoon salt

Ingredients for Cooking Carrots
and Green Papaya
3 candlenuts *or* 5 blanched almonds
1 teaspoon dried shrimp paste
6 shallots
4 red chillies
6 tablespoons oil
200 g (6⅔ oz) dried prawns, pounded finely
2 tablespoons sugar
⅓ teaspoon salt

Rempah
10 cm (4 in) piece turmeric
20 shallots
4 candlenuts *or* blanched almonds
2 stalks lemon grass
8 slices galingale *or* green root ginger
25 dried chillies, seeded

Vinegar Mixture B
750 ml (1¼ pints) vinegar
1.25 L (2¼ pints) water
300 g (10 oz) sugar

Other Ingredients
12 tablespoons oil
6 tablespoons roasted sesame seeds
20 tablespoons roasted ground peanuts *or* pounded
    peanut candy

Quarter cucumbers lengthwise. Cut away soft centre and slice into 4 × 1 cm (1½ × ½ in) strips. Rub with salt, wrap in a clean flour sack and weigh down with a mortar. Leave overnight. The next morning, squeeze out excess liquid and sun the whole day.

Cut cauliflower into small pieces. Sun for a day. Cut cabbage into 2½ cm (1 in) square pieces. Rub in salt and sun for a day. Shred carrots into fine long strips. Sun the whole day. Grate green papaya, season with salt and sun.

Bring Vinegar Mixture A to a boil in an enamel pot. Scald shallots first and remove when colour changes to a pinkish red. Use a perforated ladle to scoop up shallots. Scald each vegetable in turn for 7-8 seconds. Cucumber and cabbage should be dipped in boiling mixture for only 1-2 seconds. Chillies should not be scalded at all as they tend to be too limp after scalding. Throw away vinegar.

Prepare the ingredients for cooking carrots and green papaya. Grind candlenuts, dried shrimp paste, shallots and chillies finely. Heat oil in wok till hot, then stir-fry ground ingredients till fragrant. Add dried prawns and seasoning. Mix well. Turn off heat and add shredded carrot and grated papaya. Toss to mix ingredients.

Slit chillies from the centre down the length till the tip is almost reached. Use a narrow pointed knife to scrape away seeds. Stuff chillies with carrot and papaya mixture.

Heat an earthen pot till hot, add 12 tablespoons oil and stir-fry *rempah* till fragrant. Add Vinegar Mixture B. Bring to a boil then turn off heat and allow to cool. Remove excess oil floating on the surface.

Add prepared vegetables, including remaining carrot shreds and papaya. When completely cooled to room temperature, bottle and leave to pickle for 2 days.

After this time, mix in roasted sesame seeds. Add roasted ground peanuts just before serving.

Note: This pickle will last for 4-5 months refrigerated if peanuts are not added.

Penang Acar Awak

Preparation: 1½ hours
Cooking: 25 minutes

Vegetables
(a) 150 g (5 oz) cauliflower, cut into small pieces
(b) 1 medium-sized carrot, cut into 3 mm (⅛ in) thick, 4 cm (1½ in) long pieces
(c) 150 g (5 oz) long beans, cut into 4 cm (1½ in) lengths
(d) 150 g (5 oz) yam bean, cut into ½ cm (¼ in) thick, 4 cm (1½ in) long pieces
(e) 150 g (5 oz) French beans, each cut into 3 pieces at a slant
(f) 30 shallots
(g) 5 cloves garlic, sliced
(h) 300 g (10 oz) cabbage, cut into 2½ cm (1 in) squares
(i) 3½ kg (7¾ lb) cucumbers, each cut into 6 lengthwise
    3 tablespoons salt
(j) 100 g (3⅓ oz) aubergines
(k) 10 red chillies, cut into 3-4 pieces at a slant
(l) 10 green chillies, cut into 3-4 pieces at a slant
(m) 2½ cm (1 in) piece ginger, shredded

Vinegar Mixture for Scalding Vegetables
350 ml (12 fl oz) vinegar
1 L (1¾ pints) water
1 teaspoon ground turmeric

Rempah
1 teaspoon ground chilli
7½ cm (3 in) piece turmeric
4 red chillies
1 tablespoon dried shrimp paste
1 stalk lemon grass
4 cm (1½ in) piece galingale *or* green root ginger
5 candlenuts *or* blanched almonds
15 shallots
2 cloves garlic

Other Ingredients
350 ml (12 fl oz) oil
120 g (4 oz) dried prawns, pounded
175 ml (6 fl oz) vinegar
15 tablespoons fine granulated sugar
4 tablespoons salt
tamarind juice strained from 2 tablespoons tamarind blended with 8 tablespoons water
300 g (10 oz) roasted ground peanuts
180 g (6 oz) roasted sesame seeds

Cut all vegetables as instructed in the list. Cut cucumbers into 6 lengthwise, remove soft centres and cut at a slant to 1 cm (½ in) pieces. Rub with 3 tablespoons salt, then squeeze out excess water. Wrap in cloth and weigh down with a heavy object for 1 hour. Cut aubergines crosswise into 4 cm (1½ in) cylinders. Halve lengthwise, then cut each half lengthwise into 3-4 pieces.

Bring vinegar mixture to a boil in a clay or an enamel pot. Scald vegetables in the order listed: 30 seconds for cauliflower, carrot, long beans and yam bean; French beans, shallots, garlic and cabbage 15 seconds each; cucumbers and aubergines 4-5 seconds each. Do not scald chillies and ginger. Discard vinegar mixture.

Heat oil in a wok and stir-fry *rempah* for about 3 minutes till fragrant. Fry dried prawns for 2 minutes.

Pour in 175 ml (6 fl oz) vinegar with sugar, salt and tamarind juice. Taste and season as desired, then add vegetables except cucumbers and aubergines. Add these only after 30 minutes.

Leave vegetables overnight in the pot, stirring once or twice for even pickling.

Before serving the next day, stir in roasted ground peanuts and sesame seeds. Bottle and sprinkle more ground peanuts and sesame seeds on top.

This very tasty pickle, which goes well with rich foods and liquor, is usually prepared during the festive season. It is commonly called the "one-day pickle" but will keep refrigerated for up to 2 weeks.

Pickled Green Chillies

Preparation: 5 minutes

15 green chillies
1 teaspoon salt
120 ml (4 fl oz) vinegar

Cut chillies crosswise into 1 cm (½ in) thick pieces. Mix chillies with salt and vinegar and leave for at least 2 days before serving.

Indian Cucumber Pickle

Preparation: 1 hour
Cooking: 10 minutes

2½ kg (5½ lb) cucumbers
1½ teaspoons salt
4 tablespoons water
6 tablespoons oil
6 cloves garlic, sliced thinly lengthwise
15 shallots, sliced thinly lengthwise
5 cm (2 in) piece ginger, shredded
1 tablespoon dried shrimp paste, ground to a paste
   with a little water
600 ml (1 pint) vinegar
10 red chillies, quartered lengthwise
5 green chillies, quartered lengthwise

Rempah
8 tablespoons ground coriander
3 tablespoons ground chilli (less if desired)
2 tablespoons ground turmeric
12 tablespoons granulated sugar
2 teaspoons salt

Quarter cucumbers, remove soft centres, then cut into 2½ cm (1 in) lengths. Cut each piece lengthwise into ½ cm (¼ in) thick pieces. Mix with 1½ teaspoons salt and ¼ cup water. Leave for 30 minutes, then place seasoned cucumber in a cloth and squeeze out excess water. Dry.

Heat oil and fry garlic and shallots. Remove to a dish.

Use the same oil to fry *rempah* and seasoning mixed with 120 ml (4 fl oz) water, shredded ginger and shrimp paste.

Pour in vinegar and bring to a boil. When cool, put in cucumber and chilli strips.

Sprinkle fried garlic and shallots over pickled cucumber.

Note: This pickle goes very well with any Indian curry.

Mango Pickle

Preparation: 1 hour
Cooking: 8 minutes

1.6 L (2¾ pints) water
110 g (4 oz) rough salt
8 small green mangoes
cool boiled water
1 L (1¾ pints) water
450 g (1 lb) sugar
1 teaspoon *kamchor* powder
4 pieces *kamchor*

Boil 1.6 L (2¾ pints) water with rough salt. Allow to cool, then strain. Put in whole mangoes. Water should cover mangoes. Leave mangoes in salt solution for 3 or 4 days.

When skin turns yellow, remove mangoes and soak in cool boiled water to remove excess salt. Drain away water after 4 hours. Peel and halve mangoes lengthwise. Discard seeds.

Prepare syrup. Boil 1 L (1¾ pints) water with sugar over very low heat in a non-stick pot till thick and syrupy. Stir in *kamchor* powder and *kamchor* pieces. When syrup cools, add mangoes.

This pickle is best eaten after 2 or 3 days. Keep refrigerated.

Note: Kamchor and *kamchor* powder are obtainable from Chinese medicine shops.

Long Chinese Cabbage Pickle

Preparation: 10 minutes
Cooking: 6 minutes

450 g (1lb) long Chinese cabbage
boiling water
2 teaspoons salt
2 red chillies
5 tablespoons sugar
½ teaspoon salt
120 ml (4 fl oz) water
2 tablespoons vinegar
1-1½ teaspoons sesame oil

Discard leafy portions of long Chinese cabbage and use only white stalks. Shred into thin 5 cm (2 in) long pieces. Scald in boiling water mixed with 2 teaspoons salt for 5 minutes. Drain dry.

Seed chillies and cut into long thin strips.

In a small enamel saucepan, mix sugar, ½ teaspoon salt, water, vinegar and sesame oil. Boil for 1 minute, stirring till sugar dissolves. Pickle vegetables in this solution for 1 day before serving.

Kuakchye Pickle

Preparation: 15 minutes

900 g (2 lb) *kuakchye*
1 tablespoon salt
20 slices ginger
¾ teaspoon salt
2 tablespoons sugar
3 tablespoons Chinese vinegar
2 teaspoons mustard

Cut *kuakchye* stalks into thin 5 cm (2 in) long strips. Cut leaves into 5 cm (2 in) pieces. Rub in 1 tablespoon salt till vegetable becomes limp. Squeeze dry.

Shred ginger and rub in ¾ teaspoon salt. Squeeze out liquid.

Mix vegetable with ginger, sugar, vinegar and mustard. Pickle for at least a day before serving.

Note: Kuakchye Pickle is a famous accompaniment for Hati Babi Bungkus (p.59).

Kiamchye, Carrot and Cucumber Pickle

Preparation: 18 minutes

2 cucumbers
3 red chillies
1 teaspoon salt
½ long radish, scraped and sliced thinly
1 carrot, sliced thinly
450 g (1 lb) *kiamchye*
hot water
8 tablespoons vinegar
juice of 1 lemon
1 teaspoon sesame oil
6 tablespoons sugar

Quarter cucumbers lengthwise. Remove soft centres, then cut at a slant into ½ cm (¼ in) thick, 4 cm (1½ in) long pieces.

Seed chillies and shred into long thin strips. Rub salt into cucumber, chillies, radish and carrot.

Soak *kiamchye* in hot water for a few minutes. Squeeze dry and shred. Mix with vinegar, lemon juice, sesame oil and sugar. Leave to soak overnight. Mix with the other vegetables before serving. Adjust taste by adding more sugar or salt if desired.

Chinese Restaurant Style Pickles

Preparation: 15 minutes

4 big cucumbers
½ teaspoon salt
1 carrot
2 radishes
2 red chillies
1 tablespoon salt
175 ml (12 fl oz) vinegar
225 g (8 oz) sugar

Slice off about 2½ cm (1 in) from the rounded ends of cucumbers. Rub cut ends with sliced-off pieces to bring up the sap. Quarter lengthwise, then remove soft centres. Slice into 1 cm (½ in) thick, 2½ cm (1 in) long pieces. Season with ½ teaspoon salt and leave aside.

Slice carrot and radishes into 2½ cm (1 in) lengths. Halve, then slice thinly lengthwise.

Seed chillies, halve crosswise, then cut into long thin strips. Rub 1 tablespoon salt into chillies, carrot and radishes. Leave for a few minutes, then wash away salt and squeeze dry.

Pickle sliced carrot, radishes and chillies in vinegar and sugar for a day. Add cucumber about an hour before serving so that they remain crisp.

Note: If desired, add shreds of young ginger (from a 5 cm/2 in piece). Pickle this with carrot, radish and chillies.

Penang Salt Fish Acar

Preparation: 10 minutes
Cooking: 5 minutes

450 g (1 lb) salt fish
350 ml (12 fl oz) vinegar
75 g (2½ oz) tamarind
175 ml (6 fl oz) oil
15 red chillies, seeded
20 shallots, cut into ½ cm (¼ in) thick slices
5 cloves garlic, sliced thinly
4 stalks curry leaves (use leaves only)
5 tablespoons sugar
1½ teaspoons salt

Rempah
25 dried chillies, seeded
10 cloves garlic
3 tablespoons ground turmeric
30 g (1 oz) cummin
15 black peppercorns

Cut salt fish into ½ cm (¼ in) slices. Wash first in hot water, then in cold. Drain dry and sun for at least 2 hours.

Grind *rempah*, using 1-2 tablespoons vinegar to sprinkle over *rempah* ingredients while grinding.

Mix tamarind with remaining vinegar. Squeeze and strain. Discard pulp and seeds.

Heat oil and fry salt fish till crisp. Remove to a dish. Add chillies, shallots and garlic to hot oil and fry for just 30 seconds before adding curry leaves and *rempah*. Fry for 2 minutes.

Put in sugar, salt, tamarind vinegar mixture and fish. Adjust taste by adding more salt or more sugar.

Leave them for some hours, then pack into airtight bottles. This pickle lasts for a few months refrigerated.

Malay Fish Acar

Preparation: 20 minutes
Cooking: 20 minutes

600 g (1⅓ lb) Mackerel
5 red chillies
5 green chillies
4 tablespoons vinegar
120 ml (4 fl oz) water
4 teaspoons sugar
¾ teaspoon salt
13 tablespoons oil
2½ cm (1 in) piece ginger, shredded
3 cloves garlic, sliced

Rempah
4 red chillies
4 candlenuts *or* blanched almonds
12 shallots
3 cloves garlic
1 cm (½ in) piece ginger
2½ cm (1 in) piece turmeric

Cut fish into 4 pieces. Halve chillies lengthwise, seed, then cut into 8 long strips each.

Boil vinegar with water for 5 minutes. Stir in sugar and salt.

Heat 6 tablespoons oil in a wok and fry fish till crisp. Remove fish to a deep bowl.

Heat 4 tablespoons oil and fry *rempah* till fragrant. Add this to fish and pour in boiled vinegar mixture.

Heat remaining 3 tablespoons oil and fry garlic and shredded ginger. Add to pickled fish together with red and green chillies.

Leave *acar* for at least 2 days before serving.

Blacan

Preparation: 45 minutes
Roasting: 8-10 hours

4½ kg (10 lb) small shrimps
225 g (8 oz) salt

Trim the shrimps and discard any twigs, leaves, etc. Blend with salt and pass through a meat grinder. Mould into balls, then flatten to 2½ cm (1 in) thick patties.

Put shrimp paste on aluminium trays and cover with a fine wire mesh.

Sun for a few days, or bake in a moderate oven for 4 hours, then in a slow oven for another 4-6 hours.

Sambal Blacan with Variations

Preparation: 10 minutes
Roasting: 6 minutes

2 pieces dried shrimp paste, each 2½ cm (1 in)
  square and ½ cm (¼ in) thick
12 red chillies *or* 10 bird chillies
¼ teaspoon salt
6 limes

Flatten dried shrimp paste and roast in a dry pan over low heat for 6 minutes till aromatic. Pound roasted shrimp paste, chillies and salt together. Chillies should be pounded coarsely.

Put Sambal Blacan in a saucer and squeeze in lime juice just before serving.

Variations
For a change of flavour, mix with 3-4 pounded lime leaves or 3-4 pounded small sour starfruit. During the mango season, serve Sambal Blacan mixed with thin slivers of nearly ripe mango.

Fried Sambal Blacan

Preparation: 30 minutes
Roasting: 4-5 minutes
Cooking: 18-20 minutes

50 dried chillies, seeded
6 pieces dried shrimp paste, each about 2 mm ($\frac{1}{16}$
    in) thick and 6 cm (2½ in) square
20 red chillies, coarsely sliced
1½-2 teaspoons salt
8-9 tablespoons oil

Soak dried chillies in boiling water for 5 minutes, then drain in a colander.

Roast shrimp paste in a dry pan over low heat or under an electric grill. Toast each side for 2 minutes. Scrape away burnt portions, if any.

Grind dried chillies, then add red chillies with shrimp paste and salt. Grind coarsely.

Alternatively, pound dried chillies with shrimp paste, adding salt gradually. Then add red chillies and pound steadily for about 3 minutes.

Heat oil in a non-stick pan and fry pounded ingredients over moderate heat, stirring all the while with a wooden spoon. Cook for 18 minutes.

Store in a glass jar when cooled to room temperature.

Sambal Blacan Timun

Preparation: 15 minutes

1 cucumber
¼ pineapple
1 teaspoon roasted dried shrimp paste
⅓ teaspoon salt
juice of 6 limes
1 dessertspoon black shrimp paste (*heiko*)
2-3 tablespoons pounded dried prawns
1 onion, sliced finely
1 dessertspoon sugar

Quarter cucumber lengthwise, remove soft centre then slice thinly. Discard hard core of pineapple and slice thinly.

Pound dried shrimp paste and mix well with salt, lime juice and black shrimp paste, pounded dried prawns, onion, cucumber, pineapple and sugar.

Sambal Blacan Timun goes very well with fried noodles.

Chin Char Loke

Preparation: 45 minutes

1¼ kg (2¾ lb) small shrimps (*grago*)
4 tablespoons salt
110g (4 oz) cooked rice
420 ml (¾ pint) Chinese rice wine

Wash and trim the shrimps. Add salt and mix well.

Pour into an earthen or glass jar. Add cooked rice and Chinese rice wine. Stir with a clean dry wooden spoon. Stretch a piece of clean muslin over top of jar and secure with string or rubber bands. Gas released during fermentation will escape through the muslin.

On the second day, give a few stirs with a clean dry wooden spoon and cover again. After the third day, when Chin Char Loke is mellow, bottle and refrigerate.

Note: Chin Char Loke is an appetiser served either in its raw state as a dip for boiled streaky pork or cooked in a favourite Asian dish like Sambal Grago with Samchan. Both recipes are given on p.141.

Chin Char Loke Dip with Samchan

Preparation: 10 minutes
Cooking: 20 minutes

2 tablespoons Chin Char Loke (p.140)
1 teaspoon sugar
3-4 shallots, sliced finely
2 red chillies (*or* 1 red and 1 green), sliced finely
juice of 3 limes *or* ½ lemon
2.25 L (4 pints) water
300 g (10 oz) streaky pork

Mix Chin Char Loke with sugar in a saucer. Top with shallot and chilli slices, then squeeze lime or lemon juice over these ingredients.

Bring 2.25 L (4 pints) water to a boil, add streaky pork and cook for 20 minutes. Cut into ½ cm (¼ in) thick slices and serve with Chin Char Loke dip.

Sambal Grago with Samchan

Preparation: 20 minutes
Cooking: 25 minutes

1.2 L (2 pints) water
150 g (5 oz) streaky pork
2 tablespoons oil
6 shallots, sliced
2-3 tablespoons Chin Char Loke
4 tablespoons juice of limes *or* thick tamarind juice
sugar to taste
2 red chillies, sliced

Bring water to a boil and cook pork for about 15 minutes. When cool, cut into thin pieces.

Heat oil in an enamel or earthern pot. Fry shallots, Chin Char Loke and pork for a minute, then add lime or tamarind juice. Stir in sugar and sliced chillies and serve immediately.

Vinegar Chilli Sauce

Preparation: First method, 5 minutes
            Second method, 10 minutes

20 red chillies
110 g (4 oz) sugar
120 ml (4 fl oz) vinegar
1 teaspoon chopped garlic
2 teaspoons salt
juice of 1 lemon

First Method
Blend all the above ingredients except chillies in an electric blender for 3 minutes till sugar dissolves. Add chillies and blend till chillies are coarsely chopped.

Second Method
If no blender is available, pound chillies coarsely, then add other ingredients and stir well to dissolve sugar.

Malay Satay Sauce

Preparation: 15 minutes
Cooking: 25 minutes

750 ml (1¼ pints) water
2 coconuts, grated
250 ml (8 fl oz) oil
25 shallots, pounded coarsely
4 tomatoes, quartered
6 small sour starfruit, halved lengthwise
3 tablespoons sugar
1 teaspoon salt
450 g (1lb) roasted ground peanuts

Rempah
3 tablespoons ground chilli *or* 35 dried chillies,
    seeded
4 red chillies
10 bird chillies (optional)
6 slices galingale *or* root ginger
2 cloves garlic
4 candlenuts *or* blanched almonds
¾ teaspoon ground turmeric
15 black peppercorns
1 teaspoon ground fennel
1 teaspoon ground cummin
2 tablespoons coriander, roasted and pounded
    coarsely

Add 120 ml (4 lf oz) water to coconut, squeeze to obtain 175 ml (6 fl oz) thick coconut milk. Add 600 ml (1 pint) water to solid residue and squeeze to obtain 750 ml (1¼ pints) thin coconut milk.

Heat oil in a wok till smoking hot and fry shallots till golden brown. Add *rempah* and stir-fry for about 2 minutes till fragrant.

Add a little of the thin coconut milk, simmer and keep adding thin coconut milk till all is used up. This will take about 10 minutes.

Add the tomatoes, starfruit, sugar and salt. Pour in thick coconut milk and simmer for a few more minutes till oil floats to the surface. If a thicker gravy is preferred, simmer longer. Finally add roasted ground peanuts, bring to a boil and turn off heat.

Nonya Satay Sauce

Preparation: 15 minutes
Cooking: 25 minutes

½ coconut, grated
420 ml (¾ pint) water
½ pineapple
150 ml (¼ pint) cooking oil
3 tablespoons sugar
¾ tablespoon salt
3 tablespoons crunchy peanut butter
180 g (6 oz) roasted ground peanuts

Rempah
15-20 dried chillies *or* 1½ tablespoons ground chilli
20 shallots
1 tablespoon ground coriander
2 stalks lemon grass
1 tablespoon dried shrimp paste

Mix grated coconut and water. Squeeze and strain to obtain coconut milk.

Quarter pineapple lengthwise. Cut away hard core. Grate finely. Refrigerate grated pineapple if not used immediately.

Heat oil in a pot and fry *rempah* till fragrant. Add coconut milk, sugar, salt and crunchy peanut butter.

Stir for 7 minutes till oil floats to the top. If gravy is too thick, add boiling hot water and adjust taste accordingly. When cooked, add ground peanuts.

Serve sauce in individual bowls with a little grated pineapple.

Curry Powder

Meat Curry Powder

Preparation: 30 minutes
Roasting: 5 minutes

1.8 kg (4 lb) coriander
450 g (1 lb) fennel
300 g (10 oz) cummin
225 g (8 oz) white peppercorns
75 g (2½ oz) black peppercorns
675 g (1½ lb) dried chillies, stems removed
225 g (8 oz) turmeric
40 g (1⅓ oz) cardamoms
20 g (⅔ oz) star anise
15 g (½ oz) cloves
30 g (1 oz) cinnamon sticks
10 whole nutmegs

Pick out sand and twigs from coriander seeds before use. Wash and sun in large sieves for 2 days, stirring once in a while for even sunning. Roast in a dry pan for 3-4 minutes till aromatic. Stir constantly to distribute heat evenly.

Do the same for fennel and cummin seeds, but roast only 1-2 minutes.

Mix all the ingredients and grind well. Allow curry powder to cool for 3 hours before packing into plastic or glass containers.

Kurmah Curry Powder

Preparation: 30 minutes
Roasting: 5 minutes

2.4 kg (5⅓ lb) coriander
300 g (10 oz) fennel
300 g (10 oz) cummin
450 g (1 lb) black peppercorns
150 g (5 oz) white peppercorns
450 g (1 lb) turmeric
10 whole nutmegs
45 g (1½ oz) cloves
75 g (2½ oz) cardamoms
30 g (1 oz) star anise
60 g (2 oz) cinnamon sticks

Pick out sand and twigs from coriander seeds before use. Wash and sun in large sieves for 2 days, stirring once in a while for even sunning. Roast in a dry pan for 3-4 minutes till aromatic. Stir contantly to distribute heat evenly.

Do the same for fennel and cummin seeds, but roast only 1-2 minutes.

Mix all the ingredients and grind well. Allow curry powder to cool for 3 hours before packing into plastic or glass containers.

Fish Curry Powder

Preparation: 30 minutes
Roasting: 5 minutes

1.8 kg (4 lb) coriander
450 g (1 lb) fennel
450 g (1 lb) cummin
450 g (1 lb) black peppercorns
1 kg (2¼ lb) dried chillies, stems removed
200 g (6⅔ oz) turmeric
30 g (1 oz) cardamoms
30 g (1 oz) star anise
20 g (⅔ oz) cloves
20 g (⅔ oz) cinnamon sticks

Pick out sand and twigs from coriander seeds before use. Wash and sun in large sieves for 2 days, stirring once in a while for even sunning. Roast in a dry pan for 3-4 minutes till aromatic. Stir contantly to distribute heat evenly.

Do the same for fennel and cummin seeds, but roast only 1-2 minutes.

Mix all the ingredients and grind well. Allow curry powder to cool for 3 hours before packing into plastic or glass containers.

Vegetable Curry Powder

Preparation: 30 minutes
Cooking: 20 minutes

450 g (1 lb) dried chillies
750 g (1⅔ lb) coriander
30 g (1 oz) cummin
100 g (3⅓ oz) dried turmeric
60 g (2 oz) mixed black and white peppercorns

Discard chilli stems. If a milder curry is preferred, remove seeds.

Wash and dry coriander. Sun for at least 2 days, turning seeds a few times for even sunning, then roast over low heat, stirring constantly till fragrant.

Roast cummin slightly over very low heat.

Send all ingredients to a mill to have them ground, or grind at home in an electric mill. When cooled to room temperature, store in an airtight jar.

Use this curry powder for cooking Sothi (p.89).

Desserts and Savouries

Creamy Corn Javanese Flan Pudding

Preparation: 10 minutes
Cooking: 8 minutes

2 coconuts, grated
1 L (1¾ pints) water
120 g (4 oz) mung bean flour *or* green bean flour
270 g (9 oz) sugar
¼ teaspoon salt
½ teaspoon vanilla essence
1 tin (480 g/17 oz) cream corn
1 white coconut, grated and mixed with ⅓ teaspoon salt
1 tin (480 g/17 oz) whole kernel corn
5 green cherries
5 red cherries

Mix 2 grated coconuts with water. Squeeze and strain to obtain coconut milk.

Blend flour with 120 ml (4 fl oz) coconut milk till smooth, then stir in remaining coconut milk.

Add sugar, salt and vanilla essence. Bring to a boil over medium heat, stirring for 4 minutes till mixture thickens.

Pour in cream corn, stir briskly and cook for another 4 minutes till quite thick and white.

Pour into a wet jelly mould and leave to cool and set.

When set, turn out jelly onto a bed of grated white coconut, pour on whole kernel corn and top with cherries.

Thai Pumpkin Dessert

Preparation: 20 minutes
Cooking: 25 minutes

900 g (2 lb) pumpkin
2 coconuts, grated
1.75 L (3 pints) water
¾ teaspoon salt
10 tablespoons sugar
300 g (10 oz) palm sugar
4 screwpine leaves, knotted in pairs

Peel pumpkin and dice into 5 cm (2 in) cubes.

Mix grated coconut with 120 ml (4 fl oz) water. Squeeze and strain to extract thick coconut milk. Add 600 ml (1 pint) water to residue. Squeeze and strain to extract thin coconut milk.

Put pumpkin and thin coconut milk in a pot. Bring to a boil. Add salt, sugar, palm sugar and screwpine leaves. Boil for 30 minutes, stirring constantly.

When pumpkin is tender, add thick coconut milk and more sugar if desired. As soon as it bubbles, remove from heat.

Refrigerate if serving cold.

Kuih Talam

Preparation: 20 minutes
Cooking: 50 minutes

Green Batter
175 g (6 oz) sugar
250 ml (8 fl oz) hot water
12 screwpine leaves
60 g (2 oz) damp rice flour
1 tablespoon tapioca flour
1 tablespoon mung bean flour *or* green bean flour
extra warm water
1 teaspoon water
a few drops green colouring

White Batter
1 coconut, grated
4 tablespoons damp rice flour
1 tablespoon mung bean flour *or* green bean flour
¼ teaspoon salt
extra water

Green Batter
Dissolve sugar in hot water. Cool syrup. Pound and strain screwpine leaves to extract juice.

Put rice flour, tapioca flour and mung bean flour in a bowl. Knead with screwpine juice. Knead in syrup, then add sufficient warm water to obtain 3 cups batter. Stir in 1 teaspoon water and green colouring before straining batter through thin muslin.

White Batter
Squeeze and strain grated coconut to obtain 1 cup coconut milk. Mix with rice flour and mung bean flour. Stir in salt and sufficient water to get 350 ml (12 fl oz) batter. Strain batter.

Cooking
Test-steam the batters for consistency. (This is essential as the liquid content of damp rice flour varies greatly.) In small enamel plates, steam 2 tablespoons of each batter separately for 10 minutes. The cooked green batter should look and feel like soft jelly. The cooked white batter should be very soft and barely able to hold itself up. If batters are too thick, resulting in thin layers which can be peeled off the plates, more water or coconut milk should be added.

Heat a 20 cm (8 in) steaming tray. Pour in green batter and stir over boiling water till batter thickens and flecks can be seen floating in it. Cover and steam for 20 minutes until top is bubbly.

Using a damp absorbent cloth, dab surface of cooked green layer to mop up any liquid floating on top.

Gently pour white batter on top. Cover and steam for 10 minutes over medium heat. When cooked, the white layer should be set but not wrinkled.

Cool thoroughly before cutting.

Note: For a brown and white Kuih Talam, omit screwpine juice. Chop half a piece of palm sugar and mix with granulated sugar to make ¾ cup sugar.

Lepat Pisang

Preparation: 20 minutes
Cooking: 15 minutes

6-7 banana leaves
5 ripe bananas (*pisang rajah*)
⅓ white coconut, grated
2 tablespoons plain flour
3 tablespoons sugar
⅓ teaspoon salt
2 screwpine leaves, cut into 5 cm (2 in) lengths

Scald banana leaves in boiling water and cut into 17½ × 12½ cm (7 × 5 in) pieces.

Mash bananas with a fork. Add coconut, flour, sugar and salt. Mix well.

Put 2 tablespoons of the mixture on a piece of banana leaf. Place a piece of screwpine leaf on top and wrap into a 7½ × 10 cm (3 × 4 in) rectangle.

Steam for about 12-15 minutes over moderate heat. Serve cold.

Note: Lepat Pisang can also be grilled for 2-3 minutes and served hot.

Pengat

Preparation: 30 minutes
Cooking: 20 minutes

450 g (1 lb) yam
1 kg (2¼ lb) sweet potatoes
8 large ripe bananas (*pisang rajah*)
2 coconuts, grated
2 L (3½ pints) water
450 g (1 lb) palm sugar
1 durian (optional), about 1 kg (2¼ lb) with skin
1 tablespoon rice flour ⎫
2 tablespoons water ⎬ if durian is not used
6-8 tablespoons sugar
2 screwpine leaves

Peel yam and cut into 5 × 2½ cm (2 × 1 in) pieces. Peel sweet potatoes, halve lengthwise and cut into wedges.

Cut each banana into 3 pieces at a slant. If the extra large bananas are used, cut at a slant into 2 cm (¾ in) slices.

Mix coconut with 300 ml (½ pint) water. Squeeze and strain to obtain 350 ml (12 fl oz) thick coconut milk. Add 1.6 L (2¾ pints) water to residue. Squeeze and strain to obtain thin coconut milk.

Cut palm sugar into small pieces. Put half in a saucepan with 120 ml (4 fl oz) water and melt sugar. Keep aside till Pengat is ready to serve.

If durian is used, peel flesh from seeds. If not used, make a paste of rice flour and water.

Put yam, sweet potato and thin coconut milk in a pot with sugar, remaining palm sugar and screwpine leaves knotted together.

Bring to a boil, cook for 5 minutes, then add bananas, and durian if used. Cook about 3 minutes till bananas are tender, stirring once in a while.

When Pengat is ready add 1 cup thick coconut milk. If durian is not used, add rice flour paste as well. Simmer over low heat till bubbles form. Remove from heat.

Serve Pengat cold with a little jug of thick coconut milk and another of palm syrup for those who desire a richer and sweeter dessert.

Rainbow Abok-Abok Sago

Preparation: 15 minutes
Cooking: 45 minutes

8 screwpine leaves
340 g (¾ lb) pearl sago
¾ white coconut, grated
8 tablespoons granulated sugar
¼ teaspoon salt
3 drops pink cochineal
2 drops rose essence
2 drops green colouring

Shred, pound and strain screwpine leaves for clear green juice.

Soak sago in water for an hour, then drain. Mix with grated coconut, sugar and salt. Divide into 3 portions.

Colour the first portion pink with cochineal and flavour with rose essence. Leave the second portion white. Add green colouring and screwpine juice to the third portion.

Spread the green portion in a greased cake tin. Level and press firmly with the back of a spoon. Steam for 15 minutes.

Pour white portion over green layer. Spread and press firmly. Steam till sago is transparent.

Finally, pour on pink portion, level and press, then steam till set.

Remove from steamer, allow to cool and when quite firm, cut into diamond or square slices.

147

Sago Coconut Pudding

Preparation: 5 minutes
Cooking: 30 minutes

225 g (8 oz) pearl sago
180 g (6 oz) sugar
1 L (1¾ pints) water
1 egg white
¼ teaspoon salt
⅓ teaspoon rose essence
¼ teaspoon cochineal *or* red colouring
½ white coconut, grated
¼ teaspoon salt

Soak pearl sago in water for 1 hour then drain.

Boil sugar and water for about 10 minutes till sugar dissolves. Pour in sago and cook for about 10 minutes till transparent.

Drain off liquid by pouring into a sieve.

Beat egg white with ¼ teaspoon salt and stir into sago. Add rose essence and cochineal. (Other flavours and colours may be used if preferred.)

Press sago into small jelly moulds. Refrigerate for 3 hours to set. Loosen moulds and roll each little pudding in grated coconut mixed with salt.

Serve as a dessert after a hot curry meal.

Bubor Cha-Cha with Ice Shavings

Preparation: 20 minutes
Cooking: 40 minutes

600 g (1⅓ lb) sweet potatoes
600 g (1⅓ lb) yam
3 white coconuts, grated
¼ teaspoon salt
1.25 L (2¼ pints) water
225 g (8 oz) rock sugar
340 g (12 oz) granulated sugar
2 screwpine leaves
200 g (6⅔ oz) tapioca flour
6 tablespoons cold water
boiling hot water
½ teaspoon green colouring
½ teaspoon blue colouring
2 tablespoons extra tapioca flour
1 L (1¾ pints) water

Cut sweet potatoes into 1 cm (½ in) slices, then into diamond shapes about ½ × ½ cm (¼ × ¼ in). Cut yam into 2 cm (¾ in) cubes.

Squeeze and strain grated coconut to obtain thick coconut milk. Add salt and refrigerate.

Add 125 L (2¼ pints) water to coconut residue. Squeeze and strain to obtain thin coconut milk.

Steam sweet potatoes and yam for 15 minutes or till cooked. Set aside.

Boil rock sugar and granulated sugar with screwpine leaves for about 10 minutes. When sugar has melted, add thin coconut milk and boil for 5 minutes. Cool to room temperature and refrigerate.

Mix tapioca with sufficient cold water to dissolve it. Pour in enough boiling hot water to make a thick starch. Cook, stirring briskly.

Divide cooked tapioca into 3 equal portions. Colour portions green, red and blue. Knead each portion of dough separately, adding more tapioca flour while kneading if necessary.

While still warm, roll into thin strips of ½ cm (¼ in) width. Cut strips into triangles.

Bring 1 L (1¾ pints) water to a boil in a saucepan and cook coloured tapioca triangles separately. They float when cooked. Scoop out and plunge into cold water. Keep aside.

To Serve
Put 1-2 tablespoons each of sweet potato and yam and 2 teaspoons coloured tapioca triangles into individual serving bowls.

Add 4 tablespoons cold sweet coconut milk and top with ice shavings. Pour 1 tablespoon thick coconut milk on top. Serve immediately.

Clockwise from bottom left: Javanese Cendol (p.153), Bubor Pulot Hitam (p. 154)
and Pengat (p.147)

White Fungus with Loquats (p.158)

150

Wu Tau Koh (p.164)

Hokkien Bak Chang (p.165)

Javanese Cendol

Preparation: 20 minutes
Cooking: 15 minutes

20 screwpine leaves
15 Javanese screwpine leaves
750 ml (1¼ pints) water
a few drops green colouring
1 packet (150 g/5 oz) mung bean flour *or* green bean
    flour
450 g (1 lb) palm sugar
6 tablespoons granulated sugar
175 ml (6 fl oz) water
3 white coconuts, grated
420 ml (¾ pint) warm water
¼ teaspoon salt

Shred both kinds of screwpine leaves and blend with 420 ml (¾ pint) water. Strain to obtain clear juice. Add green colouring and boil in a non-stick saucepan.

Mix 300 ml (½ pint) water with mung bean flour or green bean flour and stir into boiling screwpine juice. Cook over moderate heat, stirring constantly with a wooden spoon till mixture is transparent and leaves pan.

Prepare a basin of ice-cold water with a few ice cubes floating in it. Place a cendol frame over water and pour cooked mixture into frame.

Press down mixture so that little drops or strips are squeezed through perforations in frame. Let green strips soak in water for 5 minutes, then drain and refrigerate.

Cut palm sugar into small pieces and boil with granulated sugar and 175 ml (6 fl oz) water till thick and syrupy.

Mix coconut with warm water. Squeeze and strain to obtain coconut milk. Add salt and refrigerate.

To serve, place Cendol in a glass, add palm syrup and coconut milk. Top with ice shavings or ice chips.

Banana Custard Dessert

Preparation: 10 minutes
Cooking: 10 minutes

1½ white coconuts, grated
420 ml (¾ pint) evaporated milk
225 g (8 oz) custard powder
¼ teaspoon banana essence
280 g (10 oz) granulated sugar
3 drops yellow colouring
2 red cocktail cherries
2 green cocktail cherries

Extract 750 ml (1¼ pints) coconut milk from grated coconut. If necessary, add a little water to residue and extract more milk to make up the required amount.

Combine coconut milk and evaporated milk to make 1.2 L (2 pints) milk.

Dissolve custard powder in 250 ml (8 fl oz) milk. Stir into remaining milk and strain.

Stir in banana essence, sugar and colouring. Cook over moderate heat, stirring constantly. When mixture thickens, lower heat and continue stirring for a minute.

Pour custard into sundae or champagne glasses.

Cut bananas into ½ cm (¼ in) rings. Slice cherries thinly.

When custard is cool and about to set, place slices of banana on top and decorate centre with a slice of cherry.

Bubor Pulot Hitam

Preparation: 7 minutes
Cooking: 2 hours

300 g (10 oz) black glutinous rice
5 L (11 pints) water
300 g (10 oz) sugar
2 screwpine leaves
1 tablespoon tapioca flour *or* cornflour
2 tablespoons water
1 coconut, grated
3 tablespoons water
⅓ teaspoon salt

Boil rice with 3.75 L (8 pints) water over moderate heat for 1 hour. When liquid has reduced to 250 ml (8 fl oz) add remaining 1.5 L (2½ pints) water and continue boiling for 30 minutes.

Add sugar and screwpine leaves knotted together. Turn heat down and simmer for another 30 minutes till rice grains are swollen and liquid is thick.

Mix flour with 2 tablespoons water and stir paste into contents of pot. Bring to a boil and remove from heat.

Mix coconut and 3 tablespoons water. Squeeze and strain to obtain thick coconut milk. Add salt.

Serve Bubor Pulot Hitam in individual bowls with 1-2 tablespoons thick coconut milk.

Tapeh (Fermented Glutinous Rice)

Preparation: 10 minutes
Cooking: 1 hour

1⅓ kg (3 lb) glutinous rice
4½ teaspoons *ragi* (locally made yeast), crushed
2 teaspoons sugar

Soak glutinous rice for 2 hours in water. Drain.

Steam rice for an hour till cooked but grainy. Cool by spreading in a sieve.

While still a little warm, sprinkle crushed yeast over rice grains. Mix well with very clean hands.

Place rice in a large glass jar with a wide mouth. Cover opening with a piece of muslin stretched across and secured by rubber-bands.

Put jar in a carboard box lined with cloth or flannel. Leave for 3 days to ferment.

Scoop out Tapeh after this time and refrigerate.

Serve cold sprinkled with sugar. This makes a refreshing dessert on a hot day.

Note: Tapeh may be served wrapped in banana leaf.

Pandan Kuih Sarlat

Preparation: 30 minutes
Cooking: 2 hours

600 g (1⅓ lb) glutinous rice
1 teaspoon salt
4 screwpine leaves
1¼ coconuts, grated
400 ml (14 fl oz) water
¼ teaspoon salt

Pandan Custard Topping
450 g (1 lb) granulated sugar
12 eggs
2½ coconuts, grated
500 ml (18 fl oz) water
½ teaspoon salt
3 tablespoons tapioca flour
2 tablespoons plain flour
12 screwpine leaves
2 teaspoons green colouring
3 teaspoons vanilla essence

Soak glutinous rice with 1 teaspoon salt overnight in water 5 cm (2 in) above rice.

Cut each screwpine leaf into 4 pieces.

Mix coconut with 175 ml (6 fl oz) water. Squeeze and strain to obtain thick coconut milk. Add ¼ teaspoon salt to thick coconut milk and refrigerate till ready to use. Add 250 ml (8 fl oz) water to coconut residue. Squeeze and strain to obtain thin coconut milk.

Wash and drain glutinous rice. Remove brown husks. Put rice with thin coconut milk in a 25 cm (10 in) round cake tin. Steam for 15 minutes.

When rice is almost cooked, stir in thick coconut milk. Steam till rice grains are tender. Sprinkle on more water if rice is dry but not cooked.

Press rice down firmly with a wooden spoon. Steam for a few more minutes.

Pour custard topping over rice and steam for 1 hour over high heat. Lift cover a few times during steaming to wipe away water collected on under surface of cover. Drops of water on custard topping cause spotty discolouration.

When custard sets, insert a knife through the centre. If it comes out clean, custard is cooked.

Cool tray in a basin of cold water. Refrigerate for an hour or so to firm topping before cutting into 5 × 2½ cm (2 × 1 in) pieces.

Pandan Custard Topping

Beat sugar with eggs till frothy or blend just 5 minutes at low speed.

Mix grated coconut with water. Squeeze and strain to obtain coconut milk. Add salt.

Mix both kinds of flour with 175 ml (6 fl oz) coconut milk. Set aside.

Shred and pound screwpine leaves. Squeeze and strain for juice. Add remaining coconut milk to screwpine juice. (Alternatively, blend pieces of screwpine leaves with coconut milk in a blender then strain.)

Add green colouring and vanilla essence to coconut milk.

Cook egg and sugar mixture over low heat in a non-stick saucepan or a double boiler, stirring constantly till sugar dissolves.

Remove from heat, add both coconut milk mixtures and stir till mixture thickens. Strain to remove lumps of flour.

Kacang Hijau with Coconut Milk

Preparation: 10 minutes
Cooking: 1 hour

600 g (1⅓ lb) palm sugar
140 g (5 oz) grated white coconut
350 ml (12 fl oz) water
600 g (1⅓ lb) green mung beans *or* green bean flour
10 tablespoons granulated sugar
2.75 L (5 pints) water
2 screwpine leaves
¼ teaspoon salt

Cut palm sugar into small pieces.

Add 120 ml (4 fl oz) water to grated coconut. Squeeze and strain to obtain thick coconut milk. Add 250 ml (8 fl oz) water to residue. Squeeze and strain for thin coconut milk.

Put beans, sugar and water in a pot and boil for 20 minutes over moderate heat. Add screwpine leaves and palm sugar. Continue boiling for another 20 minutes before adding thin coconut milk.

Simmer over low heat, stirring now and then, for about 15 minutes or till beans are soft and liquid reduced to half the original amount.

Add thick coconut milk and salt. As soon as mixture bubbles, turn off heat.

Serve either hot or cold for tea.

Agar-Agar with Santan Topping

Preparation: 15 minutes
Cooking: 20 minutes

1 packet (30 g/1 oz) agar powder
120 ml (4 fl oz) cold water
1.25 L (2¼ pints) boiling water
280 g (10 oz) sugar
2 screwpine leaves, knotted together
140 g (5 oz) grated coconut
120 ml (4 fl oz) water
½ teaspoon green colouring

Dissolve agar powder in cold water. Pour dissolved agar into hot water. Add sugar and screwpine leaves. Boil for 15-20 minutes, stirring every now and then. There should be about 5 cups liquid left after that time.

While agar is boiling, mix coconut with 120 ml (4 fl oz) water. Squeeze and strain to obtain 175 ml (6 fl oz) thick coconut milk.

Divide agar liquid in the ratio 3:2. Add green colouring to 750 ml (1¼ pints) liquid and pour into a mould.

Boil remaining 420 ml (¾ pint) agar liquid till reduced to 250 ml (8 fl oz). Add coconut milk. Bring to a boil and remove from heat at once.

Test plain green agar by shaking mould. It should be just about to set but still shaky. Gently pour ladlefuls of coconut milk mixture over green agar, taking care not to break through surface.

Leave to set. When cooled to room temperature, refrigerate.

Note: If green agar sets before coconut milk topping is ready, scratch the surface with a fork before pouring on coconut milk topping.

Dorothy's Popular Coconut Candy

Preparation: 10 minutes
Cooking: 1 hour

5 white coconuts, grated
900 g (2 lb) sugar
350 ml (12 fl oz) evaporated milk
250 ml (8 fl oz) condensed milk
1½ tablespoons butter
½ teaspoon salt
2 teaspoons vanilla essence
1 egg white, beaten

Mix grated white coconut with sugar, evaporated milk, condensed milk, butter and salt.

Put mixture in a brass pan or a non-stick pan and stir constantly over low heat till candy mixture bubbles.

Add vanilla essence and continue stirring till quite dry. Briskly stir in beaten egg white.

Pour candy onto greased cookie trays. Pack or press candy tightly with the back of a spoon.

When about to set and still warm, mark surface of candy into diamond shapes of desired size with a buttered knife. Let candy harden slightly then deepen grooves to separate pieces.

Remove candy carefully piece by piece. When dry and hard, pack in bottles.

Note: Vary the flavour and colour of your candy:
(a) For Strawberry Candy, add pink cochineal and strawberry essence.
(b) For Rose Pink Candy, add pink cochineal and rose essence.
(c) For Cocoa Candy, blend 5 teaspoons cocoa with 3 tablespoons hot water, stir till smooth, mix in 1 tablespoon extra condensed milk and add to candy mixture while cooking.
(d) For Green Pandan Candy, pound and strain 10 shredded screwpine leaves and add a few drops of green colouring.

Kuih Wajek (Glutinous Rice Pudding)

Preparation: 15 minutes
Cooking: 1 1/3 hours

600 g (1 1/3 lb) glutinous rice
2 1/2 coconuts, grated
600 ml (1 pint) water
900 g (2 lb) palm sugar
3 screwpine leaves, cut into 5 × 2 1/2 cm (2 × 1 in)
   strips
340 g (12 oz) granulated sugar
pinch of salt
4 screwpine leaves, knotted in pairs

Soak glutinous rice in water overnight.

Mix grated coconut and water. Squeeze and strain to obtain coconut milk.

Scrape palm sugar into fragments with a knife.

Line a steaming rack with a cloth. Place strips of screwpine leaves on the cloth. Spread glutinous rice on cloth and steam for 45 minutes till cooked.

Mix steamed rice with coconut milk, palm sugar, granulated sugar and knotted screwpine leaves in a bowl.

Cook over low heat, stirring constantly, till mixture becomes rich, oily and brown.

Spread Wajek evenly on a tray and let it cool to harden slightly, then cut into 5 cm (2 in) squares and serve.

Homemade Soybean Milk

Preparation: 15 minutes
Cooking: 1 hour

150 g (5 oz) soy beans
8 L (14 pints) water
450 g (1 lb) castor sugar
225 g (8 oz) rock sugar

Soak soy beans overnight in 3.50 L (6 pints) water

Blend soy beans for about 15 minutes in an electric blender. Pour into a pot with remaining 4.5 L (8 pints) water. Bring to a boil, stirring constantly.

Remove from heat and strain to obtain clear soybean milk. Add sugar and boil for about 45 minutes over moderate heat. Stir frequently.

Strain once again when cool for smooth soybean milk. Serve hot or cold with crushed ice.

Soybean Almond Jelly

Preparation: 10 minutes
Cooking: 20 minutes

1 packet (15 g/1/2 oz) or 5 teaspoons agar powder
1.6 L (2 3/4 pints) soybean milk (recipe above)
110 g (4 oz) granulated sugar
4 tablespoons evaporated milk
1/2-1 teaspoon almond essence
1 tin (587 g/1 1/3 lb) loquats in syrup
1 tin (587 g/1 1/3 lb) longans or lychees in syrup
3 red cherries
3 green cherries

Blend agar powder with a little water to a paste, then add soybean milk and sugar. Boil over moderate heat, stirring constantly, for 20 minutes till liquid is reduced to 1.5 L (2 1/2 pints). If less, add hot water to make up required quantity.

Pour in milk and almond essence. Stir well then sieve or strain into a wet mould. Refrigerate till set.

Serve cold with loquats, longans or lychees, cherries, and a little syrup. Add crushed ice.

Mah Tai Koh (Steamed Water Chestnuts)

Preparation: 15 minutes
Cooking: 1 hour

450 g (1 lb) water chestnuts
750 ml (1¼ pints) water
6 tablespoons rough granulated sugar
225 g (8 oz) water chestnut flour
400 ml (14 fl oz) water
pinch of salt
3 tablespoons tapioca flour
oil for deep-frying

Soak chestnuts in water for a few hours. Skin and chop coarsely. Boil in 750 ml (1¼ pints) water for about 8 minutes to soften and cook chestnuts. Add sugar during this time.

Blend flour with 400 ml (14 fl oz) cups water in a non-stick pot. Stir constantly over low heat till mixture becomes clear and smooth. Add cooked water chestnuts.

Transfer contents of pot to a cake tray and steam for about 20 minutes till set. Cool to room temperature then refrigerate. When cold, cut into 5 × 2½ cm (2 × 1 in) rectangular pieces and serve.

If serving hot, sprinkle pieces with tapioca flour and deep-fry for a minute or so to brown.

White Fungus with Loquats

Preparation: 7 minutes
Cooking: 30 minutes

45 g (1½ oz) white fungus
2.5 L (4½ pints) boiling hot water
450 g (1 lb) rock sugar, crushed
150 g (5 oz) granulated sugar
1 can (567 g/1¼ lb) loquats

Soak white fungus in 750 ml (1¼ pints) hot water. When swollen, pluck out black stems and roots. Drain.

Boil white fungus in remaining hot water till quite soft. Add rock sugar and granulated sugar. Simmer over low heat for 10 minutes.

Serve cold with loquats and crushed ice after a heavy meal.

Durian Ice-cream

Preparation: 20 minutes
Cooking: 6 minutes
Freezing: 3-4 hours

2½ coconuts, grated
225 g (8 oz) granulated sugar
2 teaspoons vanilla essence *or* 1 teaspoon durian essence
1 tin (450 g/1 lb) durian jam
225 g (8 oz) durian pulp, mashed
4 tablespoons mung bean flour

Squeeze and strain grated coconut to extract 900 ml (1½ pints) thick coconut milk. If necessary, add a little water to residue and extract enough coconut milk to make up the required amount.

Add sugar and vanilla or durian essence to coconut milk.

Take out a little coconut milk. Blend with durian jam, durian pulp and flour. Stir into remaining coconut milk.

Cook over moderate heat, stirring constantly, till mixture thickens.

Freeze mixture, then whip in an electric blender to a smooth texture. Refreeze.

Lychee Ice-cream

Preparation: 15 minutes
Cooking: 10 minutes
Freezing: 3-4 hours

2 tins (567 g/1¼ lb) lychees
1 coconut, grated
250 ml (8 fl oz) water
4 tablespoons cornflour
6 tablespoons water
45 g (1½ oz) gelatin
5 tablespoons water
4 tablespoons condensed milk
8 tablespoons evaporated milk
¼ teaspoon salt
10 tablespoons sugar
1 teaspoon ice-cream soda essence

Drain lychees and chop. Set aside chopped lychees and syrup separately.

Blend coconut and water. Squeeze and strain to obtain coconut milk.

Blend cornflour with 6 tablespoons water. Stir into coconut milk.

Dissolve gelatin in cold water, sprinkling in a little at a time. Add to coconut milk mixture with condensed milk, evaporated milk, lychee syrup, salt and sugar. Stir thoroughly.

Cook over moderate heat, stirring constantly with a wooden spoon till thick. Add chopped lychees and essence.

Freeze mixture. When frozen, whip in an electric blender till smooth and refreeze.

Serve with whole lychees if desired.

Homemade Chocolate Ice-cream

Preparation: 30 minutes
Cooking: 10 minutes
Freezing: 3-4 hours

2 tablespoons gelatin
4 tablespoons water
3 tablespoons cocoa
5 tablespoons boiling hot water
140 g (5 oz) cornflour
2 tablespoons mung bean flour *or* green bean flour
175 ml (6 fl oz) water
2 tablespoons condensed milk
1 teaspoon chocolate essence
7 egg yolks
3 egg whites
450 g (1 lb) sugar
1 tin (180 g/6 oz) cream
7 cups evaporated milk

Dissolve gelatin in 4 tablespoons water and melt cocoa in boiling hot water.

Blend cornflour and mung bean flour or green bean flour with 175 ml (6 fl oz) water to a smooth paste. Pour cocoa and gelatin into this paste. Add condensed milk and chocolate essence. Stir well.

Beat eggs and sugar together till creamy. Add cream and continue beating for a few minutes.

Pour in evaporated milk and flour mixture. Mix and cook in a non-stick pot till mixture thickens. Stir constantly.

Cool by surrounding pot with cold water for 45 minutes.

Pour mixture into a tub and freeze, then whip in an electric blender to a smooth texture. Refreeze.

Creamy Corn Coconut Milk Ice-cream

Preparation: 10 minutes
Cooking: 6 minutes
Freezing: 3-4 hours

2½ coconuts, grated
30 g (1 oz) mung bean flour *or* green bean flour
4 tablespoons condensed milk
3 tablespoons Maizena powder *or* cornflour
1 tin (480 g/17 oz) cream corn
340 g (12 oz) sugar
1 tablespoon ice-cream soda essence

Squeeze and strain grated coconut to extract 900 ml (1½ pints) coconut milk. If necessary, add water to residue and extract enough coconut milk to make up the required amount.

Blend mung bean flour, condensed milk and Maizena powder with a little of the coconut milk. Stir into remaining coconut milk.

Mix in cream corn, sugar and ice-cream soda essence.

Cook mixture over moderate heat, stirring constantly till it thickens.

Freeze mixture, then whip in an electric blender till smooth. Refreeze.

Singapore Island Coconut Cake

Preparation: 30 minutes
Baking: 45 minutes
Oven setting: 175°C, 350°F, Gas Regulo 6

225 g (8 oz) butter or margarine
340 g (12 oz) granulated sugar
7 eggs
450 g (1 lb) self-raising flour
1 teaspoon baking powder
8 tablespoons fresh milk
1 cup white grated coconut

Lemon Icing
2 egg whites
juice of 2 lemons
450 g (1 lb) icing sugar, sifted
3 drops yellow colouring
½ teaspoon cream of tartar

Coloured Coconut
1 white coconut, grated
3 drops pink cochineal
3 drops green colouring

Cream butter and sugar till light. Add eggs one at a time and continue beating at moderate speed till batter has a smooth, creamy texture.

Sift flour and baking powder together. Fold flour into batter, alternating with milk.

Add coconut and stir for 1 minute.

Pour into a greased 15 cm (6 in) square cake tin. Bake in a moderate oven for 45 minutes. Test with a thin skewer or a satay stick.

Cool on a wire rack, spread with lemon icing and scatter coloured grated coconut over icing.

Lemon Icing
Beat egg whites with lemon juice till frothy. Add sugar a little at a time and beat till icing is stiff, then add colouring and cream of tartar.

Continue beating till icing stands in stiff peaks.

Coloured Coconut
Divide white grated coconut into 3 equal portions. Leave one portion white. Colour another portion pink with cochineal and the third portion green.

Spekkoek (Indonesian Rich Layered Cake)

Preparation: 20 minutes
Baking: 45 minutes
Oven setting: 175°C, 350°F, Gas Regulo 6

500 g (1 lb 2 oz) butter
340 g (12 oz) castor sugar
19 egg yolks
6 egg whites
180 g (6 oz) plain flour, sifted twice
1 teaspoon vanilla essence

Mixed Spices
1½ teaspoons ground nutmeg
12 cloves, ground
2 teaspoons ground cinnamon
1 segment star anise, ground
3 cardamoms (discard husk and use only seeds),
    ground

Grease a 22 × 17½ cm (9 × 7 in) cake tin and line bottom with greaseproof paper. Set oven at required temperature. Note that only an oven with 2 elements, a bottom heating element and a grill element, can be used.

Cream butter with 120 g (4 oz) sugar for 7 minutes till creamy. Beat egg yolks with the same amount of sugar and beat egg whites with remaining sugar till stiff.

Mix beaten egg yolks with butter cream. Fold in flour, mixed spices and vanilla essence and lastly egg whites. Mix well.

Spoon 4 tablespoons batter into the prepared tin, spread with the back of the spoon. Bake for 5 minutes or until cooked. Brush each layer with melted butter.

Spread 4 tablespoons batter over first layer in the same manner. Bake for 3 minutes, then press lightly all over with the flat bottom of a heavy glass tumbler. Remove air bubbles by pricking with a toothpick. Continue in this manner till batter is used up.

Cool cake on a wire rack then cut into thin square slices with a sharp knife. Spekkoek keeps well in an airtight container for up to a week.

Tropical Durian Cake

Preparation: 15 minutes
Baking: 1 hour
Oven setting: 200°C, 400°F, Gas Regulo 8

570 g (1¼ lb) self-raising flour
225 g (8 oz) plain flour
2 teaspoons baking powder
½ teaspoon salt
675 g (1½ lb) butter
560 g (1¼ lb) granulated sugar
12 eggs
1 teaspoon vanilla essence
2 teaspoons cream of tartar
280 g (10 oz) durian pulp, mashed

Grease two 17½ cm (7 in) round cake tins and line with greaseproof paper.

Sift together self-raising flour, plain flour, baking powder and salt.

Beat butter and 450 g (1 lb) sugar at moderate speed till creamy.

Separate egg yolks from egg whites. Add egg yolks and vanilla essence to creamed butter and sugar. Continue beating till smooth.

In another bowl, beat egg whites with remaining 225 g (8 oz) sugar till white. Add cream of tartar and beat at high speed till stiff.

Fold egg white mixture into creamy batter. Fold in sifted dry ingredients a little at a time.

Spoon in mashed durian pulp leaving 4 tablespoons behind. Stir to distribute evenly.

Pour batter into prepared cake tin. Spread the remaining 4 tablespoons durian pulp on top, burying slightly to prevent burning.

Bake at 200°C (400°F, gas regulo 8) for 40 minutes, then turn to 175°C (350°F, gas regulo 6).

If cake browns on top before it is ready, cover with a round piece of greaseproof paper or foil with a hole cut out in the middle.

Continue baking till centre of cake is cooked. Test with a skewer.

Cool on a wire rack before cutting.

Rich Banana Cake

Preparation: 20 minutes
Baking: 45 minutes
Oven setting: 190°C, 375°F, Gas Regulo 7

250 g (8½ oz) butter
225 g (8 oz) sugar
5 eggs
3 tablespoons evaporated milk
3 teaspoons vanilla essence
2 teaspoons lemon juice
6 green bananas (*pisang hijau*), mashed
340 g (12 oz) self-raising flour
1 teaspoon bicarbonate of soda

Grease two 20 cm (8 in) round cake tins with 1 teaspoon butter. Line tins with greaseproof paper.

Beat butter and sugar till creamy white. Add eggs one at a time and beat till fluffy.

Add milk, vanilla essence, lemon juice and mashed bananas. Beat continuously for 2 minutes. Fold in flour and 1 teaspoon of bicarbonate of soda.

Bake in a moderately hot oven – 190°C (375°F, gas regulo 7) for 45 minutes. Test by running a thin skewer or satay stick in centre of cake. If it comes out clean, cake is done.

Pineapple Tarts

Preparation: 45 minutes
Cooking: 18 minutes
Baking: 15 minutes
Oven setting: 175°C, 350°F, Gas Regulo 6
Makes: 35

200 g (6⅔ oz) butter
330 g (11 oz) plain flour
1 egg yolk, beaten
½ egg white, beaten
1 teaspoon lemon juice
pinch of salt
2 egg yolks, beaten
1 teaspoon melted butter
1 tablespoon fresh milk
2 tablespoons extra butter

Pineapple Jam
2 Mauritius pineapples, grated
370 g (13 oz) sugar
juice of ½ lemon
6 cloves
4 segments star anise
¼ teaspoon ground nutmeg

Rub butter into flour till it resembles breadcrumbs. Add beaten egg yolk, then egg white. Knead for 2 minutes. Knead in lemon juice and salt.

Roll dough to 2 cm (¾ in) thickness. Use tart cutters to cut into small round shapes with a slightly depressed centre.

Pinch edge of each pastry round with tart pincers. Fill each centre with 1 teaspoon pineapple jam. If desired, brush with a mixture of beaten egg yolks, melted butter and fresh milk.

Place tarts on cookie trays greased with extra butter and bake for 15 minutes in a preheated oven till light golden. Cool before storing in airtight containers.

Pineapple Jam
Leave grated pineapple in a sieve to drain. Retain 1 cup pineapple juice.

Put all ingredients for jam in a heavy aluminium pot and cook for 15-18 minutes over high heat, stirring all the while with a wooden spoon.

Cool before using. If not using immediately, refrigerate.

Kuih Bangket

Preparation: 1 hour
Cooking: 20 minutes
Baking: 20 minutes
Oven setting: 200°C, 400°F, Gas Regulo 8

1¾ kg (3⅘ lb) sago flour or tapioca flour
2½ coconuts, grated
350 ml (12 fl oz) water
1 teaspoon salt
400 g (14 oz) granulated sugar
2 screwpine leaves
5 egg yolks
3 egg whites
2 teaspoons vanilla essence
1 tablespoon extra flour
120 g (4 oz) sesame seeds
2 egg whites, beaten

Fry sago or tapioca flour in 2 batches in a dry non-stick pan over low heat for 8-10 minutes. Leave aside to cool.

Mix coconut and water. Squeeze and strain to obtain coconut milk. Add salt.

Put coconut milk, sugar and screwpine leaves knotted together in a pan. Cook over moderate heat, stirring constantly till sugar dissolves. Set aside for 15 minutes to cool a little. Remove 5 tablespoons and keep aside to soften dough when it gets too dry.

Beat egg yolks and egg whites together at moderate speed for 8 minutes or till creamy white. Pour in coconut milk mixture. Continue beating at low speed for 5 minutes, then stir in vanilla essence.

Fold in flour a little at a time and knead with hands on a smooth working surface sprinkled with about 2 tablespoons flour. Knead for at least 5 minutes. If dough is still sticky, add a little more flour till a smooth pliable dough is formed.

Roll out dough to ½ cm (¼ in) thickness. Sprinkle sesame seeds over pastry. Use special Kuih Bangket biscuit cutters to cut dough in a variety of patterns.

Bake on 4 trays sprinkled with tapioca flour for 20 minutes till cookies are pale brown.

Cool on wire racks and pack into airtight containers. Separate layers of cookies with brown paper cut to fit containers.

These cookies will keep crisp for at least 1 month.

Kuih Keria

Preparation: 15 minutes
Cooking: 20 minutes

450 g (1 lb) tapioca
150 g (5 oz) white grated coconut
4 tablespoons cooked glutinous rice, mashed
½ teaspoon salt
oil for deep-frying
340 g (12 oz) granulated sugar
5 tablespoons water

Peel tapioca and halve lengthwise. Remove hard core and grate finely.

Mix grated tapioca, grated coconut, glutinous rice and salt in a big bowl.

Mould into 4 cm (1½ in) balls, flatten and poke a hole in the centre with the index finger.

Heat oil in a wok. Slide in doughnuts and fry over high heat for about 8 minutes till golden brown. Leave on absorbent paper.

Remove oil from wok. Use the same wok to boil sugar and water till syrup is thick.

Turn heat down to very low and put in doughnuts. Remove wok from heat. Continue to turn doughnuts till sugar dries up to form white sugary coating.

Cool Kuih Keria slightly on a rack and serve warm.

Goreng Pisang (Fried Banana Fritters)

Preparation: 10 minutes
Cooking: 10 minutes

9 tablespoons self-raising flour
11 tablespoons rice flour
1 tablespoon tapioca flour
250 ml (8 fl oz) water
1 rounded teaspoon lime paste
4 tablespoons water
1½ teaspoons sugar
14 bananas (*pisang rajah*)
oil for deep-frying

Sift 3 kinds of flour into a large bowl. Make a well in the centre and pour 1 cup water into well gradually, blending with flour as you pour. Batter should be thick enough to coat bananas. If too thin, add a little more rice flour.

Dissolve lime paste in 4 tablespoons water. Add sugar and lime paste to flour and mix well.

Peel bananas.

Heat oil in a wok till smoking hot. Coat each whole banana with batter and slide into oil. Fry in batches of 6 bananas for 5 minutes till golden brown. Adjust heat if they brown too quickly.

Drain in a sieve.

Wu Tau Koh (Savoury Yam Cake)

Preparation: 30 minutes
Cooking: 1½ hours

9 tablespoons oil
20 shallots, sliced
90 g (3 oz) dried prawns, soaked and pounded
   coarsely
225 g (8 oz) minced pork
6 tablespoons light soy sauce
4 teaspoons sugar
1½ teaspoons pepper
½ teaspoon salt
200 g (6⅔ oz) Char Siew (p.37), diced (Red Pork
   Roast)
4 Chinese sausages, diced
225 g (8 oz) rice flour
85 g (3 oz) tapioca flour
60 g (2 oz) plain flour
1 L (1¾ pints) water
2 teaspoons salt
1 kg (2¼ lb) yam
150 g (5 oz) roasted ground peanuts
2 stalks spring onion, chopped
2 sprigs Chinese parsley, cut into ½ cm (¼ in)
   lengths

Heat 4 tablespoons oil in a wok and fry shallots till crisp. Remove half the oil and half the shallots to a dish and set aside for garnishing.

Add remaining 5 tablespoons oil to contents of wok. Fry dried prawns till crisp, then add minced pork and seasoning ingredients (light soy sauce, sugar, pepper and ½ teaspoon salt).

Add Char Siew and Chinese sausages. After stir-frying for 5 minutes, dish out ingredients.

Blend rice flour, tapioca flour, plain flour, water and 2 teaspoons salt till smooth. Add three-quarters of cooked meat to flour mixture, leaving the rest for use as a garnish.

Peel yam and cut into 5 cm (2 in) cubes. Steam in a 25 cm (10 in) shallow round cake tray. After 10 minutes, pour in flour and cooked meat mixture. Steam till set.

Leave aside to cool. If necessary, expedite cooling by placing cake tray in a shallow basin of cold water.

When cool, cut into diamond or oblong shapes, garnish with crispy shallots, remaining cooked meat, roasted ground peanuts, spring onion and Chinese parsley.

Serve with Vinegar Chilli Sauce (p.141) and coffee or Chinese tea after a meal, for breakfast or tea.

Hokkien Bak Chang

Preparation: 1 hour
Marinating: 30 minutes
Cooking: 4 hours

1 kg (2¼ lb) glutinous rice
30 dried chestnuts
750 ml (1¼ pints) water
10-12 dried Chinese mushrooms
1 kg (2¼ lb) pork (front trotter meat)
14 tablespoons oil
7 cloves garlic, chopped
20 shallots, sliced
50 bamboo or *chang* leaves
string

Seasoning for Meat
2 tablespoons light soy sauce
3 tablespoons black soy auce
1½ tablespoons sugar
¾ teaspoon five-spice powder
¾ teaspoon salt
¾ teaspoon pepper

Seasoning for Rice
3 teaspoons light soy sauce
2 tablespoons black soy sauce
2 teaspoons sugar
½ teaspoon salt
½ teaspoon pepper

Soak glutinous rice for 3-4 hours in sufficient water to cover. Drain.

Boil dried chestnuts in 750 ml (1¼ pints) water for 30 minutes till soft. Remove traces of skin and chop coarsely.

Soak mushrooms overnight. Squeeze dry and dice.

Dice meat and mix with seasoning ingredients for meat. Leave to marinate for 30 minutes.

Heat 6 tablespoons oil in a wok and fry three-quarters of the chopped garlic. When soft, add shallots.

After stir-frying for 10 minutes over moderate heat, add chestnuts and meat. Fry for 5 more minutes or till meat is cooked. Remove to a dish.

Heat remaining oil in a clean wok and fry remaining chopped garlic till crisp. Add rice and seasoning ingredients for rice. Stir-fry over moderate heat for 10 minutes.

Soak bamboo leaves in cold water for 30 minutes. Wipe dry.

Shape two leaves like a cone, put in some rice, pressing some along the sides. Add a few teaspoons cooked meat and chestnuts in the centre and cover with more rice.

Wrap and bind with string.

Cook in a large pot of boiling water for 2½-3 hours. Hang up in bunches to drip dry.

Muruku Twist

Preparation: 10 minutes
Cooking: 15 minutes for each batch

340 g (12 oz) flour
1 rounded teaspoon ground chilli
4 teaspoons sesame seeds (optional)
1 teaspoon cummin
½ coconut, grated
water
1 dessertspoon salt
1 egg, beaten
oil for deep-frying

Toast rice flour lightly in a dry pan over low heat, stirring constantly.

Mix rice flour, chilli and sesame seeds, if used, in a large bowl. Crush cummin into bowl by rubbing between palms of hands.

Add enough water to coconut to extract 900 ml (1½ pints) coconut milk. Bring to a boil with salt.

Boil for 2 minutes. Turn heat down and bring to a boil again and boil for another 2 minutes. Do this 3 times.

Pour boiling hot coconut milk over dry ingredients. Mix with a wooden spatula till a soft ball of dough is formed.

Mix in beaten egg. When dough is cool enough to handle, knead well.

Put dough into a muruku mould (sold in Indian cutlery shops). Press out strips of dough into hot oil. Deep-fry till golden brown. Use a slotted spoon to transfer Muruku to absorbent paper on a wire rack.

When cooled to room temperature, store in airtight tins.

Nonya Roti Babi

Preparation: 15 minutes
Cooking: 10 minutes

2 big onions
700 g (1½ lb) small prawns, shelled
450 g (1 lb) minced pork
3 eggs
3 teaspoons tapioca flour
14 slices bread
90 g (3 oz) green peas
oil for deep-frying
2 teaspoons mustard
120 ml (4 fl oz) tomato ketchup
1 tablespoon Worcestershire sauce
2 tablespoons sugar

Seasoning
2 teaspoons pepper
1 teaspoon sugar
½ teaspoon salt
3 teaspoons light soy sauce

Dice onions. Chop 300 g (10 oz) prawns with minced pork. Add diced onion and mince till fine.

Beat eggs and add to minced meat, prawns and onion. Add seasoning ingredients and flour.

Cut each slice of bread into 2 triangles or 2 rectangles. Spread about 2 rounded tablespoons of minced mixture on each piece of bread. Top with a few prawns and green peas. Press down firmly.

Deep-fry 8 pieces at a time in a wok for 2-3 minutes till golden brown. Remove to grease-proof paper or a draining rack.

Serve with a sauce made by combining mustard, tomato ketchup, Worcestershire sauce and sugar.

Sharksfin Dumplings

Preparation: 30 minutes
Cooking: 40 minutes

150 g (5 oz) prepared sharksfin
8 thin slices ginger
2 teaspoons brandy
water
370 g (13 oz) prawns, shelled and minced
1 teaspoon salt
120 g (4 oz) minced pork
120 g (4 oz) minced belly pork
1½ teaspoons sugar
30 g (1 oz) carrot, shredded
90 g (3 oz) precooked bamboo shoot, shredded
3 dried Chinese mushrooms, soaked and shredded
2 sprigs coriander leaves, chopped
2 egg whites, beaten
½ teaspoon pepper
2 teaspoons tapioca flour or cornflour
1½ teaspoons sesame oil
3 teaspoons cooking oil
30 wonton skins
1 egg yolk, beaten

Mix sharksfin with ginger, brandy and sufficient water to cover. Steam over high heat for 30 minutes. Discard ginger.

Put minced prawns and salt in a basin. Knead well by pressing prawn mixture against the side of the basin. Scoop up minced prawns and throw back into basin with some force a few times.

Add minced pork, minced belly pork and sugar. Repeat kneading procedure.

Add carrot, bamboo shoot, mushrooms, coriander leaves, egg white, sharksfin, pepper, tapioca flour or cornflour, sesame oil and cooking oil. Mix thoroughly with fingers.

Cut square *wonton* skins into circles by trimming off corners. Put 1 tablespoon sharksfin filling on each skin and fold in half. Seal with a little beaten egg yolk or pleat outer edge of skin to seal.

Oil steamer and steam dumplings over high heat for 7 minutes.

Serve with chilli sauce.

Epok-Epok (Malay Prawn Curry Puff)

Preparation: 1½ hours
Cooking: 45 minutes

Pastry
400 g (14 oz) plain flour
⅓ teaspoon salt
120 g (4 oz) margarine
60 g (2 oz) Danish lard
2 egg yolks
1 egg white
7½ tablespoons cold water
3 egg yolks
2 tablespoons milk
1 tablespoon butter
2 drops yellow colouring
oil for deep-frying

Filling
½ coconut, grated
4 tablespoons water
600 g (1⅓ lb) small prawns
120 g (4 oz) dried prawns
3 big onions
450 g (1 lb) sweet potatoes
6 tablespoons oil
300 g (10 oz) beansprouts
1 teaspoon salt
2 teaspoons sugar
2 tablespoons light soy sauce
¾ teaspoon pepper

Rempah
20 dried chillies *or* 2 teaspoons ground chilli
10 bird chillies
9 candlenuts *or* blanched almonds
3 red chillies
2¼ teaspoons ground coriander
1 teaspoon ground turmeric
2 teaspoons dried shrimp paste
3 cloves garlic
16 shallots
5 slices galingale *or* green root ginger
1 stalk lemon grass

Pastry and Assembly
Sift flour and salt into a bowl or onto a smooth working surface. Cut margarine and Danish lard into 2½ cm (1 in) cubes and rub into flour with fingertips till mixture resembles breadcrumbs.

Beat egg yolks and egg whites together.

Add cold water gradually to flour and knead. Add beaten eggs and continue kneading. If dough is sticky, add a little flour. Knead dough till it is pliable.

Roll dough into a long cylinder of 5 cm (2 in) diameter. Cut into 2 cm (¾ in) slices. Roll flat.

Place 2 rounded teaspoons filling in the centre of each circle of pastry. Wet edge, then fold pastry in half. Seal and decorate edge by pinching and folding in to form a rope pattern.

Beat 3 egg yolks, milk, butter and colouring together. Brush pastry with this glaze.

Deep-fry in hot oil for 5 minutes.

Filling
Mix half the grated coconut with 4 tablespoons water. Squeeze and strain to obtain ¼ cup thick coconut milk. Fry remaining grated coconut in a dry non-stick pan till golden brown. Set aside.

Peel prawns. Pound dried prawns. Dice onions. Cut sweet potatoes into 1 cm (½ in) cubes. Steam sweet potato cubes for 15 minutes.

Heat oil in a wok and fry *rempah* over moderate heat for 2 minutes till fragrant. Add dried prawns and stir-fry till crisp.

Put in fresh prawns and coconut milk. Cook for 2 minutes. When dry, add diced onions, beansprouts and seasoning (salt, sugar, light soy sauce and pepper).

Stir-fry for just a few seconds, leaving beansprouts half-cooked. Add steamed sweet potatoes. Mix with other ingredients. Stir in fried grated coconut, then set aside to cool.

Penang Shell-shaped Curry Puff

Preparation: 45 minutes
Cooking: 16 minutes

Outer Skin
450 g (1 lb) plain flour
17 tablespoons cold water
½ teaspoon salt
2 eggs, beaten

Inner Skin
300 g (10 oz) plain flour
10½ tablespoons lard oil
⅓ teaspoon salt

Filling
450 g (1 lb) Keema (p.81)
oil for deep frying

Outer Skin
Make a well in the centre of flour and add water and salt. Mix, then knead, pushing dough towards centre of bowl. Add beaten eggs and continue kneading dough till smooth. Pinch into 7½ cm (3 in) balls.

Inner Skin
Knead flour with oil and salt. Pinch into 6 cm (2½ in) balls.

Wrap inner skin with outer skin. Roll into ½ cm (¼ in) thick, 4 cm (½ in) wide rectangle. Roll away from you like a Swiss roll.

Cut "Swiss roll" into ½ cm (¼ in) thick slices and roll each piece out gently into a round, taking care not to smooth away concentric lines.

Put about 1 teaspoonful of filling in the centre of each round. Fold into half. Pinch and pleat open edge together, starting with one edge and working towards the other.

Heat oil for deep-frying and fry curry puffs about 8-10 each time for a few minutes till golden brown. Serve immediately.

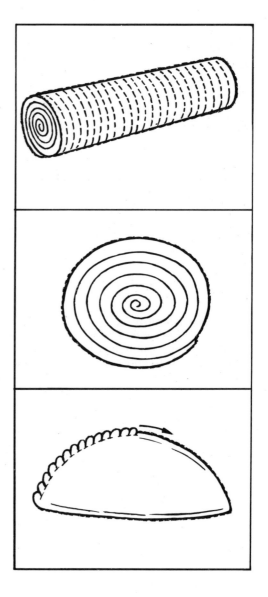

Preparing a Crab for Cooking

◀1 Use an ice-pick to kill crab. Note the narrow triangular tail which indicates crab is male. A female crab has a rounded tail ("skirt") which ends in a point. Lift tail from centre and break off.

2 Chop down the centre. Leave crab for 5 minutes to make sure it is dead. Test by putting an object (knife, scissors, etc.) between pincers. If alive, pincers will grip object.
▼

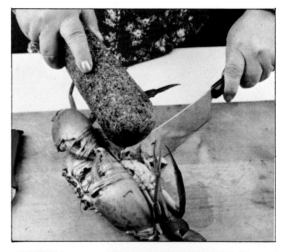

3 Cut off legs if not used.
▼

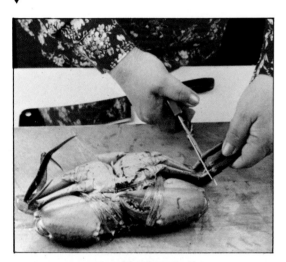

▲
4 Pry shell from body.

▲
5 Dig out spongy appendages. Keep liver. If crab is female, keep roe as well.

▶
6 Chop into two, four or six pieces.

A Selection of Ingredients for Asian Cooking

1 *Yow char kway*	12 Soaked cuttlefish	23 Fried egg noodles (fine)	33 Thick rice vermicelli	44 Sharksfin
2 Dried soybean cakes	13 Dried cuttlefish	24 Black shrimp paste	34 *Wonton* egg noodles	45 Fine rice vermicelli
3 Small dried soybean cakes	14 Fried egg noodles	25 Rice vermicelli	35 Firm soybean cake	46 Dried radish
4 Chinese sausages	15 Century eggs	26 Sesame oil	36 Soft soybean cake	47 Young corn cobs
5 Salt fish	16 Salted duck's eggs	27 Preserved soy beans	37 Flat rice noodles	48 Tamarind
6 Rice malt sauce	17 Thick yellow noodles	(light variety)	38 Soybean skin (*fu chok*)	49 Dried lily flowers
7 Black soy sauce	18 *Wonton* skin	28 Oyster sauce	39 *Teem chok*	50 Black sweet malt
8 Light soy sauce	19 Quail's eggs	29 Dried egg noodles	40 Plum sauce	51 Dried anchovies
9 Mushroom sauce	20 Dried prawns	30 *Tow-see*	41 Agar strips	52 Dried shrimp paste
10 Fish sauce	21 Dried young anchovies	31 *Hoi-sin* sauce	42 Spring roll skin	53 Transparent noodles
11 Chinese rice wine	22 Green pea flour	32 Macaroni	43 Fresh Hokkien mee	54 Dried tamarind skin

Asian Vegetables, Herbs and Fruits

1	Screwpine leaves	17	Tomatoes	32	Cucumber	45	Chinese chives
2	Banana flower	18	Bird chillies	33	Carrot		(with flowers)
3	Pumpkin	19	Yam	34	Cauliflower	46	Young ginger
4	Winter melon	20	Bamboo shoot	35	Mustard green	47	Ginger
5	Long bottle gourd	21	Yam bean		(kai choy, Chinese)	48	Small sour starfruit
6	Pisang mas	22	Lady's fingers	36	Radish	49	Chinese spinach (tong hoe)
7	Pisang rajah	23	Capsicum	37	Red & green chillies	50	Water chestnuts
8	Pisang tandok	24	Bittergourd	38	Sweet potato leaves	51	Cabbage
9	Pisang hijau	25	Vegetable marrow	39	Chinese white cabbage	52	Basil (Daun selaseh)
10	Petai	26	Pineapple	40	Leek	53	Basil (Daun kemangi)
11	Drumsticks	27	Limes (large),	41	Potatoes	54	Mint leaves
12	Lemon grass		limes (small)	42	Bunga kantan	55	Soybean sprouts
13	Tapioca	28	Lemons	43	French beans	56	Beansprouts
14	Onions	29	Angled loofah	44	Chinese mustard greens	57	Spring onion
15	Garlic	30	Green aubergine		(white stalk variety)	58	Galingale
16	Shallots	31	Purple aubergine				

59	Coriander leaves
60	Curry leaves
61	Watercress
62	Celery
63	Lettuce
64	Kiamchye
	(salted kuakchye)
65	Daun kadeok
66	Turmeric leaf
67	Long beans
68	Chinese chives
	(without flowers)
69	Daun kessom
70	Mustard green (kai choy)
71	Mustard green (choy sum)

Cardamom	Coriander	Fennel	Cummin	Cloves	Mustard seeds
Poppy seeds	Black peppercorns	White peppercorns	Fenugreek	Dried chillies	Star anise
Cinnamon	Dried turmeric	Candlenuts	Candlenuts with shell	Sesame seeds	Red kokee seeds
Soy beans	Green mung beans	Red beans	Pearl sago	Black glutinous rice	Lotus seeds
Channa dhal	Moong dhal	Thuvar dhal	Black gram	Gingko nuts	Cashew nuts

Dried chestnuts Nutmeg Indonesian black nuts Dried Chinese mushrooms *Tung chye* Cloud ear fungus

Demerara Red sugar Brown sugar Palm sugar Peanut candy Sugared melon sticks

Dried longans Chinese red dates *Kamchor* Yeast Salt fish *Papadum*

Glossary of Ingredients

English	Malay	Chinese
Agar-agar	Agar-agar	菜燕
Anchovy	Ikan bilis	江魚仔
Angled loofah	Ketola	角瓜
Aubergine (Brinjal)	Terung	茄子
Bamboo shoot	Rebong	筍
Banana flower	Jantung pisang	香蕉花
Banana leaf	Daun pisang	香蕉叶
Basil	Daun selaseh Daun kemangi	羅勒菜
Beansprout	Taugeh	豆芽
Bird chilli	Chilli padi	小辣椒
Bittergourd	Peria	苦瓜
Black glutinous rice	Pulot hitam	黑糯米
Black peppercorn	Lada hitam	黑胡椒
Black shrimp paste	Petis	蝦膏
Black soy sauce	Kicap hitam	黑醬油
Brown sugar	Gula timbang hitam	赤糖
Cabbage	Kobis	包菜
Candlenut	Buah keras	馬加拉
Capsicum	Lada Jepun	大青椒
Cardamom	Buah pelaga	豆蔻
Carrot	Lobak merah	紅蘿蔔
Cashew nut	Biji gajus	腰子豆
Cauliflower	Bunga kobis	包菜花
Celery	Selderi	芹菜
Century egg	Telur hitam	皮蛋
Chestnut	Buah berangan	栗子
Chinese chive	Kucai	韮菜
Chinese mustard greens (white stalk variety)	Sawi putih	白菜
Chinese parsley	Pasli	芫荽菜
Chinese red dates	Korma Cina	中國紅棗
Cinnamon	Kayu manis	肉桂皮
Cloud ear fungus	"Telinga tikus"	木耳
Cloves	Bunga cengkih	丁香

English	Malay	Chinese
Coconut	Kelapa	椰
Coriander	Ketumbar	芫茜仔
Cucumber	Timun	黃瓜
Cummin	Jintan putih	小茴香
Curry leaf	Daun kari "Karupillay"	咖哩葉
"Daun kadeok"	Daun kadeok	加綠葉
Dried chilli	Lada kering	辣椒乾
Dried Chinese mushroom	Cendawan Cina kering	香菇
Dried cuttlefish	Sotong kering	魷魚
Dried lily flowers	"Bunga pisang"	金針
Dried longan	Mata kucing kering	乾龍眼
Dried prawns	Udang kering	蝦米
Dried radish	Caipo	蘿蔔干
Dried shrimp paste	Blacan	馬拉煎
Dried soybean cake	Taukwa kering	油炸豆腐干
Dried tamarind skin	Assam gelugor	亞參皮
Dried young anchovy	Ikan bilis embun kering	銀魚干
Drumstick	Keloh "Murungakai"	印度長瓜
Fennel	Jintan manis	仁丹曼尼
Fenugreek	Halba	茴香花
Fine rice vermicelli	Mee sua	麵綫
Firm soybean cake	Taukwa	豆干
Fish sauce	Kicap ikan	魚露
Five-spice powder	Serbok lima rempah	五香粉
Flat rice noodles	Kway teow	粿條
French bean	Kacang buncis	烏龜豆
Galingale	Lengkuas	藍薑
Garlic	Bawang putih	蒜頭
Gelatin	Jelitin	冷盤燕菜精
Ginger	Halia	薑
Gingko nut	"Pek kway"	白果
Green chilli	Lada hijau	青辣椒
Green mung beans	Kacang hijau	綠豆
Green peas	Kacang pis	荷蘭豆
Hoi sin sauce		和新醬
Indonesian black nuts	Buah keluak	巴克拉

English	Malay	Chinese
Kale	"Kai lan"	芥蘭
"Kamchor"		甘草
"Kiamchye"	Sawi asin	鹹菜
"Kuakchye"		芥菜
Lady's fingers	Bendi	角豆
Leek	Daun bawang Cina	蒜
Lemon	Limau	酸柑
Lemon grass	Serai	葱茅
Lettuce	Salad	香菜
Light soy sauce	Kicap putih	醬清
Lime	Limau nipis	青檸檬
Lime leaf	Daun limau perot	柑葉
Lime paste	Kapur	白灰
Lobster	Udang karang	龍蝦
Local lime	Limau kasturi	酸柑
Long bean	Kacang panjang	菜豆
Long bottle gourd	Labu putih	瓠瓜
Long Chinese cabbage	Kobis Cina	中國長白菜
Lotus seed	Buah teratai	蓮子
Macaroni	Makroni	通心粉
Margarine	Marjerin (Mentega buatan)	菜油
Mint leaf	Daun pudina	薄荷葉
Monosodium glutamate	Serbuk perasa	味精
Mung bean flour	Tepung hoen kuih	綠豆粉
Mushroom sauce	Kicap cendawan	醬油(草菇老抽)
Mustard green	Sawi	菜心
Mustard seed	Biji sawi	覓菜仔
Nutmeg	Buah pala	豆蔻
Onion	Bawang besar	大葱頭
Oyster sauce	Kicap tiram	蠔油
Palm sugar	Gula Melaka	椰糖
Peanut candy	Bipang kacang	花生糖
Pearl sago	Biji sagu	沙莪粒
"Petai"	Petai	伯達
Pig's caul	Babat babi	網西油
Plum sauce		甜梅醬

English	Malay	Chinese
Pork (front trotter meat)		前腿肉
Potato	Ubi	馬鈴薯
Preserved soy beans	Taucu	豆醬
Preserved soybean cake	Tempe	酵豆
Pumpkin	Labu	金瓜
Quail's egg	Telur burung puyuh	鳥蛋
Radish	Lobak Cina or Lobak putih	蘿蔔
Red beans	Kacang merah	紅豆
Red chilli	Lada merah	紅辣椒
Red kokee seed		枸杞
Red snapper	Ikan merah	紅魚
Red sugar	Gula timbang merah	紅糖
Rice malt sauce		甜醬
Rice vermicelli	Meehoon	米粉
Rock salt	Garam kasar	粗鹽
Salt fish	Ikan asin	鹹魚
Salted duck's eggs	Telur asin	鹹鴨蛋
Screwpine leaf	Daun pandan	香葉
Sesame oil	Minyak bijan	蔴油
Sesame seed	Bijan	蔴
Shallot	Bawang kecil	葱頭
Silver belly	Ikan kekek	丹曼魚
Small sour starfruit	Belimbing buloh	小洋桃
Soaked cuttlefish	Sotong kembang	泡水魷魚
Soft soybean cake	Tauhu lembik	豆腐
Soy beans	Kacang soya	黃豆
Soybean skin	Kulit tauhu	豆皮
Soybean sprouts	"Taugeh besar"	大頭豆芽
Soybean sticks	Tauhu kering	腐竹
Spanish mackerel	Ikan tenggiri	馬駿魚
Spinach	Bayam	莧菜
Sprat	Ikan tamban	丹曼魚
Spring onion	Daun bawang	青葱
Spring roll skin	Kulit popiah	薄餅皮
Star anise	Bunga lawang "Buah pekak"	茴香

English	Malay	Chinese
Sweet black malt		黑甜醬
Sweet potato	Keledek	蕃薯
Sweet potato leaf	Daun keledek	蕃薯葉
Tamarind	Assam	亞參
"Tang aw"		冬窩
Tapioca	Ubi kayu	木薯
"Tee taukee"		甜腐竹
Thick rice vermicelli	Laksa meehoon	粗米粉
Threadfin	Ikan kurau	午魚
Thuvar dhal	Kacang kuda	印度黃豆
Tomato	Tomato	蕃茄
Transparent noodles	Tunghoon	冬粉
Turmeric leaf	Daun kunyit	黃薑葉
Vegetable marrow	Labu Cina	毛瓜
Vinegar	Cuka	醋
Wonton skin	Kulit wantan	云吞皮
Water chestnut	Sengkuang Cina	馬蹄
Water convolvulus	Kangkung	甕菜
Watercress	Pengaga	西洋菜
White glutinous rice	Pulot	糯米
White peppercorns	Lada putih	白胡椒
Wild ginger flower	Bunga kantan	干冬花
Winter melon	Labu kundur	冬瓜
Wolf Herring	Ikan parang	西刀魚
Yam	Keladi	芋頭
Yam bean	Sengkuang	莎葛
Yeast	Ibu roti Ragi	酒餅
Yellow noodles	Mee	麵
Yellowstripe trevally	Ikan kuning	君令魚
Young corn cob	Jagung muda	嫩玉蜀黍
Young ginger	Halia muda	子薑
"Yu char kway"	"Yu car kway"	油條

Menu Suggestions

Dinner or Lunch

Plain Rice	
Duck Padre	84
Fish Curry with Dorothy's Curry Powder	86
Indonesian Prawn Cutlet	30
Fried Spinach	55
Rasam	117
Kacang Hijau with Coconut Milk	155

Plain Rice	
Penang Curry Kapitan	23
Claypot Corn Soup with a Difference	121
Indian Cucumber Pickle	136
Thai Pumpkin Dessert	145

Mee Rebus Java	107
Sotoh Ayam	128
Taukwa Goreng	32
Javanese Cendol	153
Fresh Fruit in Season	

Tomato Rice	98
Malabar Mutton Curry	79
Ayam Panggang	21
Cucumber Salad with Coconut Milk	90
Mango Chutney	92
Fresh Fruit in Season	

Plain Rice	
Mutton Rendang	19
Cuttlefish in Soy Sauce	50
Soybean Sprouts with Prawns	54
Fresh Fruit in Season	

Nasi Lemak	100
Ikan/Udang Goreng Assam	63, 70
Otak-Otak Bakar	70
Kangkung Masak Lemak Udang	75
Banana Custard Dessert	153

Compressed Rice for Lontong	100
Indonesian Beef Rendang	19
Belimbing and Prawn Sambal	76
Sambal Sotong	31
Sambal Telur	24
Sayur Lodeh	31
Tempe Goreng	32
Coconut Serondeng	32
Durian Ice-cream	158

Plain Rice	
Pork with Sweet and Sour Sauce	37
Steamed Chicken and Longans in Yunan Pot	121
Bittergourd with Preserved Soy Beans	54
White fungus with Loquats	158

Plain Rice	
Duck Vindaloo	83
Indonesian Fish Frikkadels	24
Bittergourd with Turmeric	89
Pineapple and Raisins Chutney	91
Fresh Fruit in Season	

Fried Rice	101
Mixed Vegetables in Clay Pot	121
Winter Melon Soup	112
Soybean Almond Jelly	157

Hot Singapore Laksa Lemak	105
Penang Loh Bak	132
Singapore Chinese Rojak	132
Bubor Cha-Cha with Ice Shavings	148

Beef and Asparagus in Yunan Pot	118
Sharksfin Soup with Crabmeat	111
Cantonese Fried Kway Teow	105
Bubor Pulot Hitam	154